TAKE YOUR PLACE

Stepping into a Life of Miracles

Angela Kline

PRESS

ENDORSEMENTS

I once saw a bumper sticker on a beat up, rusty hulk of a car with a cloud of smoke billowing out of its exhaust like a diesel locomotive. As it rattled by I laughed at the message on the sticker, "God is my Source". My immediate thought was, "If God is your source, you need a different God."

How many times have you seen people who testify to God's goodness but fail to demonstrate it in real life? As I read Angela Kline's book, *Take Your Place*, I immediately realized that her life and message is the real deal; a journey from brokenness to wholeness. Transformed from a shattered life of abuse, addiction, depression, and suicide, she now lives a life of victory, supernatural power and healing miracles.

Angela is a practitioner of the truth and an adept teacher. Her story will give you hope and real answers. If you have been knocked down by life's struggles and failures, Angela is proof that you can get up again. It will give you fresh motivation to **Take Your Place** as one of God's loved and anointed servants to bring hope and healing to others.

— DR. DALE A. FIFE
Author: The Secret Place, *Passionately Pursuing His Presence*

If you are desiring to experience more from your Christian life than you currently are, this book is for you. *Take Your Place* is a training manual to help equip you to do the works of Jesus. It contains the keys to walking in your God given destiny and fulfilling the call of God on your life. You will find personal fulfillment as you begin to practice the truths presented here.

Angela Kline is a living testimony of what she presents in this book. I know her as one who is passionate in her pursuit for more of Him. Her zeal is contagious! *Take Your Place* will help you become all God created you to be.

— GARY OATES
Author: Open My Eyes, Lord
International Conference Speaker

We live in a day when Christianity often lives as if the Trinity is the Father, Son and Holy Scriptures instead of the Holy Spirit. Angela Kline is a person who lives the reality of one who experiences the daily, contagious Holy Spirit-directed life that impacts others wherever she goes. *Take Your Place* is a book that will not only help you understand God's desire for healing, but you will learn what it means to experience His daily presence-whether on the job or at your next visit to Walmart! This book challenged me to experience more of His presence in the routine of life. So will you.

— OS HILLMAN
President, Marketplace Leaders and International Coalition of Workplace Ministries
Author: TGIF Today God Is First and The 9 To 5 Window

Angela Kline has captured some amazing things in her new book, *Take Your Place*. I found much of the teaching on Healing and the Kingdom of God very important for a foundation for every believer and something that I will highly recommend to others who are pursuing that place of destiny in God. Some of the profound impact for me was in some of the very direct words to the Church. When Angela said, "Bad teaching and disappointment have robbed many people of the reality of the supernatural realm," it gave a launching pad for so much of what is carried in this book. It is filled with good teaching and hope and gives people the reality of the supernatural realm!

When she declares "we're supposed to be emptying out the drug houses...," she heralds the message that Jesus brought to the world. Christians have the answers; indeed, we carry the answer in us in the Person of Jesus Christ, and this book demonstrates Jesus living in the world today through the lives of ordinary believers who have stepped into their destinies and are releasing His Power. How true it is that "the Kingdom remains a mystery to people who don't really want it"... and how many they are. But this book will cultivate a hunger for the Kingdom, a hunger for God, and a hunger for the purposes of God in anyone who reads it!

On a personal note, I have watched the hunger of Angela. It is real... it is contagious... it is a life that has absolutely found destiny and purpose! Angela has taken her place in this great battle at the end of the ages. Read this book, and it will encourage you to take your place alongside her and many others who are pressing through into the harvest that is breaking across the nations of this world! Brilliant, Angela, brilliant!

— DANNY STEYNE
The Mountain, Columbia SC, www.TheMountain.org
Author: These Walk on Water and When Bruised Reeds Break

What a wonderful book! It is so exciting to see the fruit of a life laid down totally for the purposes of God, and to have Angela share with the world, the secrets that she has learned in how to have a dynamic and victorious Christian life. From the first day that Angela attended Heart for the Nations Bible School over a decade ago, we knew that she had "The good hand of the Lord upon her!" She wasted no time as a newly saved child of God in putting her feet to the gospel and began immediately preaching in nursing homes. She would preach and testify of those things that she was seeing God do, and then she would give an altar call for salvation. Her message was so compelling, and the love of God flowed through her in such a special way, that most times everyone would give their lives to the Lord. Then they wanted her to pray for them for healing! **Angela's book will change your life!** *You won't be able to put it down*, and in very practical ways she shows you how you can **Take Your Place**, and do the works of Jesus. You too can be a world changer and a history maker, and inspired by Angela's passion, we suspect that her book will stir up in you the very gift of God that you carry, and that you will be compelled to **Take Your Place!**

— JIM RICKARD
Apostle, RAIN – Resurrection Apostolic International Network

— RAMONA RICKARD
Pastor of Church of the Resurrection
Founders, International Association of Healing Ministries,
www.rainministries.org, www.laguerison.org

Angela Kline has done a fantastic job of weaving together the very powerful, personal testimony of her life and the heart of the Lord, especially as it regards the subject of healing. This book will impart to you the faith, the hope and the love for you to **Take Your Place** in the manifestation of the kingdom of God on earth. The testimony of her own life and the serious hurdles Angela had to overcome will give you the faith to not disqualify yourself because of your own past. Her teachings on the kingdom of God will cause your heart to overflow with hope and love. I highly recommend this book and I believe all who read this will find themselves positively affected by Angela's passion for His kingdom. This book is an equipping book but it also carries an impartation of igniting fire. As Angela's pastor the last several years I can tell you that she in fact does live out what she reveals of herself in this book. This is a book for all to read and then "pass it on".

— JOHNNY ENLOW
Sr. Pastor of Daystar International Christian Fellowship
Author: The Seven Mountain Prophecy

I have known Angela Kline for a number of years and have observed her passion for the Lord and His healing and delivering power. She also has a strong desire to see the saints raised up to do the work of the ministry and has demonstrated this through her ministry with Healing Rooms which I have personally experienced. I am so pleased and excited she has written the book, *Take Your Place* where she explains her personal background to her passion and calling, and the maturing and growth of the anointing in leadership, and ministry. She has done an excellent job of confirming the authority and the anointing that is for God's people to set the captives free and to be change agents for the Kingdom of God. This book will teach, train, inspire and influence you in the power of prayer, prophetic deliverance, and healing of the body and soul. It is a blessing!

— DR. W. PAUL "BUDDY" CRUM
Sr. Apostle, Life Center Ministries, Dunwoody, Georgia
Author: Much More than a Job and Pressing on With Joy

Angela Kline has unpacked a critical message for all Christ followers today. Where is your place in the Kingdom? We hear the Spirit say "**Take Your Place**." But where do we do this? And how? This book helps guide you in a unique way to explore the mystery and joy of finding your place. In Jeremiah 33:3, our Heavenly Father exhorts us "Call to Me, and I will answer you, and show you great and mighty things, which you do not know." So Call out! And read this book – you will find great and mighty things which you did not know! Excellent work Angela!

— DOUG SPADA
Founder and CEO, His Church at Work

Finally a book that shows Christians of all ages the secrets of how to **Take Your Place** as a history maker and to enter into the fullness of God's purposes in the earth. Angela opens up the treasure chest of heaven and shares the supernatural jewels of the Kingdom of God so that you can walk into your destiny of ruling and reigning in the earth. Angela shows you how to be a victorious Christian and to expect miracles every day of your life. This book is a great tool for anyone that has a desire to be used by God to touch a hurting world.

— MARC BUCHHEIT
NW Regional Director for IAHR
(International Association of Healing Rooms)
Director, Shelton Healing Rooms, Shelton, Washington

Angela recognizes the urgency to equip an end time army of champions for the great harvest through the Great Commission. This book truly is an equipping manual for all believers. It answers the common questions ordinary Christians have today concerning their role in power evangelism.

— RICK TAYLOR
Region 4 Director for IAHR
(International Association of Healing Rooms)
Director, Santa Maria Healing Rooms,
Santa Maria Valley, California

Angela's real love and passion for Jesus come through in this book where she tells her amazing testimony of God's transforming power. As you read this book it will build your faith and give you a burning desire to pray for the sick and see them get healed. It is designed to inspire you to know that miracles did not stop with the apostles, but they are happening here and now. After reading this book you'll feel excited and empowered to go to the sick and the lost, **Take Your Place**, and do the stuff! There are hurting people out there just waiting for you and me to be a demonstration of His power today.

— JIM DROWN
Global Evangelistic Missions

The power of Angela's testimony along with the truth conveyed in this book stirred my faith and awakened my inner man. It is a message to help equip an 'end time army'.

— STEVE MITCHELL
Conference Worship leader

DEDICATION

I dedicate this book to my children Moriah Caitlin and Israel Christian. It is my hope and prayer that my life and my love for you will encourage you both to be all you can be for Jesus. May the Lord use you both mightily as you learn to Take Your Place and raise up your generation. I pray that the fruit of your lives will be more than a hundredfold of what God accomplishes in mine. I'm grateful that the Lord showed me that I could be a Mom and still have a shot at helping save the lost, heal the sick, and help train up a mighty army in the earth. Your love and joy have meant more to me than I could ever say! I am the most blessed Mom in all the world!

ACKNOWLEDGEMENTS

I give thanks and credit for this book to my Heavenly Father. This book was in His heart, and I was only obedient to write what He showed me and put in my heart. Everything good about this book is because of Him. I thank my loving Savior and Lord Jesus for giving it all up for you and for me. I so thank Holy Spirit for being an ever constant companion, teacher and encourager to me throughout this book and always.

To my awesome husband and greatest cheerleader, Den. You are like a cup of cold water in the desert to me. I so appreciate all you do to enable me to fulfill my destiny of helping raise up an army to bring in the harvest. You are the best husband and such a great dad to Moriah and Israel. I praise the Lord for your loving support!

To my children, Moriah and Israel. Thank you so much for being the "best" kids in the world. I couldn't have written this book without your understanding the call of God on my life. You have given up a lot of time with me so that this project from God could be accomplished. I so appreciate and cherish both of you.

There are several people in my life who have helped me fulfill my destiny in God. First of all I would like to acknowledge my dear friends Herb Mjorud who went home to glory nine years ago and his beautiful wife, Thelma, who is now 95 years young, for taking me under their wings and teaching me about Jesus.

I want to thank pastors Jim and Ramona Rickard, for living a selfless life of serving our King Jesus and for helping the saints of God learn about their inheritance. Thank you for paying the price for revival and for starting Heart for the Nations Bible School. I will be forever grateful for your love and teaching.

Special thanks to Elaine and Bud Bonn for taking Den and me under your wings and teaching us about the Lord. Your love and teaching gave us a strong foundation and we are grateful.

Special thanks to Cal and Michelle Pierce, my spiritual Dad and Mom for loving me like a daughter. I'm so grateful for your love, your encouragement and your support. With loving parents like you, I know that there's nothing I cannot do. I really love you with all my heart!

There are a few great men of God who have really shaped what I teach regarding the kingdom of God and healing. As one of his daughters in the Healing Rooms, I teach some of the same things that Cal Pierce does while being flavored with some of the teachings of Bill Johnson and Kris Vallotton. I first sat in one of Bill's meetings at Jim and Ramona's church about 12 years ago, and have listened to many of the things he has taught through CDs or books since then. What these men teach has so become a part of who I am and what I teach that I don't always remember where I learned it. If I remember who I heard it from, I will mention it in this book. Regardless, I'd recommend everything that Cal, Bill, and Kris have written to be a part of your library. Just as their teachings have helped me, so they will help you Take Your Place.

Special thanks to my very special friends and pastors, Johnny and Elizabeth Enlow. You are the *tops!* I have learned so much from both of you. I'm grateful that the Lord has given you both to me in order to help shape many of the things I believe and the way I minister. I feel so very honored and favored by the Lord to be able to walk this journey with both of you this side of eternity. Truly we have been joined at the hip for "such a time as this." I honor the calling on both of your lives and love you both with all my heart! Everyone should have the privilege of having awesome spiritual leaders like you to submit to and to walk alongside.

I'm extremely grateful to Chris Tiegreen for his editing expertise with this book! He was able to take my almanac and help break it down into a readable fashion for you all to learn and enjoy! Thanks Chris, you're the best!

Thanks to Marla Boole, my precious and faithful assistant for her countless hours of serving Jesus by helping me with the Healing Rooms and for pre-editing this book. You rock, and I love you girl!

Thanks to Jill Wilkinson and Brenda Cannon for helping me proofread this book prior to being printed.

To our Healing Rooms staff and team: Thank you for stepping out to Take Your Place to heal the sick in Atlanta and beyond. You are an example to the world that "Greater is He that is in us, than he who is in the world." Because of you, others have been healed and encouraged that they too can take their place and heal the sick.

CONTENTS

FOREWORD

Angela Kline's new book, Take Your Place, comes at a time in church history where God is positioning the body of Christ from a rapture mentality to a harvest theology.

This book is a *must read* for every warrior in God's army. I would call it, not just a motivational manual, but a how to get started manual that is inspiring and practical for stepping into your destiny by taking your place. Jesus said that we are not to just be hearers but to become doers of His will. You cannot become a doer unless you take your place.

Angela's passion for the lost and the sick shines through this entire book. She reminds us to take our place so that the Kingdom of God can come upon the earth. She reminds us that the Kingdom of God must come through us to a lost generation. That the lost and sick are worth our life! We must take our place in order to reach them. She reminds us that by the power of the Holy Spirit in us, we battle from victory, not for victory.

Every once in a while a book is published that doesn't just give us good information, but is an expression of how God moves through someone's life. This is one of those rare books. What you read here will come to you as a testimony of how God's will has changed Angela's life. Her life has not only been healed of the past, but is an expression of what you will read.

As a Regional Director of Healing Rooms Ministries, she teaches, casts vision, equips, prays for the sick and evangelizes the lost everywhere she goes. I fully endorse her apostolic vision to raise up the saints to do the work of the ministry. Her passion for Jesus is what the body of Christ needs in this hour. Now is the time to equip the body of Christ so that we can see our cities transformed.

It is a blessing and encouragement to read a Kingdom book that is first written in a life before it is written on a page. As you read this book, allow what is written on a page to be written in your life. I've been *greatly impacted* by Angela's life and message and I know you will be too!

Cal Pierce
International Director
Healing Rooms Ministries
Author: Preparing the Way and Healing in the Kingdom

INTRODUCTION

My friend, you were created to be a world changer and a history maker. You have been called to receive the very life of Jesus Christ and to enter into the same supernatural power that He walked in. You and I have the awesome opportunity and responsibility to change the world by displaying the kingdom of heaven upon the earth, causing everything to come under His Lordship. Jesus came to reveal the love of our Heavenly Father and supply us with the supernatural power needed to bring total restoration into our lives and the lives of people around us. As you shine your light in this dark world and do the very works that Jesus did – you will be like a lighthouse that shows people the path to life.

The world needs a sign that our God is real and that He is *all-powerful!* The world needs to know the one and only true God and that Jesus alone is the way to Him. People need real solutions to real problems; they need health, wholeness, provision, peace and love. Your life can be like a lifeline for others to grab hold of to pull them out of their storms and onto the Rock, which is Jesus. Let's start showing them who He is and what He is like. The Lord promises to confirm His Word with healings and miracles (Mark 16:15-18). Healing is a sign to unbelievers that reveals His compassion and His kingdom. He wants us to demonstrate His miraculous power every-where we go. Even if you aren't yet seeing His power demonstrated in your own life, read on – this book is for you!

Before I came to know Jesus as my Lord and Savior, I was a basket-case. My life was in shambles. I was depressed and physi-cally sick all the time. I was in constant pain in my back and neck, and I had no hope. But Jesus came to save, deliver, and heal me. If you need healing, He will heal you too! Now He's using me not only to heal the sick through His power, but to help train others to do it too! It is my heart's cry to see individuals and churches moving in the power of God and in His fullness. Honestly, if God can use me, He can use *anybody.*

In 2007, the Lord gave me an actual vision of a book entitled *Take Your Place.* It was already published and it had my name on it. I'd never had a desire to write a book and argued with the Lord that I didn't want to write one. Then He showed me through this vision that He wanted to use my life as an example to teach others how they are to take their place to advance His end-time army. It was a week later that I shared this vision at our staff meeting at church. My pastor, Johnny Enlow, told us that he had just started writing a book called *The Seven Mountain Prophecy.* Interestingly enough, both of our books are about how, as Christians, we are to take our place as lights in the world in order to transform society and those around us.

Saints of God, our job in the earth is to take back everything the enemy has stolen from us and to help those around us do the same. Did you know that you are a saint? If you've received Jesus—you are.

In Genesis, God created Adam and Eve with the purpose of filling planet earth with His abundance and His life. He told them that He wanted them to be fruitful and multiply, to subdue the earth and take dominion because they were His royal family. In other words, they had the keys to the kingdom, they were in authority, and what they said came to pass. Everything belonged to them. As God's kids, they had a wonderful relationship with Him and were to expand His great kingdom and His rule upon the earth, showing others who their awesome Dad was.

But then one day, . . . you know the story. Eve ate the fruit from the tree that she wasn't supposed to eat. Then Adam ate it, and the *shekinah* glory that covered them vanished in thin air. Immediately they noticed that they were no longer clothed. But, *eek!* They were naked. So they hid themselves.

We see here that when they sinned, it caused them to be separated from God and His glory presence left them. This sin brought the curse, and the results were pain, sickness, poverty, and disease, which would eventually bring death. That was the progression: Sin—Curse—Disease and Death.

Our Heavenly Father loved us so much that even though Adam and Eve sinned, He told them of His master plan of redemption and restoration. As we know, He sent the most precious thing He had, His only Son, Jesus. Jesus came as the light in the world to show us what His Father was like and the wonderful kingdom that He has for us to live in here upon the earth.

When He went to the cross, *He saw your face* and shed His blood so that you could live an abundant life.

> "He has delivered us from the power of darkness and conveyed us into the kingdom of the Son of His love, in whom we have redemption through His blood, the forgiveness of sins" (Colossians 1:13-14).

He also hung on the cross to redeem us from the curse so that we might receive the blessing of Abraham.

> "Christ has redeemed us from the curse of the law, having become a curse for us (for it is written, *'Cursed is everyone who hangs on a tree'*) that the blessing of Abraham might come upon the Gentiles in Christ Jesus, that we might receive the promise of the Spirit through faith" (Galatians 3:13-14).

Before He died, He completed His work by saying, "It is finished!" He redeemed us from sin, the curse that came from the sin, and then the effects of the curse, which include sickness and disease.

Isaiah prophesied that this would happen.

> "He was wounded for our transgressions,
> He was bruised for our iniquities;
> The chastisement for our peace was upon Him,
> And by His stripes we are healed" (Isaiah 53:5).

Then the New Testament verifies that this was to pay for our healing.

> "When evening had come, they brought to Him many who were demon-possessed. And He cast out the spirits with a word, and healed all who were sick, that it might be fulfilled which was spoken by Isaiah the prophet, saying:
> *'He Himself took our infirmities and bore our sicknesses'"*
> (Matthew 8:16-17).

> "Who Himself bore our sins in His own body on the tree, that we, having died to sins, might live for righteousness—by whose stripes you were healed" (1 Peter 2:24).

Friends, He did it all for us so we can live an abundant life now the way Adam and Eve lived prior to sin. He even went down to hell and stomped on the devil's head and took away the keys (authority) of the kingdom and gave them back to us. The enemy had gained authority when Adam and Eve sinned, but now that their sin was paid for, Satan's authority over God's people was destroyed.

We are now in charge again, as Jesus gave back to us the dominion in the earth that had been lost. Jesus is our Savior, but He also came as our role model to show us what we can have restored back to us. Upon entering into His earthly ministry at age 30, Jesus started displaying kingdom power by healing the sick, casting out demons, raising the dead and doing miracles. He walked the walk, talked the talk, and showed people who His Father was, what He was like and how they were to walk in the earth.

Jesus said in Matthew 10:7,8

> "And as you go, preach, saying, 'The kingdom of heaven is at hand.' Heal the sick, cleanse the lepers, raise the dead, cast out demons. Freely you have received, freely give."

When you received Jesus, you freely received all He had to give. Now He wants you to give it away to others. He promoted you into His army and desires for you to enforce His victory on the earth.

We are in a battle, and in order to win, we must understand spiritual warfare. In the kingdom of God, our weapons are not of the flesh but spiritual and supernaturally powerful (2 Corinthians 10:4).

The power of God that resides in us as believers is the *dunamis* (dynamite or miraculous) power of God and is greater than the power of the devil in the world. It's time that we start teaching others by our example the victorious life that God has for us is for ALL of us—today. We are a victorious army, and God wants you to learn His ways so you can win. This is for your own life and for those in your family. But God doesn't want you to stop at that.

As Christians, we are called to be as the light in the world—not to hide our light but to be positioned on the high place for others to see and glorify our Father in heaven (Matthew 5:14-16). We are to *re*-present our loving Heavenly Father to all those around us by displaying His love and awesome power to everyone we come across, just as Jesus did. Many in the world are sick, in pain and are dying. So many are lost and they are crying out for help. As we have our spiritual antennas up, Holy Spirit will direct us to those around us so we can deliver God's message of love, hope and healing to them. Or God may send them to your door.

Today while I was writing this introduction, the FedEx man came to my door to deliver a package. I asked him how he was doing, and he told me that he had just come back to work after being off for two months. When I asked him what was going on, he explained that he had a pinched nerve in his neck and a torn rotator cuff. He said he didn't want surgery, so he had prayed and asked God to heal him. He had come back to work, but still couldn't lift his arm without pain.

Needless to say, even a blind person would have seen this divine appointment a million miles away. I told him that he could be completely healed and asked him if I could pray for him. "Sure," he said. I laid my hand on his shoulder and prayed for him, and guess what? He was healed! He got so excited because he could raise his arm without any pain. So to prove it, he kept lifting his arm up and shouting, "Hallelujah, Hallelujah!" I was so excited and was hoping that my neighbors would hear him giving God all the glory for healing him. That, my friend, is a "GO JESUS!"

Friends, the world is getting darker. It is time to shine our lights! We must stop believing the lies of the enemy and rid ourselves of all fear. We must understand our job in the kingdom is not to come to church just to sit there, but we go there to get equipped so that we can be the hands, the feet and the voice of Jesus to those around us. This isn't something we do as a 9-5 "job", but this is our life 24/7 as we are called to display the wonderful works of God in the earth.

Isaiah 60:1-3 says,

"Arise, shine. For your light has come! And the glory of the Lord is risen upon you. For behold the darkness shall cover the earth, and deep darkness the people. But the Lord will arise over you, and His glory will be seen upon you. The Gentiles shall come to your light, and kings to the brightness of your rising."

A new day has come in which the saints of God are waking up. They are throwing off the things of the world that are holding them down and are taking their place of dominion in the kingdom of heaven upon the earth.

They are discovering that the harvest field is not in the church but outside its four walls. Have you ever had aspirations of being in ministry? Well guess what? You are! Remember, you are the light in the world now. Those in the five-fold ministry — apostles, prophets, evangelists, pastors, and teachers, according to Ephesians 4:11 — are called to equip the saints so you can do the works of Jesus. It used to be that only a few great men and women of God walked in awesome power to heal the sick. But today the saints are coming to understand the truth that Jesus commissioned everyone to lay hands on the sick and heal them. He said that we would do the same things and greater things than He did when He walked upon the earth (John 14:12). He healed the sick, cast out demons, and raised the dead, so that is what we should all be doing as well.

I so appreciate my spiritual Papa, Cal Pierce, who is the director of Healing Rooms Ministries in Spokane, Washington. He has been used by God to call ordinary believers to co-operate with Holy Spirit by releasing His power to heal the sick through Healing Rooms all around the world. At this time, there are 946 Healing Rooms in 46 nations and the number changes weekly. Our vision is to have a Healing Room in every city in every nation. I get to help with this as I travel to other cities to train up the saints to take their place in the marketplace as well as helping people start their own Healing Room. In the Healing Rooms we are seeing people healed from every kind of sickness, pain and affliction - including some receiving new body parts from heaven. Terminal cancers and even AIDS are being healed by Jesus through ordinary men, women and children. The Healing Rooms are like lighthouses in a city that prophesy that Jesus is the Healer, drawing all men to Him and then to Papa God.

This book goes beyond praying for the sick in healing rooms or in churches and will take each believer into the harvest field where the light of Jesus is so needed. As each of us reach out in the love of Jesus and share our testimonies with people, His light will shine on them to show them God's plan of restoration. As we take our place, it will help God's children learn about their full inheritance and start living in the abundance He planned from the beginning. Then they can shine their light more brightly to those around them. If they have fallen, we can be there to pick them up and help them stand so that their light will shine brightly once again.

I encourage you to open your heart and your mind to the truths taught in this book as I share what the Bible says about your inheritance and taking your place in this world. Jesus said, "As long as I am in the world, I am the light of the world" (John 9:5). Then He taught believers that we are to be the salt and the light (Matthew 5:13-16).

The parable of the sower gives us some insight into being a light for God (Mark 4). The seed was sown on four different types of ground. This speaks of how we hear God's Word. We must not only hear the Word of God concerning how to "Take Our Place" in the world, but we must do something with what we hear. The word *hear* means to attend to and to understand. I believe that the Lord is trying to get us to understand that we must not just hear His Words about our inheritance or His commission to each of us about being a light in the world. We must be people who hear His words with a good heart and not only accept His words but bear fruit for Him. Truly His message to you today is that you are called to Take Your Place.

The enemy will come immediately to try to take the word that is sown in your heart (Mark 4:4). Therefore, you must guard the Word of God that you hear. Some people will gladly receive the truths in God's Word, but because they don't have a deep foundation, when problems or persecution arise for the word's sake, they will immediately stumble (Mark 4:5). It's important to find like minded Christians who can help you learn, grow and who will pray for you. Then you must dig into the truth of the Word of God about your inheritance because your victory will bring many others into victory also. ✗ *Key*

Still yet, others will hear the word, and the cares of the world, the deceitfulness of riches, and the desires for other things will enter in, choking the word, so that it becomes unfruitful (Mark 4:7). Jesus warned us that we cannot serve God and mammon. He tells us not to worry about our lives, for our heavenly Father knows what we need. But we are to seek first the kingdom of God and His righteousness, and all these things will be added to us (Matthew 6:25, 33). It's important to prioritize Jesus and His call on your life to take your place as a light in the world. Eternal destinies are at stake!

But when the word is sown on *good ground,* the crop will spring up and produce increase. These are the ones who hear the word, accept it, and bear fruit: "some thirty-fold, some sixty, and some a hundred" (Mark 4:8). As we listen and accept what He says with a good heart, we will bear fruit with patience (Luke 8:15). Not just a little fruit either, but up to a hundred-fold.

As you read this book, you will be learning how to live a victorious life and how you too can shine your light so the lost will come running home. We need to be like Jesus, our "Good Shepherd" who would leave the 99 to go find the "one" who was lost. We need to view each "one" as special, important and worth our time, wherever we go, because that's how Jesus sees them.

This is not just another book but a training manual for every believer. It will better equip you to fulfill God's commission as a light in the world as you take your place! My prayer is that you will open your spirit and be able to enter into the fullness that He has prepared before the foundation of time for you to walk in. Remember that God doesn't show favoritism. What He has done for me and through me, He'll do for and through anyone. I hope that this book encourages you to soar with Him in new ways and that you will understand the awesome depth of His love for you personally! That's why He wanted to me to write this book for you—so you will know His heart and walk in His power.

Arise, my friend, and Take Your Place!

Angela Kline

CHAPTER 1: My Story

One month after Dennis and I got married, my friend Cherí called and told me that God loved me and that I needed to get saved.

What? God loved me? I had a really hard time believing that. I had grown up in a very dysfunctional family and I *felt* that my parents hated me. I didn't understand what Cherí was talking about, as I had never heard about getting "saved." She explained that I needed to receive Jesus in order to go to heaven. It sounded pretty simple, but I thought I had already done that. After all, I had been in church almost every Sunday since I was a baby. I believed that Jesus died for my sins, I took my first communion in second grade, and I had been taking it ever since. I had been confirmed, but I wasn't sure what that meant. I had never heard about being born again. What did that mean?

I had also never read the Bible. Our family had a huge Catholic Bible that we put wedding announcements or funeral notices in, but no one in our family ever read it. Not knowing where to look in the Bible, I asked Cherí for more information. She gave us a small book that taught us what the Bible has to say about the steps to peace with God. After reading it we prayed the prayer that was in the back of the book to receive Jesus as our Lord and Savior. We had both grown up Catholic and heard that Jesus died for us, therefore we believed. We had just never heard about praying to receive Him. To us it seemed pretty much like a no-brainer. If we needed to do something in order to go to heaven, we wanted to do it! After all, who wants to go to hell?

A couple of weeks later, I called Cherí to ask her if it was wrong to get drunk. She said it was, so I asked her to show me where that was in the Bible. You see, we grew up seeing people drink alcohol and getting drunk, even in the church hall, but for some reason that day I was questioning it. Later I found out that this was the Holy Spirit convicting me that it was wrong. I was truly amazed and asked Cherí why she used to go out drinking with me before, and she said she had been backslidden. "I don't understand," I said. "If you knew it was wrong, how could you have gone out drinking and got drunk with me?" She told me that this happens to people sometimes when they don't do what they know is right. As a born-again Christian, I just couldn't comprehend this!

All I wanted to do was to tell everyone that they needed to receive Jesus. Years earlier when I was seventeen, I was in a terrible car accident on a bridge. A lady hit me almost head on, and rescuers had to cut the roof of my car open to get me out. I had cuts a quarter of an inch from my jugular vein. Praise God His angels were protecting me, because if the jugular vein is even nicked you usually bleed to death. I was in a coma, and it's a miracle that I'm alive today. I suffered from short-term memory loss, which was restored within a few months, but was left with partial whiplash and severe back injuries. Once I received the Lord, I so rejoiced in His hand of protection because if I had died in that car accident, I would be in hell today without a chance of getting out because I hadn't received the "free" gift of eternal life through Jesus. Knowing this burned in me a deep desire to tell as many people as possible about Jesus.

Though it's good that I wanted to tell people about Jesus, it's sad that in the early years I missed so much by getting people to focus on a ticket to heaven rather than on all of the abundance that God wanted to give to them. Because I'd been in gross darkness even while going to church most of my life and being basically a nice person, I wanted to keep everyone from going to hell. No one had ever told me that I needed to receive Jesus in order to go to heaven, so I was on a mission to make sure others were told. I didn't want anyone else to hope that simply avoiding bad sins and doing good things would get them to heaven one day.

The Power of God to Deliver

Thank God I was on a fast track of learning about the whole gospel of the kingdom, not just receiving a ticket to go to heaven one day when I died. My life was in shambles and I was really wounded, both physically and emotionally. About a month later, Cherí called to tell me that she had done something that completely changed her life. She had waited a couple of weeks to tell me about it in case the changes didn't last, but they had. She said her pastor had prayed for her and all her anger was now gone. She had no desire to drink alcohol anymore, and she felt so much peace. She said it was called "deliverance". Having never heard of this, she reminded me that the Lord's Prayer says "deliver us from evil." I knew this—after all, I had been a good Catholic girl and had prayed that prayer hundreds of times. But then she told me that demons were real, which shocked me. I had always thought the devil was make-believe, a little red man with a pitchfork in cartoons. But if this kind of prayer helped her, I wanted it. The power of her testimony brought me to deliverance.

A week or so later, I went with Cherí to see her pastor for prayer. He told me that God had this on His calendar since the beginning of time and that I would be different after prayer. To be honest, I seriously doubted it would help. But I was desperate and thought to myself, "What do I have to lose?"

I had grown up in a home where both of my parents had been heavy drinkers, and I experienced a lot of abuse. My father was filled with rage and my mom with depression. My parents had been victims themselves, and knew no other way. My siblings and I lived in constant fear. When I was in high school, I had to run away because someone in my family had threatened to kill me. I was put into foster homes for a while and went through severe emotional trauma and tormenting fear. Where would I go? What would happen in my life? I was so afraid I was going to die. Those words of death caused demons of fear to torment me night and day. Needless to say, I had an extremely bad background and needed a lot of healing. So could something as simple as a little prayer set me free? It worked for Cherí, and she had grown up in a very similar home as mine. Maybe this deliverance prayer *could* help me. I sure hoped so.

I was a binge drinker and seriously wondered how I would ever be able to quit drinking when Den and I decided to start a family. It wasn't that I drank every day, but when I started drinking, I couldn't control myself. I was also a rage-aholic, was severely depressed much of the time, and thought about killing myself when the depression came over me. God created me to be a very passionate person, so when I was happy, I was extremely happy; my mountains were high. But my valleys were very, very low. I didn't really want to kill myself, of course, but the thoughts and emotions were telling me to commit suicide. I found out later that these were spirits of depression and suicide and that the devil was trying to kill me.

In addition to all that, I cussed like a sailor, I was full of anger, I had excruciating cramps every month, and I was sick all the time with chronic sinus infections and bronchitis. I was bound with fear and felt rejected and unloved by everyone around me. These were the biggest, but not all, of the many issues I suffered with.

During the prayer, the pastor stopped to ask me a few questions. The first was whether I had ever been involved with the occult or witchcraft. I told him I hadn't, but Cherí reminded me that we had a friend who had done "readings" for us with tarot cards. Cherí had thought it was okay at the time because she saw the woman as a white witch. I had even considered getting my own tarot cards to read for myself and others, but I didn't—thank God He protected me from that—because I could see the fruit in that woman's life wasn't good. She was extremely angry and acted like a rage-aholic. Even though she had told me all about these spiritual experiences that she'd had, her actions made me question her spirituality.

Our friend had told us that her dead father came to see her and told her things he couldn't possibly have known. She said he told her that everyone goes to heaven and described the amazing beauty of it all. She used to tell me that she had seen me in past lives, so I started believing in reincarnation. After all, I didn't understand salvation and didn't know that Jesus was the only way to get to heaven. I had only known of religion, not about a relationship with God. Now the pastor was telling me we were fooled and that all witches get their power from the devil. He explained that the devil often appears as an angel of light to get us to think we're on the right path. I'd always wondered how that worked.

The pastor also asked if I had ever read horoscopes, had my palm read, or played with an Ouija board. I had done all of those things. I didn't know what the Bible said and that those things were wrong. I had to renounce them and ask God to forgive me. I had to repent for drinking alcohol excessively and claim deliverance from a spirit of alcoholism and addiction. Even though the spirits came down from my ancestor's sins, I had to take responsibility for my part in them also and ask God to forgive me. Spirits of depression and suicide had also come down through my family line. I was delivered from these generational spirits that day.

Forgiveness, the Key

Then the pastor asked me if I had any unforgiveness towards anyone. I freely admitted that I hated my parents for all the years of abuse. He said I needed to forgive them if I wanted to be forgiven. "You see, it's conditional," he explained. "If we want to be forgiven, we need to forgive others." Then he asked if I knew the Lord's Prayer. Sure, I knew it! I had said that prayer hundreds, if not thousands, of times. But even though I had said the prayer a lot, I really didn't think about the words—and I certainly didn't think they applied to me. After all, my parents had really abused me. I felt that I had a right not to forgive them. For one thing, they weren't even sorry, as far as I could tell; and if they were, they never apologized. How could I forgive someone who wasn't even sorry? For another thing, what they did to me caused overwhelming pain, and I hated them for it! But the pastor reminded me that Jesus laid His life down even for those who hated and killed Him.

Wow, I had to think about this. Of course I wanted to be forgiven. This pastor went on to tell me that we aren't to judge others' sins because God is the righteous Judge. If we judge others, the same judgment will come back on us. He explained that this was keeping me bound to all my pain, and I needed to release and forgive my parents. I told him that I didn't feel like forgiving them, but he explained that forgiveness is a choice, not a feeling. Well, now I was in a quandary. How could I forgive my parents for all that they had done?

What I'm sharing here is only a tiny fraction of the abuse I went through for many years. I pondered my "right" to stay angry with them, but decided that if this was the key to my getting free like Cherí, I needed to do it. "Okay, I'll forgive them," I said. He led me through a prayer and then commanded the bitterness and unforgiveness to leave me. After prayer, the pastor told me that I was going to be a brand new person. To be honest, I doubted that very seriously.

New Life in the Morning

I awoke at 5:00 the next morning. I'm a night owl and like to sleep in, but here I found myself awake with such joy. In my heart I was singing, "Zip-a-dee-doo-dah zip-a-dee-ay. My, oh my, what a wonderful day. Plenty of sunshine heading my way. Zip-a-dee-doo-dah zip-a-dee-ay!" Wow, where was that coming from?

I had so much love in my heart. I could see my parents in my mind's eye, and I couldn't stop smiling. I found myself crying out to God to have mercy on them. I could actually see them through God's eyes as the victims that they were, and all the hatred, pain, and unforgiveness were gone. Oh, how I loved them! Though I'd been in bondage myself just a few hours earlier, the key for getting free was in forgiving them.

I remember lying in bed that morning and praying for everyone who had ever hurt me and asking God to bless them. I cried out for mercy for those who were away from Him and asked Him to reach down and touch them. This was so different for me! I'd never prayed like this in my life. The only prayers I ever prayed were when I needed something. And now, the joy in my heart—this was certainly a day of miracles! God had changed my hard heart into a ray of sunshine. He took all my pain away, and I felt like a new person. "Wow," I wondered, "what else is going to be different in my life?"

As the days and weeks went by, I noticed that my desire for alcohol was truly gone—and it stayed gone! Instead of anger and rage, I had peace and joy. And here's a biggie: when something went wrong, I found myself saying, "Shoot!" I had never used that word unless I was playing basketball. Now I couldn't have even spelled the most simple cuss word. God completely changed my vocabulary. What a miracle!

The depression and thoughts of suicide never came back, and the joy of the Lord became my inner strength. But it wasn't something that I had to work for, it was just there, oozing out of me. The fear that hung over me all my life was gone, and I had a renewed feeling of confidence. All the chronic sinus infections and bronchitis left me, and we hadn't even prayed about that. I used to be in bed every month with cramps that would have me crying in pain. Now they were all gone. All of these were rooted in the things I had just been delivered from, so when the spirits left me, I was healed. *Note*

With all the junk removed, I could now be who God created me to be. As a little girl, I had told God that I knew I loved people more than most people did. He had put His heart in me even then, and I would cry when I saw people sick, hurt, weak, poor, or abused. When I was in second grade, I remember kneeling at church after confession thinking that I would be the first female priest in the Catholic Church. Then in high school when I realized how impossible that looked, I thought I would become a nun in a convent. But since I really liked boys and wanted 12 children, that was out of the question too! It's amazing, as I look back over my life, to realize that even though I went through a lot of trauma, God's hand protected me. He put within me His love and a desire to help those who were hurt, sick, poor, or abused.

After this deliverance, I called the pastor of the Lutheran Church I'd joined a couple of years earlier and asked to meet with him. When I told him about my deliverance, he said, "Praise the Lord, Angela, that's great!"

"What do you mean?" I asked. "You knew about deliverance and never told me about it? I was bound in so much pain, and I've never even heard about this!"

I also told him I had been born again. He was shocked because he assumed that because I loved God and had been coming to church that I was saved. But this church was more of what I know now to be a "seeker sensitive" church. They never had altar calls for salvation and never talked about deliverance or healing. After what God did for me, I wanted to tell everyone.

Encounter with the Holy Spirit

Not long after that, I had a tangible encounter with the power of God and His love. I told Him that I wanted everything that He had planned for me and that I didn't want to get to heaven one day to find out that He had more that I didn't know about. God put such a hunger in my heart that I wanted everyone to know about receiving Jesus and about His power to deliver us from demons.

About a month after going through deliverance, Dennis and I heard about some classes at our Lutheran Church called the "baptism of the Holy Spirit." We didn't know what it was, but felt led to go and find out. For two Sunday afternoons we went to a class at the church to hear them teach from the Bible about the power available to Christians through the baptism of the Holy Spirit. We had never heard anything about this at all, but we were open to it because it was in the Bible. We found out that the enemy tries to keep people away from this experience. Of course he fights people to try to stop them from receiving Jesus, but his number one fight is to keep the church away from the power of God that's available to every believer. Satan fills Christians with fear to keep them from this wonderful gift that is available to us. After all, if he can prevent the church from walking in power, this alone will keep many people from ever wanting to become a Christian.

After the second Sunday of this class, they prayed with each one of us individually and laid hands on us to receive the baptism of the Holy Spirit. They told us that we could open our mouths and speak in our heavenly language. Dennis went first and started to speak in this heavenly language called "tongues."

Now it was my turn. I knew that the Bible said that this is for today and that this power is available to every believer, but Cherí's pastor who prayed for my deliverance had said that speaking in tongues was of the devil. So who should I believe? This pastor, my pastor, or the Bible? Since all these people saw the Bible differently, who was I to believe? After all, this church hadn't even told me about deliverance, but Cherí's pastor prayed for me, and now I was free. This left me with lots of questions. I decided that if God wanted to give me this free gift, then He would; and if He didn't, then it wasn't His will for me. I had hands laid on me and nothing happened. I didn't feel anything. All I heard was a couple of people praying in a strange language. After a while, when still nothing was happening, I resolved to believe that it just wasn't something He wanted to give to me.

I was sad because Dennis got it and I didn't. God had already done so much for me, so maybe He didn't want to give me anymore. *Oh well*, I thought. I got my deliverance and I loved my parents. That in itself was the most amazing miracle I had ever seen. In my book, it ranked with God parting the Red Sea.

You Shall Lay Hands on the Sick

Another month passed, and we found out that Dennis' father, Norm, had been diagnosed with colon cancer. It had spread to his liver, and he was told that he probably only had six months to live. I really loved Norm. He was a kind father who had love in his eyes — something I'd never seen in my life. I would have done anything to see him healed.

I was a financial planner at the time, and one of the guys I worked with told me about Pastor Herb Mjorud from our Lutheran church who had been healed from cancer. He told me that Herb prayed for people, and they were healed too. I said, "God doesn't heal people, that was only in the Bible!" But he assured me that God *was* still healing the sick. I got so excited! I called the church and asked to see the pastor right away, thinking that just maybe Norm could be healed.

Herb and his wife, Thelma, were glad to meet with me imme-diately in their home, where they ministered to people during the week. I was surprised when I met them; they were in their 80s and still doing the work of the Lord. They weren't weird at all. In fact, they were the sweetest elderly couple I'd ever met. Herb told me his personal testimony of how he had been attacked by cancer many times but the Lord healed him every time. He also shared many stories about the miracles of healing he'd seen as he prayed for people. One of them was the story of a man in another country who was blind and only had white in his eyes. As Herb laid his hands upon this man and prayed, he saw God form color in his eyes. The man could see instantly.

Herb taught me about the full gospel of the kingdom and that Jesus paid the price so that we could be healed as well as delivered and saved from our sins. He also explained God's plan for every believer to be filled with His Holy Spirit and to be able to heal the sick. In Mark 16, Jesus told His followers that in His name they would cast out demons; they would speak with new tongues; and they would lay hands on the sick, and they would recover.

You see, I knew demons were real and that they could be cast out. I heard that we could speak in tongues, though I still hadn't received that gift. But I had never heard that we could lay hands on the sick and they would recover.

"Are you kidding?" I said. "If that's true, I'd quit my job tomorrow and go clean out the hospitals." And I was serious! I knew this was my destiny. I now had a commission from Jesus Himself. I was to cast out demons, I would speak in tongues, and I would lay hands on the sick and they would get healed. To say I was excited was a major understatement. I couldn't stand to see people sick or in pain, and now I could do something to help them. I didn't even think of myself being in pain from my car accident. I was thinking of Norm and how Jesus paid the price so he could be healed and not die.

I told Herb that I had just been delivered from a lot of demonic spirits and oppression. When he asked if I had received the baptism of the Holy Spirit, I told him that I went to the class but hadn't spoken in tongues.

"Angela did you ask to receive the baptism of the Holy Spirit?" he asked.

"Yes, I did." I said.

"Then you have been baptized in the Holy Spirit. The manifestation of the gift of tongues just isn't evident yet." He said that just as Jesus came into my heart when I asked Him to, the Holy Spirit baptized me when I asked Him to. It didn't matter what I felt or whether I had spoken in tongues. This gift is received by faith. Herb went on to tell me that three spirits travel together: fear, doubt, and unbelief. These spirits work to keep Christians from receiving the power of God and the gift of heavenly languages (tongues) through the baptism of the Holy Spirit. I told him that I'd questioned it because Cherí's pastor said speaking in tongues was of the devil. He again reminded me of the passages in the Bible regarding this and that the enemy didn't want me to have this gift

Well, friends, let me tell you—that stinking devil had stolen 27 years of my life, and I wasn't about to let him have another minute! "Okay," I said, "I'm ready to receive this gift."

Herb rebuked the spirits of fear, doubt, and unbelief and asked me to open my mouth and speak in tongues as he and Thelma did the same. He explained that it wouldn't be my mind but my spirit praying, so I needed to open my mouth and give it some sound. The most wonderful thing happened. As I opened my mouth and started making sounds, words came out that I had never heard in my life. It was so different and a little strange, but I had the peace of God, so I wasn't afraid. It was so beautiful though. I knew that I wasn't making up the words. Herb interpreted my new prayer language—I had prayed a prayer of healing for Norm.

I started taking many of my friends to Herb and Thelma's house to be healed, delivered, and filled with the baptism of the Holy Spirit. I wanted everyone to know that Jesus not only saves but delivers us, fills us with His Spirit, and heals us from even terminal diseases. The first person I took there was Leslie, a Christian who had multiple sclerosis. She had lost vision in one of her eyes and needed a miracle. When Herb and Thelma prayed for her, I sensed the awesome presence of God and saw Jesus standing there. That evening her eyesight was completely restored and she could see. The doctors were later amazed because there were still holes in her optic nerves, yet she could see. I could go on and tell you of all the miracles I saw over at Herb and Thelma's house but that alone would take a book. Seeing miracles makes life so amazing and exciting. And you can do them too!

School of Deliverance

I was so excited about what God was doing that I thought about going to school to be a pastor, but decided instead to take a class on deliverance. Since I had gotten free from demonic oppression, I was completely different. I had almost all new friends and a new outlook on life. I quit hanging out with my old friends who went to the bars—they didn't want what I had, and I certainly didn't want to waste anymore of my life on things that didn't matter for eternity. Plus I knew that I couldn't re-open the door to the enemy with alcohol abuse. My heart was burning to tell people about Jesus and to cast out demons. I wanted everyone to experience the kind of freedom and joy that I had.

Physical Healing

Thank God that He didn't stop the work He was doing in my life and my body. A few months after meeting Herb and Thelma, I was telling Sue, a friend from church, about my back hurting. As I've mentioned, I was in a car accident when I was 17. Now at 27, I'd been walking around holding my back like a pregnant woman for the past 10 years because of the intense pain. I also was in extreme pain in my neck from whiplash. (Duh! I could have had Herb and Thelma pray for me, but I was only thinking that God would heal terminal illnesses or severe cases like blindness.)

Sue told me about some "healing revival" meetings at Church of the Resurrection that were going on every night. Sue was a nurse who had been having some problems with her eyes and was healed at one of the meetings. *If God heals people from cancer and opens blind eyes,* I thought to myself, *He can surely heal my neck and back.*

So Dennis and I decided to go to one of the meetings at this church. We had never experienced such joy in a church service or seen anything quite like this before. In our church, occasionally someone would hold their hands out in front of themselves, and a couple of people may even elevate them slightly. But I had no grid for what I was experiencing. People were dancing, shaking tambourines, and waving flags around! They were so excited. Then when the minister, Doug Stanton, preached, he would walk around and call out specific health conditions that God wanted to heal, and people would go forward for prayer. He'd lay hands on them, and they would fall down while being touched by the power of God. We had never seen or heard of this before. It was quite strange to us. But we felt God's peace and love, so we continued to go to the meetings.

After we had been to several meetings, one night Doug said God wanted to heal a young woman who had severe back and neck injuries from a car accident. I got so excited. This could be my night!

But then I thought it certainly couldn't be me—there were plenty of other young women there. Any of them could have been in a car accident too. I looked around, but no one else was responding. *Could this be me, Lord?* I asked. *Do you want to heal me tonight?* I felt a "Yes" in my spirit and got up to go forward.

If you've never done this when you were new to the things of the Spirit, it's kind of scary. I didn't know what was going to happen to me. And what would happen if I fell down? Would someone be there to catch me, or would I fall and hurt my back even worse? But as I went to the front, I saw a man there to catch me if I fell. And as Doug prayed, I did fall down. He didn't even push me either. This was for real! When I got up all the pain in my back was gone. When I returned to my seat, I looked down at my Bible for a long time. I was so excited; for ten years I hadn't been able to look down for more than a minute or two without pain in my neck, but this time there was *no pain!* This truly was a miracle! My neck was healed. God really loved me—I finally believed it because this healing was a tangible expression of His love for me.

Revival Days

Now that I had been saved, delivered, baptized in the Holy Spirit, and healed, I had a lot to tell people about. Everywhere I went, I told my testimony of how God touched my life. Some received it, and some didn't.

I still hadn't read the Bible, but in these revival meetings, I learned that God heals the sick and that He wants to use normal Christians to do the same miraculous works that Jesus did. Being a normal Christian with a desire to see people healed, I attempted to walk on the water—not literally, but by stepping out and praying for the sick. And guess what: God showed up. I saw so many miracles! Why? Because He responded to my childlike faith.

It had been only five months from the time I got saved when I started going to revival meetings. As with everything that I did, I told Cherí. I told her everything but the part about the baptism of the Holy Spirit classes and my newfound language because I knew she believed, as did her pastor, that these gifts were just for the early church. But when I started going to these meetings and got healed, I called her to tell her about it.

Cherí mailed me a letter telling me how this wasn't of God and that I had gotten involved with a cult. All I knew to tell her was that the fruit of this ministry was good and that I didn't understand how something so good where people were getting healed and filled with God's love could be bad—especially since it was in the Bible. I told her of all the things that we'd been seeing, of people being healed and marriages being restored. I had been healed and had experienced the tangible presence of God for myself.

Cherí loved me and was trying to protect me. After all, I was a baby Christian. She was just trying to help so that I wouldn't get involved in a cult. But at this point, she needed to look to the Word of God and not at what religion was telling her. Her pastor was also just trying to protect his flock from the enemy. Since some of these things I'm telling you may seem a little weird, this is a common reaction. But hold on—I'll show you where all this is in the Bible, just keep reading. You can do what I did and tell God that you want the whole truth. Be like the Bereans and search the Word of God for yourself (Acts 17:10-11). It's a treasure chest full of gold and silver, and all of God's promises are for you! He's not like us; He doesn't show favoritism. He loves us all the same and has abundance for each one of us!

Testimonies are so powerful. You can debate with people over scripture about what you believe, but people interpret the Bible in many different ways. They can't misinterpret your testimony, however—especially if they know you personally. I told Cherí that I was once in bondage, but now I was free. And she believed that because she had experienced it with me. She and I had both received deliverance. But what I was telling her was something she had never heard before. I invited her to come and see for herself, but I couldn't stop going to these meetings. Our friendship ended over this and it really grieved me.

Cherí was pregnant, and I was so sad that I couldn't be a part of her life during that season. But God continued to burn a passion deeper than anything else in my heart for Him and for truth. I just had to press into Him, even if it meant losing my best friend.

After my back and neck got healed, I went to visit Herb and Thelma again and told them about the meetings. They said that they knew pastors Jim and Ramona Rickard and encouraged me to continue to go. I told them about how I got healed and hadn't even considered asking them to pray for me. I explained that I'd thought God just healed terminal and impossible cases. I told them I had a little discomfort in my back, and they offered to pray for me. They had me sit in a chair and saw that my legs were different lengths. As they prayed, one of my legs lengthened and all the discomfort left. Then they checked my arms, and one of my arms grew out right in front of me. I had never seen anything like that before.

Someone on the outside looking in might say my healing for my back and neck or Leslie's blind eye being healed weren't true because a person could be lying. But to actually see my leg and arm grow out? That's visible. I actually saw it happen. Only God could have done that! I found I was falling more in love with Him each day as I saw these tangible expressions of His great love for me.

I went to work the next day and thought I'd put this into action. André, my financial planning partner, had just been to Toronto and was filled with the Holy Spirit. We had great prayer sessions and so enjoyed talking about the Lord and His power. I told André what happened to my arm and leg, and he said he had some back pain. I prayed for him, and right there in his office in downtown Minneapolis, God grew out his leg quite a bit and healed him. It was so cool! Wow—God could use me just like He used Herb and Thelma! It was true: God doesn't show favoritism (Acts 10:34 NIV).

I was talking with my neighbor that night, and she too had a bad back. Seeing that one of her legs was quite a bit shorter, I commanded her leg to come out. It did, and she was healed. This one was even more amazing—one of her legs was at least an inch shorter than the other, and I saw it grow out very quickly. This has become very common since then; I pray for people with back or neck problems, and they are almost always healed instantly. If there's an imbalance in the spine, I see arms and legs grow out to be equal lengths. Sometimes I haven't even needed to pray; God knows what I'm going to ask, and He does it before I even say anything. Miracles like this would make even the strongest atheist a believer! That's why each of us need to take our place.

Another Kind of Miracle

Over the next few months, I started praying for people everywhere I went and saw many amazing miracles. As I've mentioned, Cherí and I weren't talking anymore. I heard that she had her baby, and I was so sad that I couldn't see her and rejoice with her over her new gift from God. But God was about to change that.

An Evangelist from Florida, June McKinney came to the revival meetings, which were still going on daily. She told some amazing stories of what the Lord was doing through her. She would go into villages in Africa, and virtually the whole village would be healed. A person died on a plane once, and as she prayed, the person came back to life. I had read the scripture that we were to heal the sick and raise the dead, but this was the first time I'd heard of anyone other than Jesus raising the dead.

I pulled June aside after this meeting. "If God can use a woman, then He can use me," I said. "What can I do to see more miracles in my life?" She asked if I had my heavenly prayer language. I told her that I did. She then told me to start praying in tongues for an hour each day for 30 days, and that I would start seeing more miracles.

I took that challenge to heart. I asked the Lord to wake me up early every day so I could get up and pray. Somewhat to my surprise, that's exactly what He did. I knew I couldn't do this on my own because I was a late riser and didn't like to get up early. But each day, He woke me up. I would go walking, praying in tongues as I walked. Then one day as I was praying, I heard God say, "Angela, pray for Cherí!" I argued a bit with Him—she was wrong, and I didn't want to pray for her. But I gave in, and within a few days I received a letter from her telling me about her baby and how she would like to see me. She acted as if nothing had been wrong between us. I was so excited. It really had been God who told me to pray for her. This was a miracle! I called her up and scheduled a time to go and see her and her new baby, Hannah.

During our visit, Cherí told me that Hannah had a stomach disorder and would need surgery because the food wasn't getting into her stomach. Apparently Cherí also had this condition when she was a baby. As I walked into the kitchen to see little Hannah, I heard the Lord speak: "Angela, if you pray for Hannah, I'll heal her."

This was a test—a *major* test! Would I ask Cherí if I could pray for Hannah and risk losing her friendship again? Being with Cherí was already a miracle in itself. And since this was God speaking, what did I have to lose? Apparently, this is why the Lord hooked me back up with Cherí anyway. But my mind was worried. What would happen if I prayed and nothing happened? She then would have ammunition against me to tell me how wrong I was and that God didn't really heal people. What would I do?

I knew exactly what to do. I would do just as God said and pray for Hannah. I have found in the walk of faith that you need to just step out and try to walk on water right away. If you don't, you won't. So when God speaks, or when you feel Holy Spirit giving you faith for a miracle, you need to do it quickly and not think about it. If you think about it, you won't do it because your human reasoning will always cause you to sink!

So without thinking about it anymore, I quickly said, "Cherí, God just told me that if I pray for Hannah, He will heal her." She said, "Okay." But now that she said I could pray, *how* would I pray? I didn't know anything about this condition. Should I pray in tongues? *No*, I thought, *that will freak her out*. So I laid my hands on Hannah and prayed a simple prayer commanding her stomach to be healed in the name of Jesus. At this point, I don't think it mattered how I prayed. God wanted to heal Hannah, and He wanted Cherí to believe in His supernatural healing power. You know, of course, how this story ended. Hannah quit throwing up, and when Cherí took her to the doctor, they found out that she was healed. Go Jesus! Needless to say, this made Cherí a believing believer.

The Tests and the Wedding

When I had first met Herb and Thelma they recommended that I get a book by Francis McNutt on healing for Den's dad. Francis had been a Catholic priest and had a healing ministry. I got the book and read it. Since Francis had been a Catholic priest I felt that Norm *may* be open to reading it. This was very hard and scary for me. Den's family members were very devoted Catholics and were concerned that we were now in a cult. But since I had been healed, I wanted to see Norm healed too. So I chose to step out in faith and gave him the book.

About six months had passed since Norm was first diagnosed with cancer. By this time, it had spread to his liver. He was turning yellow and going downhill fast. Den's older brother was getting married, and his dad was just glad that he was still alive to be there for this special occasion.

The night of the wedding, I had a dream that I prayed for Norm and he was healed. It felt very real. When I got up in the morning, I called Herb to find out how to pray for someone to be healed from cancer. I had only been saved for about eight months and had seen quite a few miracles. But cancer? I didn't even know how to begin. And with Den's dad? Help, Lord! Although Norm really loved me I was afraid to even bring up the subject since some of his family members didn't agree with our beliefs. This would be another test, and I really wasn't feeling up to this one. At that point, this was one of the hardest things I'd ever had to do. But I believed that God had given me this dream, so I needed to be obedient.

We went to the hotel to meet Den's parents and were then going to go to brunch. Norm was weak and in a wheelchair. My heart was pounding so hard that I felt like a time bomb was about to go off—I remember it like it was yesterday. I kept praying for courage and was looking for the perfect opportunity to pray for him, but my chances were running out. We were getting ready to leave. It was either now or never! Stumbling for words, I said, "Norm could I pray for you?" He said I could, so I prayed a little prayer for him commanding the cancer to die and releasing the life of Jesus into his body.

Whew! That was done. I felt a release in my spirit. I had passed this test—thank you, Jesus! The thoughts went racing through my head. What if Norm didn't get healed? But what if he did? I decided to put my trust in God and to thank Him for healing Norm. Then off to brunch we went.

Norm had been unable to eat much, but at breakfast he had a hearty appetite and ate a lot of food. They said that he ate much more than he had been able to for quite some time. He even looked better. He had more energy, and it seemed that new life had entered him just like I had prayed.

I had encouraged Den's dad to continue to read the Word of God. Norm was certainly better that day, and everyone saw it. Even though some may have felt it was just that he was happy to see his son married now.

What I have found over the years is that the enemy comes right away to put the same symptoms on us so that we doubt that God did anything to heal us. But it didn't matter what anyone thought—I had been obedient to God. And what if I had never prayed? I would never have known whether he would have received his healing. I would have kicked myself forever wondering what would have happened, so I am glad that I prayed.

Norm did feel better over the next week or so, but then he got worse. In a couple of months, he left the earth and went on to his heavenly inheritance. I was so grieved! I loved him like a father, and now he was gone. The lies of the enemy came into my mind to try to stop me from praying for people, but God strengthened me with His Word. I learned that I had to rest my faith on His Word alone, not on my experience. I needed to continue to do as He said and to lay my hands on the sick and trust Him to heal them. After all, He said that if we would do our part, they would recover (Mark 16:17-18).

Party at Cherí's

Shortly after this experience, Cherí called to say she'd been doing a Bible study on the Holy Spirit and that she knew God had more for her. She asked me to come pray for her to receive the baptism of the Holy Spirit. Another miracle, right before my eyes! So I went to pray with her, and she received this wonderful gift. She then invited me to come over to tell some of her friends about it and to pray for them as well. Wow—my own little revival meeting at Cherí's. God most certainly was a miracle worker! Who would have thought this would ever happen? Months earlier she thought I had been in a cult.

I took my friend Kris with me over to Cherí's, where about six of her friends were gathered. I shared my testimony about what the Lord did for me, and I prayed for the girls to receive the baptism of the Spirit. They all began to speak in tongues, and one of her friends fell out in the Spirit onto the couch. Cherí's husband was walking through the living room and probably thought we were crazy. I prayed for him too, and one of his limbs lengthened and he was healed. Experiencing a miracle like that for himself made him no longer a skeptic; he too was a believing believer. What a glorious day! God certainly was weaving things together.

Salvation for All

After only being saved a year or so, I asked June McKinney if she had ever asked God to show her hell or at least to hear the cries of those who are there. (Only those who have a passion for souls would understand this.) June was one evangelist who I knew would understand my heart. You see, I used to cry out to God to show me hell so I would stop at nothing to make sure that every person around me escaped the fires of hell. June told me that she understood and that she too had asked him, but after she started hearing their cries, she asked God to stop it. She then told me that I should read *Divine Revelation of Hell* by Mary K. Baxter, in which the author tells how Jesus had taken her into hell so she could tell people about the reality of it.

Friends, let's make our lives count for all eternity. There are more than four billion people who right now are on their way to hell. If we don't reach out to them with God's love, they will be forever separated from God, His love, and His abundance. Some people think that if and when they go to hell, they will be partying with their friends. But this is not so; they will be all alone, and instead of partying, they will be tormented day and night forever and forever. Now if that doesn't make you want to be full of God's light and love, I don't know what will.

I could go on and on to tell you about the things the Lord has done in my life, but that alone would take a whole book. My testimony is very powerful, and so is yours! Go out and share your testimony everywhere you go and see the Lord duplicate miracles in the lives of those around you. Believe it or not, unbelievers are usually the easiest to pray for. As you continue to step out and share the testimony of the things the Lord has done in you and through you, even unbelieving believers will believe. That is Christians that don't believe in the fullness of the kingdom of God that is available here on earth. So ask yourself what God has done for you that you could share with others. Someone out there, actually *a lot* of someones out there, need what you have.

Matthew 10:8 tells us to heal the sick, cleanse the lepers, raise the dead, and cast out demons. Freely you have received, freely give. So take inventory of what you have freely received and give it to anyone who comes your way. It's not about talking people into what you have, but telling your testimony of what God has done for you and then freely giving it to them. As Paul wrote, he came not in persuasive words, but in demonstration of the power of God (1 Corinthians 2:4).

To this day, I believe one of the reasons God is using me to help raise up the saints to do the work of the ministry is because I said "yes" and continue to do so. When the tests come, I'm willing to go for it with all my heart. I hadn't even read the Bible when I started praying for the sick. I just learned a couple of healing scriptures, and God used my raw faith to heal the sick and those in pain. It wasn't *what* I knew, but *who* I knew.

By reading this book, you will know much more than I did. So I expect you to step out in boldness, by taking your place and step into a life of miracles!

CHAPTER 2: The Kingdom of God

I once heard a minister share a story about a poor man who lived his life scraping along just to pay his bills. No matter what he attempted, it seemed he could never get ahead. One day he received notification that a distant relative had died and left him an exquisite mansion. Obviously, this man was extremely elated. Finally something had gone right for him. Could something this good really be true, or was he dreaming?

Upon receiving the deed and keys to the mansion, he proceeded to his new home. As he arrived, he was struck with awe and amazement at its incredible size and magnificence. With great excitement, he inserted the key and opened the massive double oak doors stepping into the most amazing and beautiful foyer he had ever seen.

For a moment the man wondered if it wasn't him who had died and gone to heaven. How could it be that someone he had never met would leave him all this? With joy in his heart and a smile upon his face, he walked out and returned to his meager dwelling. All week long, he lived his life barely getting by while dreaming of his new mansion. He told his friends about it, yet each day he returned to his same old home.

One week later, this excited young man returned to his mansion and stepped into the foyer again. He was in awe of its beauty and was totally amazed that it actually belonged to him. He couldn't believe how fortunate he was to have it. As he stood there, he mentally thanked this relative for this gift. Yet he still didn't go beyond the foyer to enjoy his new possession. After a short time, he returned to his old home and to his ordinary life.

Unfortunately, because he didn't venture past the foyer, he missed the envelope his relative left in one of the other rooms. Inside this envelope were instructions to access the safe in the office. In the safe were the keys to various lockboxes where all the valuables were stored, including the documents showing where all his other properties and investments were located. But these weekly visits to the mansion continued month after month until the man developed a pattern of accessing only the limited benefits of his new property.

Now we all understand this story is not real. We couldn't imagine anyone actually being that foolish, not entering in to enjoy everything they had inherited. Yet we find this happens week after week in churches throughout the body of Christ. Many of our brothers and sisters only focus on the salvation message, but this is just the entrance to the kingdom of God. We need to move beyond teaching about the entrance and move into enjoying the fruit of the kingdom of God on the earth.

Thankfully, there's more to the kingdom than the door. Jesus came preaching the gospel of the kingdom of heaven—the good news of the dominion of God's supernatural realm. Inside the kingdom, God has much more for us than we could ever imagine. There's provision, protection, peace, joy, power, and demonstration. We need to venture deeper into our Father's house and seek what He has placed there for us. It's much more than just entering in; He fully expects us to come to the banquet table and eat all of His delicacies.

What Is the Kingdom of God?

The kingdom of God—the divine rule in human hearts, lives, and situations—was a prominent theme in Jesus' teaching. Jesus demonstrated and taught the kingdom through the Spirit's power (Luke 4:18-19), and He transferred that power and responsibility to His disciples by baptizing them in the Holy Spirit.

Bill Johnson wrote one of the best books I have ever read on this subject: *When Heaven Invades Earth*. The kingdom is more than a good method or a great message. It consists not of eloquent words but is a demonstration of the power of God so that we don't trust in our own wisdom but in His power (1 Corinthians 2:4-5). Jesus was focused on one thing: announcing and establishing the kingdom of God on earth. He announced it with His preaching, teaching, and healing, and He established it through His death and resurrection. Jesus desires that we not only step into the kingdom when we receive Him, but that we come on in and enjoy all of the benefits He provided for us.

In the Gospels and Acts, there are at least 20 direct references to preaching "the gospel of the kingdom" from John the Baptist (Matthew 3:1-2), throughout Jesus' ministry (Mark 1:14-15), in the disciples' ministry under Jesus (Luke 9:1-2), and throughout Acts. Jesus prophesied that this same message would be taken to the ends of the earth (Matthew 24:14), commissioning His disciples for that task and promising the Holy Spirit's power (Mark 16:15-18; Acts 1:3-8). It's clear that the early church proclaimed the same message Jesus preached, that is, "the gospel of the kingdom of God" (Acts 8:12; 19:8; 20:25; 28:23, 30, 31). They also experienced the same confirming evidences that were present in His ministry.

There is only one gospel. Jesus preached it, transmitted it to His disciples, and committed it to His church. Paul warned against ever receiving any other gospel. "Any other" may be either a message of outright error or a nominally Christian but diluted message devoid of power. Jude 3 urges us always to contend for the original, "the faith which was once for all delivered to the saints." We are to hold to the full "gospel of the kingdom" and expect the Lord to confirm that "word" with the signs He promised (Mark 16:15-18).

In order to understand what God has given us regarding His kingdom, let's start at the beginning. In Genesis 1:22, we see that when God created the sea creatures, birds, and land animals, He blessed them, saying, "Be fruitful and multiply." When He created human beings, however, He added, "Fill the earth and subdue it; have dominion over the fish of the sea, over the birds of the air, and over every living thing that moves on the earth" (Genesis 1:26-28).

He not only wanted us to be fruitful and multiply, but He commanded His children to subdue and have dominion over the earth. What does it mean to subdue and have dominion?

Subdue: to conquer and bring into subjection
Dominion: to have rule, control, and domination

So quite simply, we are to conquer by bringing everything into subjection, and we are to dominate with God's rulership.

We were born to dominate planet earth and everything in it. We are of the royal bloodline, and as princes and princesses, we are in charge in the kingdom. This was and still is God's plan for His children, for He gave earth to us to enjoy. Even though Adam and Eve's sin caused them to lose the keys of the kingdom to the devil, our awesome, loving Father told them He would provide a Redeemer. When Jesus came, He brought us back into right relationship with our heavenly Father again. Our sins, sicknesses, and poverty were taken by Jesus. He redeemed us from the curse (Galatians 3:13) so we can be free—not just when we get to heaven one day, but today. He then went to hell and stomped on the devil's head and took away the keys from Him. When we receive Jesus and the abundant life that He provided for us, we receive all authority and all power over all the power of the enemy.

Jesus told Peter that He would build His church and that the gates of hell would not prevail against it. He then told Peter that He was going to give him the keys of the kingdom of heaven, and whatever he bound on earth would be bound in heaven, and whatever he loosed on earth would be loosed in heaven (Matthew 16:18-19). This means, thank God, that we aren't stuck in the kingdom of darkness under the devil's dominion anymore. We've been redeemed, and now we're in control again. Saints, it's time that we "take our place" by subduing the earth and exercising dominion again!

Jesus came to destroy not only the devil but all his works (1 John 3:8). When Jesus was here, He cast out demons and reversed the work of the devil by healing everyone who came to Him, even raising the dead. Everywhere He went, He told people to repent because the kingdom of God was at hand (Matthew 4:17). The Greek word for repent here is *metanoeo*, which means to change one's mind. He was saying, "Please, change the way you're thinking because the kingdom of God is here. It is within arm's reach, and if you don't change your mind, you're going to miss it!"

The religious leaders were looking at the physical world with their natural eyes. They had a different expectation of their Messiah, therefore they misinterpreted what He would look like. For instance, they thought He would overthrow the Roman government when He set up His kingdom on the earth. We know that He did come the first time to set up His earthly kingdom, but it was a spiritual kingdom. Even though you can't see the kingdom of God, you can see the effects of the kingdom. Those who believed the gospel were healed and made whole. But those who didn't believe were not.

Many of you too have been looking in the physical realm to see the kingdom of God, and you've missed it. But you don't have to keep missing out. As you continue to read this book, you will learn how to take your place as a son or daughter—a royal prince or princess—and how to rule in the earth. Ask the Lord to reveal *His* truth to you.

The kingdom of God is within us because Holy Spirit now lives inside of us. It's His power that flows out of us to heal the sick and do the works of the kingdom. It has always been God's plan for His children, who were made in His image and in His likeness, to rule. Jesus came to show His disciples what it means to operate with all authority and dominion in the kingdom of God. Because He came as a man like them, they would be able to do the works He did. Now we can too.

Preach the Gospel of the Kingdom

Jesus gave his followers a clear assignment:

"He said to them, 'Go into all the world and preach the gospel to every creature. He who believes and is baptized will be saved; but he who does not believe will be condemned. And these signs will follow those who believe: In My name they will cast out demons; they will speak with new tongues; they will take up serpents; and if they drink anything deadly, it will by no means hurt them; they will lay hands on the sick, and they will recover.' So then, after the Lord had spoken to them, He was received up into heaven, and sat down at the right hand of God" (Mark 16:15-19).

We see that Jesus said we are to share the gospel, but what gospel are we to share? This is where most of us in the body of

Christ have dropped the ball. If we look closely, we see that Jesus preached the gospel of the kingdom and told His disciples to do the same. According to this scripture, if we preach the gospel the sign of healing the sick will follow. Jesus did not just preach the gospel of salvation to merely get people into the kingdom, though in the church today this is often the main focus. We must understand that the gospel Jesus and His disciples preached was the full gospel. We must preach the gospel of the kingdom, not just the gospel of salvation. The gospel of salvation is wonderful, but the sacrifice of Jesus' life was for much more than just getting you to heaven one day when you die. What kind of loving God would He be to give us a ticket to heaven one day, but leave us here in the meantime to live a life of hell upon the earth?

Jesus taught extensively about the kingdom of God. Even after His resurrection, He appeared to His disciples over a period of 40 days and spoke about the kingdom (Acts 1:1-3). This message must have been pretty important if He spent His last days on the earth preaching it. Jesus taught his disciples how to live in the kingdom of God while they were here on earth. This is something we are missing in our churches today. When we receive this revelation and start to walk in it, we will also begin to see the kingdom at work in the earth, even in our own lives.

If you are telling people about the Lord but aren't seeing signs and wonders, ask yourself this question: What gospel am I preaching? If you will preach the gospel of the kingdom, the signs of healing the sick and casting out demons will accompany it. Start telling people that God loves them and that Jesus came to give back to them everything they have lost. Tell them a testimony of how God met your need or the need of someone you know.

If this is new for you, then you just need to choose what you're going to believe. Will you believe what you've experienced, what you've been taught, or what the Word of God says? We need to stop basing our beliefs on what we see with our natural eyes or on what others have told us and allow the Word of God to change the way we think.

Renew Your Mind

Bill Johnson teaches that we must have our minds renewed if we want to be used to release the kingdom of God on the earth. Romans 12:2 says that we must not think as those in the world think, but we need to be transformed by having our minds renewed. Then we will be able to prove what is the good, acceptable, and perfect will of God.

To "renew" is "to renovate," meaning to restore or bring back to an original state. We are not to accept the pattern of the world, whose god is the devil (2 Corinthians 4:4). We are to be transformed by having a renewed mind. We should be committed to seeing the Word of God and His kingdom displayed here and now!

"Prove" means to test and practice in everyday life that God's will for us is good, acceptable and perfect. Do you practice God's will every day? If not, don't feel condemnation over it, but recognize the challenge God is putting before us. It's always good to ask yourself, "What did Jesus do?" He walked around and loved everyone everywhere He went. He came to earth on a mission in order to represent our Heavenly Father to us. Then He met people's needs as they came to Him. Some needed to be healed or to have a demon cast out, others needed a word of knowledge, and some just needed to be loved. No matter where you go, you can be a channel of God's love to people, and Holy Spirit will show you what each person needs. All of His gifts will flow through you so that His kingdom will manifest on the earth.

Has it ever occurred to you that one of your jobs on earth is to prove the will of God and reveal His kingdom? Our job is to show other people what He is like by destroying the works of the devil and bringing forth His kingdom in their midst. Most people don't really know what God is like, or that His power is available today to do miracles, signs, and wonders. Even though the Bible says God is love, many don't know Him as a truly loving, passionate, and kind God and Father. So it's our job as ambassadors of the kingdom to put His works on display. As we show people heaven on earth, we will be revealing the heart of our Heavenly Father towards them.

My quest for living in the kingdom all began when my friend Herb told me his testimony about what he had seen and been a part of. If you truly want to lead people to the Lord, I commend you for that. My hope is that you will learn how to do it more effectively by sharing the full gospel of the kingdom. I also hope you will see in this book that it's much easier to do than perhaps you thought because it's about Him doing the works through us.

You may mostly be around Christians who are already saved, and that's okay. Most Christians don't know the full gospel or that God heals people today. Don't judge them; just reach out in His love because they are His precious children. If they try to get into a debate with you, just drop it and love them.

Are you excited yet? You should be. God wants to use you because there's no one else in the world just like you. No one else can reach all the same people that you can reach for Him. He's calling you to engage in this romance of a lifetime and to run with Him through the pages of history as you help change your world through one act of random kindness at a time.

So if you are like me and you want to make a huge impact for the kingdom of God, don't wait any longer. A lot of times, we wait for something to happen on the outside, when actually everything you need has already been deposited on the inside of you. Remember, He lives in you, and your body is the temple of the Holy Spirit. When Daddy God looks at you, He sees you as perfect through the blood of Jesus. It's time to step out of the boat and attempt to walk on water! Keep your eyes on Jesus, and trust Him for the results. You aren't responsible for what happens, you're only responsible to be faithful with what He has given you. So let's get going on an adventure of a lifetime!

Arthritis Healed at Walmart

One day my children and I went to Walmart. My son, Israel, is my eagle eye and always tries to spot someone who needs to be healed. As we were getting some milk, Israel said, "Hey, Mom, look over there." I looked and saw an older couple; the wife was in a motorized cart. The compassion of Jesus welled up in me, and I felt drawn to her. Leaning into Holy Spirit, I listened to see what He would have me do. Israel was concerned because I wasn't moving toward them, and he was worried they would get away. But I explained to him that we needed to ask God if this was a divine appointment and if they would be open to this. Sad to say, some people aren't and can be rude. I felt that Holy Spirit was giving me a yes in my spirit, so I watched and waited for an opportunity to approach them. Remember it's best to step out in love and see what God will do. Then depending on how open they are, will determine how much of His love and power you can pour out into them. As I looked over toward her sweet little husband, I saw he was trying to reach something that was too high for him. So I walked over, greeted him, and asked him if I could help. He said, "Oh, yes, that would be great!" I reached up and grabbed the item for him and he was very appreciative. (I love elderly people. He was so cute—I really just wanted to hug him!) I started making small talk with him as we walked down the next aisle. His wife was waiting for him, and I smiled at her and said hello. I lingered in the aisle trying to pretend that I was looking for something else I needed as I waited for the next thing Holy Spirit would have me do.

I have to confess, I was a little embarrassed as we were in the beer and wine aisle of the store. I hoped no one I knew would see me. As I started talking with her she warmed up to me very quickly. I took the opportunity to ask her if she needed prayer. She told me that her husband's sister was sick with cancer and needed prayer. What I have learned is that most people don't think you will pray right there—but do it anyway! I asked for her sister-in-law's name and prayed right there for her. When I was done, I asked her why she was in the motorized cart. She said she had arthritis and that she had pain in her knee. So I asked her if I could pray for her too. She said, "Sure, I don't know why not."

I then introduced her to my secret weapons, Israel and my daughter, Moriah, and asked her if we could touch her as we prayed. I think having my children with me makes me look innocent and normal. (I am, but what I mean is that I don't seem as intimidating when I have my sweet little children with me!) So we laid our hands on her, rebuked the arthritis and all the pain, and commanded it to leave. Then we asked Holy Spirit to come and release His healing virtue into her knee. We declared that Jesus paid the price for her to be healed and commanded her body to receive healing in His name.

I then saw a picture of Peter getting out of the boat as he attempted to walk on water. I told her the picture I saw and encouraged her to try to walk. She got up and walked, and all the pain was gone. Go Jesus!

Daily Life

This was just one of the many ministry times that have happened as I go about my daily life as a Mom. This is what God wants all of us to do—to bring His kingdom into every situation no matter where we are. You can live a supernatural life naturally. In fact, moving in the supernatural realm and praying for people to be healed should be as routine as brushing our teeth. Healing, deliverance, and other signs and wonders are all part of our inheritance as Christians.

We are a people who can be led by Holy Spirit. He lives in us, so anywhere we go, He goes too. Another time we were at the mall and my eagle-eyed son said, "Look, Mom, let's get this lady. She's coming down the escalator." I looked, and sure enough, her husband was holding her crutches. But I remembered that I needed to ask Holy Spirit because He knows if these people would be open to this or not. I asked Him, and He said "No!" To confirm this, after they got off the escalator I smiled and said hello to them just to see how they would respond. They barely looked at me and off they went. Israel was extremely bummed out! He really wanted for us to pray for this lady, so I sat down and explained to him that Holy Spirit knows everything, and He alone knows if this couple would have been open or not. They weren't open and hardly even looked my way as I tried reaching out in God's love to them. Honestly, God doesn't want us to be rejected, but to be accepted. Since then, I've learned even more about how to press into Holy Spirit and ask Him if I am to pray for someone. This beats stepping out and being rejected.

So this is how I live my life. I reach out in love and give them what they are hungry for, never pushing things down their throat. As I mentioned, I used to tell everyone everything about Jesus whether they wanted to hear about it or not. Have you ever heard about how we shouldn't give what is holy to the dogs or cast our pearls before swine (Matthew 7:6)? If you start asking Him, you'll be surprised to find out that He will reveal things to help and protect you. Plus you'll be more fruitful in your attempts.

If you haven't noticed, I'm giving you examples of people who wanted prayer and were healed and those who wouldn't receive it. This way you'll know you will see both sides of this as you take your place by stepping into a life of miracles.

Hunger for the Impossible

God has put an insatiable hunger inside each of us to see the impossibilities of this world become possible. That's what kingdom life is all about. It's supernatural — releasing heaven into the earth. In order to do this, we must stop following our natural senses. We need to switch over into the spiritual realm and operate out of our spiritual senses. Because most Christians don't understand the spiritual kingdom and how it operates, the enemy works really hard to get us locked into what we see and hear in the natural. But God tells us to walk by faith and not by sight (2 Corinthians 5:7). We are to move by what He says, and not by what our senses tell us.

Deep down, we know there's so much more to life than what we can see with our physical eyes. Many people get involved with the New Age because they are looking for more power. I started thinking one day about how people who are involved in New Age beliefs often have a lot more spiritual encounters than most Christians. If the kingdom of darkness offers supernatural experiences, how much more should Christians be operating in the Spirit and having heavenly encounters!

This thought led me to start asking questions of Christians who had come out of the New Age movement. What they told me was that they know how to yield themselves to the spirit realm more than Christians do by using meditation and other methods. This is why they have spiritual encounters and even out-of-body experiences. When I asked the Lord why, He showed me it was because their God-given hunger for power had been unfulfilled in the church, so they turned to the kingdom of darkness for it.

Let's get in the game and start entering God's supernatural realm by connecting with Holy Spirit. King David knew how to do this and was known as a man after God's own heart. Maybe we can learn a thing or two from his life. He wrote in Psalms about how he meditated on God, on all His works and His Word. This is the essence of biblical meditation (Psalm 63:6; 143:5; 119:148). Notice that true biblical meditation is different than Eastern meditation. As believers, we don't just empty our minds, we fill them with God, His Word, and His works.

Bad teaching and disappointment have robbed many people of the reality of the supernatural realm. Christians see the New Agers and occultists operating in things of the spirit, and then when believers try to meditate or get into the Spirit, they get scared that a demon is going to jump on them. But we can't leave everything supernatural to the kingdom of darkness. We need to wake up. It's time we stand up and take our place in the spiritual kingdom of God and take back what is legally ours!

We live in a day when people are hungering for and stepping into their destiny in greater numbers, fulfilling the purpose of God for mankind on the earth. The body of Christ is beginning to fulfill the original plan of God to take her place. Won't you join us? I've heard it said that if Jesus' disciples had their choice, they would probably rather be alive today than any other time in history. Whether that's true or not, you and I were born for such a time as this, and we get to be in on the action.

To be effective in taking dominion in the kingdom, we must redefine what we consider to be "normal" Christianity so that it lines up with God's idea of normal. We should always measure ourselves with the Word of God and not those around us. Otherwise, we get into trouble and settle for less than what God promised. The problem is that many of us are led by our soul and our physical body. In actuality, however, we are spirits who live in a body and possess a soul. We should be led by the Holy Spirit through our human spirit, and our soul and body should follow.

The Lord's Prayer

Most Christians know the Lord's Prayer. But let's take a closer look to see what Jesus was *really* trying to teach us. We are to pray and release His kingdom and His will to be done here on earth as it is in heaven. Many people don't understand His kingdom or His will. They pray for the sick with, "If it's your will, Lord, please heal Bob." However, when we pray this way, we're saying we don't know what God's will is and are leaving it up to Him to do what He wants. Remember, He put us in charge, and we must use our authority and command sickness to go and release the power of God so the life of heaven will touch those who are sick.

Are you still questioning what His will is? If so, ask yourself this question: What things are free to operate in heaven? That's what should be free to operate here on earth. In heaven there is joy, peace, wisdom, health, wholeness, and all the other good promises we read about in the Bible. What doesn't fit into His will? Well, whatever isn't allowed in heaven—sickness, disease, bondage, and sin, for example—shouldn't be allowed here either.

Friends, this is the kingdom Jesus transferred to us. This is our assignment on the earth and must become our focus. As ambassadors of the kingdom, we are to destroy the works of the devil. When we make God's will our primary understanding and do it, everything else will fall into place.

Jesus said it over and over again: we are to preach the gospel of the kingdom. When we make this our life mission, people get delivered and filled with the joy of the Lord. Bodies get healed, bondage and oppression lift from people's minds, and the works of the enemy are destroyed. Businesses get prosperous, marriages get restored, saints from different churches become unified, and cities get transformed because the kingdom of God is in operation. This is what we see happening in the Healing Rooms and many other places in the body of Christ when we come together in unity to lift Jesus up.

Cities Transformed

When we become carriers of the kingdom, our cities will truly be transformed. I love the story that Cal Pierce tells about a young woman who had been healed of HIV in the Healing Rooms in Spokane. She had been on drugs for 20 years, and after she was healed, she started bringing women in off the streets and working with them. She had a vision to take Christmas baskets to some lady strippers at a nightclub in Spokane, and then later took them roses for Valentine's Day. God used this to soften the heart of the bar owner, who later confessed to her that he had once been a pastor. He told her that when his wife died, he blamed God and fell away. He also told her that he knew God would one day come and get him.

This woman convinced the pastor-turned-bar-owner to use the bar for an Easter service one year, and they fed the homeless, prostitutes, and anyone else who came in that day. Some of the ladies who had been addicted to drugs got up and gave testimonies of how God delivered them. Some people on the streets threw their crack pipes down and said they were done with drugs. A mighty steel punch from heaven went into the darkest part of the city and lit it up. The bar owner said that he never had so many people in his bar and wanted to know if they could do it again the next year. Shortly afterward, the Healing Rooms started receiving a monthly check from this man.

Teen Challenge and many other ministries, including a women's shelter, moved onto the strip after this. The bars began to close as the light of Jesus came into Spokane's darkest corners. About the same time, the city of Spokane started a redevelopment program to change the look and atmosphere of the strip. No longer will the sins of the forefathers dictate to sons and daughters what they have to live with in the city of Spokane. The testimony of Jesus prophesies into darkness and illuminates it. It changes the atmosphere in our cities.

Do you want to see your city transformed by the kingdom of God too? When you're willing to do as Jesus said and step out to do the works of the kingdom, miracles happen and cities are changed. The Christian life becomes the most exciting thing in the world when people's lives are rescued out of the grasp of the enemy. I know because I was one of those lives. I was bound, but now I'm free and helping others get free. The key is to get back to the basics. We must understand that we are to preach the gospel of the kingdom, not just the gospel of salvation. So start proclaiming the whole gospel. You'll see your city changed and individual's lives delivered from darkness and carried into the light!

His Ways are Higher

In order to benefit from all that Jesus has provided, we must know what He has done and then see it from His heavenly perspective. We must stop limiting God by our small viewpoint.

"For My thoughts are not your thoughts, nor are your ways My ways," says the LORD. "For as the heavens are higher than the earth, so are My ways higher than your ways, and My thoughts than your thoughts" (Isaiah 55:8-9).

Most of us are familiar with the work of the enemy. Have you ever been stolen from? Do you know anyone who has died before their time or had their life destroyed? Well, that's the job description of the devil himself. He also lies to us, causes terrible things to happen, and then tries to ascribe them to God. He comes to us with a partial truth but then twists it. He'll say, "If God loved you, He could have stopped that from happening." Yes, God is Sovereign and He could have stopped it because He can do anything. But He doesn't normally stop what we allow. If we allow the enemy to steal from us, the enemy will indeed take everything we relinquish. Remember, God has given us authority over the works of the enemy.

If there are times in your life when you don't see God's hand, remember that you can always trust His heart. My Bible says that God cannot lie (Titus 1:2) and that He gives good and perfect gifts to His children (James 1:17). Jesus came to reverse the curse and give us back dominion, but we must take our place and enforce it.

Build an Ark

This is how you can help save people from death. In Noah's day he built an ark in order to save himself, his family, and all of the animals. Through your life you too can build an ark for people in order to help save them from the enemy. Think of "ARK" as "Acts of Random Kindness." Can you be a light to everyone you come into contact with? Can you treat them like Jesus would? He would treat them as if they were the most important person who ever lived because that's how He sees each one of us. Love is the answer. I encourage our Healing Rooms team to love everyone with the compassion of Jesus and to treat them as if they were the most important person in the world.

When I was in Bible school, one of my teachers, Bud Bonn, taught a class on Compassionate Caring—Personal Evangelism. I really loved Bud, but I thought he had a lot to learn about evangelism. I'd already had the privilege of leading many people to the Lord and told people about Jesus everywhere I went. But I always tried to get everyone to pray the sinner's prayer the first time I saw them and would try to hammer them until they accepted the Lord—all because I was motivated out of fear and didn't want anyone to go to hell.

Bud's way was to make each person feel loved, and he truly treated everyone as if they were the most important person he had ever seen. He was very different than me. While I was in and out in a flash, he took a lot of time with each person. I'd pray for them to be healed, see a miracle, then lead them to the Lord, and out the door I would go. Bud would always find someone who was sweeping the floor or working to thank them for their work and tell them how much he appreciated them. In my early days of being a Christian, I didn't understand him. But I sure loved his heart for people.

Bud was so awesome, and Dennis and I became like family with him and his wife, Elaine, who was the healing instructor at the Bible school. Like mama and papa eagles, they took us under their wings and helped mentor us. I learned so much from both of them. Elaine taught me the Word of God on faith and healing, and because of the great foundation she laid in me, I'm able to now teach others.

As I look back so many years later, I can see how much Bud taught me about loving people, appreciating everyone and meeting them where they are. Through him I saw a picture of what Jesus must have been like when He walked on the earth, and finally I learned about Compassionate Caring—Personal Evangelism.

A couple of years ago, I was crying out to God for the keys to bringing healing to the sick and I heard, "Love is the answer!" And it really is. Everything we need comes from the One who is love. He's always pouring it out, so the more we can open up to receive His love, the more healing we'll receive. The call of God on your life gives you a special part in God's glorious plan for revival in this hour. His primary purpose in the last days is to reach the ends of the earth with the full gospel of the kingdom—*all through love as we rise up and take our place!*

CHAPTER 3: The Healing Word

The greatest love story of all time was written by the hand of God with the blood of His only Son, Jesus. Our Father was extremely grieved when mankind was separated from Him in the garden. So He chose to sacrifice Jesus that we might know His great love for each of us and His desire for us to be restored back to Him. He bankrupted heaven to send His only Son to take our place and receive our punishment. Since Jesus did this for us, we can now take our place by standing up healed and restored. As God's righteous and innocent children, we are to tell the world who our God is by showing them what He's done for us and what He will do for them.

To understand how much love our Father has, think about what it would be like to send your only child to die for a sinner in prison. I don't know anyone who could do that. Yet that's exactly what our Daddy in heaven did for us. It was the greatest example of love ever displayed since the beginning of time. He sacrificed Jesus for you because of His great, passionate love for you! Even if you were the only person to ever live, He still would have sent Jesus just for you—and Jesus would have gladly come. Our Father loves you so much that He sent Jesus to die a sinner's death so you could be free and so your sins could be forgiven once and for all, never to be remembered again as they were thrown into the sea of forgetfulness.

Prior to being crucified, Jesus was severely beaten at a Roman whipping post. To perform the scourging, they used a short-handled whip with nine leather straps that were imbedded with small bits of metal and bone. As this whip hit the victims, it would tear their flesh from their bodies. Traditionally they hit their victims 39 times.

I've read somewhere that medical doctors divide all diseases into 39 different categories. If Jesus was beaten 39 times, this would represent one "stripe" for each kind of disease (see Isaiah 53:5). Just as Jesus took all sin upon Himself, He took all sickness and disease for everyone too.

We don't ask God to heal people; He already did that when Jesus was beaten 2,000 years ago. Our healing is a spiritual reality that is received by faith, just as salvation is. Jesus told believers to *heal* the sick. To do this, we use our authority to command the sickness to leave, and then we release His anointing into their bodies to bring restoration just as Jesus did. Whether or not a person receives the manifestation of healing when you pray doesn't determine whether they will be healed or not. You need to know that healing is already settled in heaven, and the manifestation will come forth if they continue to stand in faith and resist the enemy and his lies.

Jesus agreed to go through His suffering so that you could live an abundant life here on earth as well as in heaven. God could have had Him die in an instant, but He had Jesus beaten first so we could receive healing. The Bible actually says that it *pleased* the Lord to crush Him for us (Isaiah 53:10 NAS). Now if that's not great love, I don't know what is!

Foundations

It's very important to know that healing is not only possible, it's part of the salvation package Jesus provided for all mankind. Since the enemy will try to get you to operate by what you feel and see, you must understand this in order to press in for your own healing as well as the healing of others. In order to build something that will last, it's important to have a strong foundation. This also applies to our desire to be healed and see others healed. We must have a foundational understanding of His will for healing in order to move in the power of God. Otherwise, the enemy will be able to use what you don't know against you.

"My people are destroyed for lack of knowledge," says Hosea 4:6. It doesn't do you any good to have something if you don't know you have it. I once read a story about a poor Irishman who came to America on a boat many years ago. He spent everything he had to buy his ticket and only had a few cents left to buy some day-old bread to bring on his journey. Every mealtime, he would go to his quarters quietly to eat so that no one would ask him to share what he had. When he was finished eating his old bread, he would stand outside the dining hall and watch as other passengers ate three delicious meals each day. The last night on the boat, an elderly gentleman asked the Irishman to join him for dinner. Ashamed that he didn't have any money, he told the man that he would have to decline because he couldn't afford to dine there. Surprised by his remark, the elderly gentleman said, "Haven't you been eating these wonderful meals in the dinner hall all week? All the meals were included in the price of your ticket."

This penniless Irishman had sat alone in his room eating a small piece of crusty old bread when he could have been eating delicious meals with the other passengers. That's what it's like with us. If we don't know what is paid for, then we'll go without. It's essential to know what has been provided on the menu that our Father has for you!

Complete Package

Healing is part of our salvation, which is free. It's by His grace—God's unmerited favor and His undeserved blessing. The Greek word for being saved is *sozo*. This means that it isn't just to go to heaven, but that we can also be "healed and delivered." *Sozo* is the whole package of being made whole or well. We see this word show up in many contexts in the New Testament. It's translated into English with a variety of different words, but in the original text, it's all the same word.

Salvation:

"That if you confess with your mouth Jesus is Lord and believe in your heart that God raised Him from the dead you shall be saved [*sozo*]" (Romans 10:9 NIV).

"For the Son of Man came to seek and to save [*sozo*] what was lost" (Luke 19:10 NIV).

Healing:

"But Jesus turning and seeing her said, "Daughter, take courage, your faith has made you well [sozo], and at once the woman was made well [*sozo*]" (Matthew 9:22 NAS).

Deliverance:

"And those who had seen it reported to them how the man who was demon-possessed had been made well [*sozo*]" (Luke 8:36 NAS).

Learning How to Kiss

I'm going to teach you how to KISS—Keep It Simple, Saint! We want to focus on the simple truth of the gospel so that people can receive the manifestation of their healing. Not only do we need to know the truth, we must get rid of all the things that block our thinking. Much of the church today has been influenced by the theology of cessationism.

What is cessationism? It's the belief that the power gifts like, tongues, prophecy, healing, and other miracles were only for the early church to help get it started. But that doesn't even begin to explain all of the people that we see healed on a regular basis. It also confines Jesus' instructions about laying hands on the sick and healing them to a very short period of history. But we've been doing exactly what Jesus said, and He heals people. Mark 16:17-18 says, "And these signs will follow those who believe: In My name they will cast out demons; they will speak with new tongues . . . they will lay hands on the sick, and they will recover." This has been our experience, in spite of what cessationists say.

The enemy has deceived much of the church and caused them to believe a lie. Since many Christians pray for people to be healed and don't see God heal anyone, they decide that God must not heal the sick anymore—or at least not as often as He used to. With these kinds of lies being taught from many pulpits, it makes Christians believe that we're without power to heal the sick. These lies push the gifts and weapons of our warfare back 2,000 years. Without the power gifts of God, some believe that the only power that is released is the power of the enemy. That, sad to say, describes what we are experiencing today in countless churches. But laying hands on the sick is an elementary teaching of Christ (Hebrews 6:2).

The lies of the enemy cause us to filter the Word of God through the mindset of a fallen nature rather than a redeemed nature. This fallen perspective causes people to see themselves as sinners, not as redeemed royal princes and princesses in the kingdom of God. The scriptures clearly tell us that Jesus became the curse that belonged to us and He redeemed us (Galatians 3:13). We're not under law but under grace. So if we have been redeemed from the curse and healed by the stripes of the beatings that literally tore His flesh from His body, then why are we living as if we haven't? If we live our lives as sinners rather than as redeemed saints, the enemy will get us to believe that we have to take whatever he serves us. The problem with this mindset is that it treats the devil as if he's bigger than God!

Cal Pierce says that this kind of thinking will try to explain why we're the way we are rather than the way we ought to be. It produces excuses like:

- I'm sick for His glory.
- God made me sick to teach me something.
- He'll heal me someday *if* it's His will.

This puts the responsibility of healing on God because it says, "God is Sovereign and He can do what *He* wants to do!" While that is true, we're supposed to take the initiative. God tells us what His will is so that we can step into it and fulfill it. We are to be His hands and feet and take back dominion by bringing a visual demonstration of the kingdom of God on earth as it is in heaven.

Healing Basics for Everyone

If you are reading this book, you're probably a Christian and have heard this verse about our salvation time and time again: "The Lord has laid on Him the iniquity of us all" (Isaiah 53:6). Therefore you have faith and believe that Jesus died for your sins so you could be forgiven and inherit eternal life—and I bet I couldn't talk you out of your salvation, could I? That's because this is preached in most Christian churches today, and you have faith that it's true.

But we need to understand the whole salvation package. In the atonement accomplished by Jesus, forgiveness of sins is only part of the equation. The same passage says that we are healed by the stripes He received when He was beaten (53:5). Why is it that we are so convinced that our sins are forgiven, but the enemy can so easily get us to question the truth about healing? It's because faith comes by hearing the Word of God over and over again, and this truth is not preached very much in churches today.

He Carried Our Sicknesses

Let's take a close look at this in the Word of God. The Amplified Bible puts Isaiah 53:4-5 this way: "Surely He has borne our griefs (sicknesses, weaknesses, and distresses) and carried our sorrows and pains . . . and with the stripes [that wounded] Him we are healed and made whole."

These scriptures describe our healing. Isaiah clearly teaches that bodily healing is included in the atoning work of Christ, His suffering, and His cross. The Hebrew words for "griefs" and "sorrows" (v. 4) specifically mean physical affliction. This is verified by the fact that Matthew 8:17 says this text in Isaiah was fulfilled when Jesus healed people from sicknesses and other physical needs. "He healed all who were sick, that it might be fulfilled which was spoken by Isaiah the prophet, saying: He Himself took our sins and bore all of our sicknesses and diseases."

Further, the words "borne" and "carried" refer to Jesus' atoning work on the cross. They are the same words used to describe Christ's bearing our sins in Isaiah 53:11. This is also seen in the New Testament in 1 Peter 2:24: ". . . who Himself bore our sins in His own body on the tree, that we, having died to sins, might live for righteousness— by whose stripes you were healed." We also see forgiveness of sins and healing of physical diseases linked together in Psalm 103:2-3: "Bless the LORD, O my soul, and forget not all His benefits: Who forgives all your iniquities, who heals all your diseases."

Did you know that if you were to look up "all" in your concordance that you would find out that it means *all*? It's that simple; "all" means all. Let's KISS—Keep It Simple, Saint!

Neither forgiveness nor healing is automatically appropriated, though. Each provision—a soul's eternal salvation and a person's temporal, physical healing—must be received by faith. If I asked you if Jesus died for everyone to be saved, I'm sure that you'd probably say "yes." But will everyone be saved? No, because many won't receive the free gift of eternal life. In the same way, Jesus was beaten for everyone to be healed, but not everyone will be healed because many won't receive the free gift of healing. Some refuse to believe, some have something blocking their ability to receive, and some may even be casualties of the war we're in. But in spite of the fact that there are casualties of war, healing is our inheritance and is available for everyone who will receive it. Jesus finished the work so these are possible for every person: simple faith receives each as we choose. We need to have our minds renewed to believe what God says about the provision and inheritance He has for all of His children.

Several years ago, God spoke to me and said to tell people to change the way they think because many approach Him for healing with a lottery ticket mentality. We come to Him to be healed with our lottery ticket in hand, hoping He'll call our number and we will be healed. But to receive anything from the Lord, we must first know His will and then ask in faith. Just as you had to receive Him as your Savior, so you need to receive Him as your Healer. Proverbs 4:20-22 says, "My son, pay attention to what I say; listen closely to my words . . . for they are life to those who find them and health to a man's whole body." Believe His Word and keep it always before you. If we can believe that God laid all of our sins upon Jesus for the salvation of all, then we can also believe that our sicknesses and diseases were placed upon Jesus for our divine healing.

Because we are Jesus' body, we shouldn't have to live with sickness or pain. We should be walking in divine health, a state of total well-being. The Bible doesn't mention Jesus having any pain or sickness when He was on earth, so we shouldn't have pain or sickness either. These things will try to come on us, of course. But when they do, we must stand up and take our place, commanding them to leave in the name of Jesus. If we've opened the door to the enemy through sin, we need to submit to God and ask Him to forgive us.

We can then command the enemy to leave us in Jesus' name. Then we call upon His finished work and declare that "by His stripes we are healed."

It may take some time to resist the enemy who has brought the pain or sickness into your body, but remember that you're in charge. Don't take it! He's counting on you not knowing the truth. Just as you believe Jesus died for your sins, believe that He also took sickness so that you can receive healing today. If you don't believe the truth, the enemy will be able to pull the wool over your eyes and keep you from receiving the abundance that God planned for you from the beginning. He doesn't want you to know who's in charge so you'll allow him to keep trespassing on your body. Don't accept a victim mentality! You're not a victim but a victor! You just need to remind the enemy that God lives inside you and that you have power over him.

If you have a lottery ticket mentality, throw it away. God wants us to come with our claim ticket in hand and turn it in. As we do, we can know that our answer has been sent from heaven. Remember, we have confidence in Him that if we ask for anything according to His will, He hears us. If we know He hears us, we can know that we'll have the things we have asked of Him (1 John 5:14-15).

Emotional Healing

Emotional problems are the underlying root of many spiritual and physical problems. Many people are in hospitals today because they have a root of unforgiveness, strife, bitterness, and fear. The inner workings of these roots affect the functioning of the entire body.

Fear, for example, is a spirit that haunts individuals in order to get them to believe the lies of the enemy. I honestly believe that these spirits hang out in doctors' offices, hospitals, and nursing homes. They are looking for open doors to try to inhabit believers. They are just waiting for a doctor to give someone a diagnosis of cancer so they can convince the person to receive the diagnosis and believe the doctor's report. But you do not need to accept a bad report, even a doctor's! Reject it and don't allow that spirit to steal your life. It's up to you; you choose whose report you will believe—the doctor's or the Lord's. And the Lord says that you're healed by Jesus' stripes.

The good news is that Christ's redemptive work included emotional and mental healing as well and can overcome the fear that causes us to believe the lies of the enemy. For God has not given you a spirit of fear, but one of power, love and a sound mind (2 Timothy 1:7).

Knowing Truth Will Set You Free

One day while I was reading my Bible, I noticed that it says we're his disciples if we abide in Him. That passage goes on to say that we shall know the truth, and the truth will make us free (John 8:31-33). My next thought was that if people aren't free, there must be something they don't know. And in my spirit, I heard, "Not something, *someone!*"

The word for "truth" in this passage is the same word from Jesus' statement in John 14:6: "I am the way, the truth, and the life." *He* is the truth that sets us free. The Greek word for "abide" means to remain and to continue to be present. So if you abide (continue to be present and remain) in Him—for He *is* the Word—you shall know (experience) the truth (Jesus) and the truth (He) shall make you free. This is so important, yet so simple. *If you remain in Him, you shall experience Him and His Word, and He will make you free!*

Notice the first word: IF! That means that there's a condition. We must choose to remain in Him. Remember, He is the Vine and we are the branches. If we abide in Him, we will bear much fruit; but if we don't abide in Him, we can do nothing. If we abide in Him and His Words abide in us, we will have what we ask for.

Believe me, this isn't as easy as it sounds because our flesh will always try to just keep doing what it wants. The enemy will do everything he can to keep you so busy that you don't take time to be with Jesus. But if you can make abiding in Him a priority, He makes everything so easy.

He Healed Them *All!*

Jesus healed everyone who was sick who came to Him.

> "His fame went throughout all Syria; and they brought to Him
> all sick people who were afflicted with various diseases and

torments, and those who were demon-possessed, epileptics, and paralytics; and He healed them" (Matthew 4:24 NAS).

"When evening had come, they brought to Him many who were demon-possessed. And He cast out the spirits with a word, and healed all who were sick" (Matthew 8:16).

"When Jesus went out He saw a great multitude; and He was moved with compassion for them, and healed their sick" (Matthew 14:14).

"Great multitudes came to Him, having with them the lame, blind, mute, maimed, and many others; and they laid them down at Jesus' feet, and He healed them" (Matthew 15:30).

As you can see, it doesn't matter what a person had; all were healed! It should be the same way today. He used several different methods to bring healing to them. A woman with an issue of blood reached out and touched His cloak (Mark 5:27). For a leper, Jesus reached out to touch him and showed him a tangible expression of the Father's love for him. And "immediately the leprosy left him" (Luke 5:13). Sometimes He just sent His Word when those around Him had the faith to receive. Then Jesus said to the centurion, "Go! It will be done just as you believed it would" (Matthew 8:13 NIV).

The Disciples Healed Them All

Not only did Jesus heal everyone who came to Him, so did the disciples:

"A multitude gathered from the surrounding cities to Jerusalem, bringing sick people and those who were tormented by unclean spirits, and they were all healed" (Acts 5:16).

"It happened that the father of Publius lay sick of a fever and dysentery. Paul went in to him and prayed, and he laid his hands on him and healed him. So when this was done, the rest of those on the island who had diseases also came and were healed" (Acts 28:8-9).

Healing Through Elders of the Church

If you are an elder of a church, did you know that you're called to anoint people with oil and bring healing to them? In the Scripture passage in James we see that this is one of the methods of healing found in the Bible. Some have taken this to mean that pastors or elders are the only ones who can pray for the sick. As I have shown you in this book, that isn't true. I see ordinary believers heal the sick every week. Everyone can heal the sick if they have been baptized by the Holy Spirit because He is the one who heals them. So whether you are a new or a seasoned Christian (Elder) you can take your place and heal the sick.

> Is anyone among you suffering? Let him pray. Is anyone cheerful? Let him sing psalms. Is anyone among you sick? Let him call for the elders of the church, and let them pray over him, anointing him with oil in the name of the Lord. And the prayer of faith will save the sick, and the Lord will raise him up. And if he has committed sins, he will be forgiven. Confess your trespasses to one another, and pray for one another, that you may be healed (James 5:13-16).

One thing I find powerful about this passage is that it says if we confess our trespasses to one another and pray, we'll be healed. I am *not* saying that we have to confess to anyone other than God to be forgiven. But the Bible has this in there because getting our sins out of the dark and confessing them will allow us to be healed. The enemy entices us into sinning and then pours condemnation on us so we'll stay ashamed and keep it in the dark. This is so we won't repent. The key is to bring it into the light.

You can certainly just repent to God, but if you do that, command the enemy and whatever sickness or oppression he has put on you to leave immediately. Then always remember to ask Holy Spirit to fill up that vacated area with His love and power. The good thing about confessing it to someone else and then to God, is that they can love on you and speak truth into the situation. Let go of all unforgiveness, all bitterness, and all condemnation. You need to be like God and forgive yourself when you repent. Then do as God does and forget about it!

Miracles Glorify Christ

We've heard many testimonies of people getting their healing through a prayer cloth that we've prayed over. I remember a time when one of our Healing Rooms team members asked for a prayer cloth for one of her friends who had painful sores on her feet. We prayed over the cloth and she gave it to her friend, who put it inside her purse. When the friend went to take a bath that evening, she noticed that when she removed her socks, all the sores were gone and so was all the pain. Go Jesus!

We also had a couple ask the team to pray over a cloth for their son who had a mental illness. When they saw one of our team members at a conference, they told her they took the prayer cloth home and the son was completely and totally healed. What a miracle!

This seems weird to some people, but it's very biblical: "God worked unusual miracles by the hands of Paul, so that even hand-kerchiefs or aprons were brought from his body to the sick, and the diseases left them and the evil spirits went out of them" (Acts 19:11-12).

Healing in Communion

Our covenant communion is explained in Perry Stone's very powerful book called *The Meal that Heals.*[1] Sickness and aging came into the world with the sin of Adam and Eve. A sick person is not necessarily sick because of sin in his life but because of sin in the world. When we look at the power of the New Covenant, there is one method of covenant healing that isn't dependent upon the faith, prayer, or anointing of someone else. It's having faith in the blood and the body of Christ when we take communion. During the communion service, we are to appropriate the healing that Jesus purchased for us when He allowed His body to be broken by the beatings He took.

Before the great exodus of the children of Israel from Egypt, they were told to take the blood of a young lamb and apply it on two side posts and on the upper doorpost of the houses where they were to eat the Passover meal. The blood became a token of supernatural protection against the destroyer that was going to come at midnight to kill the firstborn in every unmarked house (see Exodus 12:1-13).

The second aspect of Passover was the meal. The lamb was to be roasted, and all of it was to be eaten. The lamb's body brought a supernatural healing because the morning after the Passover meal, the entire nation of Israel was healed! When they left Egypt to travel to their Promised Land, they carried with them the wealth of the Egyptians (Psalms 105:37). Can you even imagine an entire nation being healed in one night? Saints, that's where we're going. Many years ago, Kathryn Kuhlman prophesied that we would have healing services in which *everyone* would be healed. This is our inheritance; let's press in for it!

Just as manna rained down from heaven in the wilderness, so Jesus is the true bread from heaven. Jesus said He was the bread of life, and whoever ate of this bread would live forever (John 6:48-51).

Jesus fulfilled Passover and eliminated the need for yearly sacrificing of the lamb (Hebrews 9:26). The cup and the bread became a symbol of the completed work accomplished by Jesus' death. As we receive communion, we can actually receive the benefits of the atonement—total healing for our spirit, soul, and physical body.

Since the children of Israel ate manna daily in the wilderness, and manna represents Jesus (John 6:50-51), we too should be able to eat this meal to nourish us each day. Dr. John Miller, whose research Perry Stone cites often in his book, has received communion every day for over 20 years! Smith Wigglesworth, an early pioneer in the Pentecostal movement, also took communion daily.

If we take communion in faith, we can expect our loving Father in heaven to give us the healing it represents. Just as ancient Israel ate the lamb with the bread and was healed, so will we be healed from sickness, pain, and disease as we eat the bread that represents Jesus' broken body. The bread and cup are so powerful because communion is a reminder to God of the New Covenant that He established through the sufferings of His Son. God is always moved by His covenant. Our obedience causes Him to remember the promises He provided in the New Testament. And as the bread and the fruit of the vine become a part of our body, we are reminding God of His covenant with us.

If you are in need of healing when you take communion, start by quoting the promise "with the stripes of Jesus I am healed." Then tell the Lord you believe that the blood of Jesus was shed for your atonement, which includes your physical healing. Believe as you receive communion that the life of Christ is working in your body, driving out every sickness, disease, and weakness that is hindering your life. If you don't receive communion every day, then try to take it at least once a week. Just don't let it lose its meaning by becoming overly familiar with it.

Saints, this is how it ought to be. God doesn't need us to be sick in order for us to die to get to heaven. We ought to be able to close our eyes when we are ready to cross over into eternity with the lover of our souls, just as Wigglesworth did at the age of 87 during a church service. I think we should take communion daily and by faith believe that God wants us to experience divine health every day.

I know of people who have taken communion over the years and received healing from various infirmities and sicknesses. I've even heard stories of wrinkles being eliminated as the life of Jesus comes into their bodies and of gray hair returning to its normal color again. Could it be that communion brings about divine reversal in our bodies? In the Healing Rooms, we take communion with those who come for prayer, especially those who have terminal illnesses. Jesus provided healing by His broken body and as we take the bread we are taking what His body provided for us.

Healing Through the Word

One of the things we recommend for people to do if they want to receive the manifestation of healing is to read the Word of God concerning healing. We have a Healing Confession sheet that we give to people, and we encourage them to read it out loud three times a day just as they would take an antibiotic. I know a woman who was told that she would never walk again, but she was healed by hearing healing scriptures over and over. She read many healing scriptures aloud and recorded them on an audiotape. Then she would play the tape at night when she went to bed. Within a few months, she was up and walking because the Word of God doesn't return void. "So shall My word be that goes forth from My mouth; it shall not return to Me void, but it shall accomplish what I please, and it shall prosper in the thing for which I sent it" (Isaiah 55:11).

Walk as a Servant of God

It's not enough to know the written Word. You must also know the living Word, Jesus. One of the greatest things we can learn from Him is the principle of serving. As we serve, He gives us more responsibility, not to lord things over people but to become greater servants. The greater you are, the lower you go and the more you serve others. That's just the way things are done in the kingdom, which is why Jesus had a lot to say about serving:

"For even the Son of Man did not come to be served, but to serve, and to give His life a ransom for many" (Mark 10:45).

"But not so among you; on the contrary, he who is greatest among you, let him be as the younger, and he who governs as he who serves" (Luke 22:26).

Things in the kingdom of God are often quite opposite to the things of this world. As you know, the higher you get in this world, the more others serve you. And this is how many think it should be in the church. But that's an unbiblical view. Jesus said that we're to serve, and He became the greatest example of serving by giving everything He had for us.

Be Clothed with Humility

Jesus clothed Himself in humility. We are to remember that God has chosen the foolish and the weak things of the world to display His glory so that no flesh would receive the glory, but it would go to Him (1 Corinthians 1:27-29). Since pride comes before the fall

(Proverbs 16:18), our Father set things up so that we couldn't take credit for His works and get puffed up. He wants everyone to understand "the kingdom way." It's all about leaning into Him as the only powerful One.

That takes a lot of pressure off us, doesn't it? It's all about Him, not about us. That is such good news to me because I'm very weak in many areas. But I don't have to rely on my own strength, and neither do you. We can rely on His! For when we are weak, then He is strong (2 Corinthians 12:10). You may think at times, as I have in the past, that you can't be used by God because you aren't good enough or because you don't have enough ability. But if that is your thought, then you are *exactly* the kind of person He wants to use! He wants to show His great and awesome power through us weak, imperfect vessels. If we think we have it all figured out and that we can save the world, that's where the danger comes in. We must continue to recognize our weakness, our dependency and desperate need for Him. God will not share His glory with anyone, so if you want to carry His anointing to help change the world, you'll need to be clothed in humility.

So remember that He chose you not because of your ability but because of your *availability*. The next time you get nervous because you're asked to do something that takes you out of your comfort zone, remember that it's all about Him.

I read a book years ago about someone who had just come out of the presence of God and was shining with the Lord's glory. The glory was so bright that his vision was blurred. He thought that he could see clearly, but the glory even caused him to have blind spots. So Jesus wrapped a plain mantle around him in order for him to see clearly. This mantle wasn't elaborate or beautiful, but was needed.

This is how Jesus walked on the earth: wrapped in humility. The Bible says there was nothing about Him that would cause people to desire him—physically speaking, that is. But those who got to know Him, who saw beyond the outer casing, came face to face with true love. If their hearts were open, they received a new spirit and they were able to see clearly. But others were blinded by their pride. Let's be careful not to allow pride to blind us as well.

When the Lord starts to do miracles through you, the enemy will come right away to try to make you proud and take the praise for yourself. *Be careful!* If you do this, it *will* hurt you! When God pours out His love, His mercy, His healing power or His grace, remember that it's all about Him! You're just the available vessel that He's pouring through right then. If you want Him to keep pouring through you, make sure that you give Him *all* the praise and *all* the glory due His name. That's why I always say, "Go Jesus!" To walk in the anointing of God, the characteristic of humility must be upon us. Peter wrote that we should be clothed with humility because God resists the proud but gives grace to the humble. Therefore, we need to humble ourselves under God's hand and He will exalt us in His timing (1 Peter 5:5-6).

My experience has been that there will be many tests along the path on our journeys with the Lord. One of our frequent tests has to do with our humility. Because God loves us so much, He will allow us to be tested so we'll gain more humility and get rid of the pride in our own lives. As my pastor Johnny says, "Don't ask God if you have pride, ask Him where it is." We all have it, and God is frequently purifying us from it. He likes to use men and women who are humble.

Moses is a great example of that. The Bible declares that Moses was more humble than all the men who were on the face of the earth (Numbers 12:3). God desires to flow through us, but He's looking for humble, clean vessels.

Other Key Verses About Humility

- Forgiveness and restoration are related to humility: "If My people who are called by My name will humble themselves, and pray and seek My face, and turn from their wicked ways, then I will hear from heaven, and will forgive their sin and heal their land" (2 Chronicles 7:14 NIV).

- Humility leads to greatness: "Whoever humbles himself as this little child is the greatest in the kingdom of heaven" (Matthew 18:4); "whoever exalts himself will be humbled, and he who humbles himself will be exalted" (Matthew 23:12).

- Humility positions us for grace and defeats Satan: "God resists the proud, but gives grace to the humble. Therefore submit to God. Resist the devil and he will flee from you. Draw near to God and He will draw near to you" (James 4:6-8).

- Humility brings honor: "A man's pride will bring him low, but the humble in spirit will retain honor" (Proverbs 29:23).

Jesus, Our Example

Jesus humbled Himself as a man and was obedient even to the point of death on the cross (Philippians 2:8). In all things, we need to do what Jesus did. No we don't need to die on the cross, but we must continually go lower and humble ourselves in all things even as He did.

I don't know about you, but I think I'd much rather humble myself than be humbled. God is the potter, and we are the clay. It's His job to mold us and make us into the vessel He wants for His glory. There will be times in that process when you'll be pounded as He's molding you into the image of His Son. Then the potter puts His clay pot into the fire to harden it. It's not easy during the process, but it's necessary, and in the end, it's worth it.

Gold has to go through fire to be refined. Many people need to learn how to put to death the desires of the flesh and allow their spirits to take charge. We have to give up our own ways and rid ourselves of all pride. As we've noted, God resists the proud but gives grace to the humble. So if God is resisting you, get into a position of humbling yourself before Him and ask Him to show you what's going on.

As we humble ourselves He will give us His heart and strategies to impact the world. Friends, we can't even think big enough! God wants to do superabundantly, far over and *above* all that we [dare] ask or think [infinitely beyond our highest prayers, desires, thoughts, hopes, or dreams]—according to the action of His power that is working within us (Ephesians 3:20 AMP).

It's time that we believe His Word completely! Arise my friends and take your place with us, stepping into a life of miracles!

CHAPTER 4: Face to Face with God

I had a dream the night before I was going to preach at my church. I was in love with a young man, and we couldn't stand being apart. We spent every waking moment together—we were so passionately in love. Every thought I had was of him, and all of his thoughts were of me. We couldn't wait to get married. When I woke up in the morning, my first thought was, "I'm in love!" Then my second thought was, "Oh no, it's not my husband!" Instantly I heard Jesus say, "It's me!" What a relief to know I wasn't committing adultery in my heart!

"Oh, Jesus," I cried out. "I'm so sorry, I forgot how wonderful it is to be passionately in love with you!" He then showed me that without realizing it, I had grown lukewarm in my love towards Him. He said this was the case for many in the body of Christ. They loved Him but needed to return to their first love with Him—a passionate love. It's so easy to get very busy with life, even ministry things, and neglect the reason we do what we do. It's all about our love for the Lover of our soul, who gave everything up for us so we'd have His abundant life. You know what it says in Revelation about returning to your first love, don't you? Jesus knew the deeds of the Ephesian church, their hard work and their perseverance. Yet He was holding this against them: they had forsaken their first love. He went on to say that if they didn't repent and return to the things that they did at first, that He would remove their lampstand from its place (Revelation 2:1-7).

That's sobering. I repented and begged Him to help me keep Him close to my heart. I asked Him to help me to never allow my love to grow lukewarm again. The truth is that He is always just waiting for us to come to Him!

A few weeks later, I had another dream about this. I was again with this young man who I was passionately in love with. We would meet at a big pool and swim together. Even though there were many other people there, it was as if we were all alone. A couple of times I had to leave to do things, and when I returned he was sitting there waiting for me. His gaze was upon me and he had been very anxiously awaiting my return.

Seriously, this is a real picture of what happens. Jesus is always waiting to have time alone with each one of us. If you're married, think back to when you were a newlywed. Didn't you want to spend every moment possible with your spouse? If you're not married, imagine the most wonderful, passionate loving relationship you can.

In order to keep a marriage relationship "hot," you have to keep a log on the fire. Years ago, Dennis and I took a class that taught us how to prioritize having at least 15 or 20 minutes of alone time with each other every day. We need this with Jesus also. He's our daily bread. Can you imagine how skinny or sick we would be if we only ate once a week? Yet many Christians only come into the presence of Jesus once a week. We were created for more than this. Just as you'd schedule a regular date night with your spouse, so we should schedule regular dates with Jesus.

I'm not saying it's easy to prioritize time with Him because everything else will compete for your time. But if you put Him first, you will be amazed at how wonderful your day will actually be. His Presence causes everything to work just right. You'll get things done in record speed with precision, and your outlook on life will be much brighter. This will take discipline and the ability to say no to the flesh, but His presence is definitely worth it. There's absolutely nothing like being in His presence and experiencing Him, for it fills the longing of our souls.

If you aren't doing this already, don't feel guilty. It's a new day, so start today. The enemy always lies to us and tries to condemn us about these kinds of things. If you're feeling condemned, just remember that Romans 8:1 says there's no condemnation for those who are in Christ Jesus. We aren't supposed to walk according to the flesh, but according to the Spirit. So if you've been walking in the flesh, ask God to forgive you. Start being led according to the Spirit and receive His love and desire for you today. After all, there is no time like the present.

If you had asked me before my dream if I was in love with Jesus, I would have said, "absolutely!" But until you experience the passion of His love for you personally, you probably won't realize that your love has grown lukewarm. It's about experiencing Him and being with Him, not just having head knowledge or singing songs about Him. We don't want to sing about Him like He's not around, but to sing to Him in worship.

So step into the "secret place" with God and allow Him to reveal His love to you in an exciting and new way that will fulfill your deepest longings.

Our Purpose

Did you know you were made for God's own pleasure? The Creator of the Universe designed you for fellowship with Him, to receive His amazing love. It's true, there's nothing that He desires more than to have a close relationship with *you*! He *is* love, not a mean, angry Judge. Because so few of us have really understood who He is, we've misrepresented Him to those around us. And oh, how we need His love each day to love others!

God is pouring out His love on the earth today in an amazing way, and He desires for you to open up and freely receive it. That's our purpose—to be loved and to pour out His love to others. Love is the answer! Inside each of us is a vacuum, and it's shaped like God, who is love. Many people have tried to get that love and acceptance in so many other ways, attempting to fill that void with things: food, drugs, alcohol, sex, jobs, or even good works for God. Yet when we come to the end of ourselves and realize that we can't do it and need Him, His love floods into our soul. In *The Secret Place,*[2] Dr. Dale Fife says:

The quality of your spiritual life is in *direct* proportion to the amount of time you spend with Him!

I wish we could get this right! We've fallen so far from our purpose, striving and trying to earn our way by our works. We've gotten it all backwards. We prioritize doing things in order to be satisfied, yet true satisfaction will only be found in His presence. Dr. Dale also says:

> *Never* **confuse your purpose with your assignment.**
> **You'll never be satisfied until you fulfill your purpose**
> **of intimacy with God!**

How exciting it is to know that if we can understand and fulfill our purpose of receiving and pouring out His love, we will be fulfilled beyond our wildest imaginations. Everything should flow out of our love relationship with God. We must be able to receive His love because we can't give out what we don't already have.

Dr. Dale says that living unloved would be like clipping a bird's wings and removing its ability to fly! God wants you to fly with Him in heaven. Sure, your physical body is confined to this earth for now, but the Bible declares that we are seated with Him in heavenly places.

Intimacy Is Most Important

When I was preparing to teach a seven-week Healing School, I assumed I would start with the subject of faith. I sat down to talk to the Lord about this, and as soon as I asked Him what I should start with, I heard "Now abide faith, hope, love, these three; but the greatest of these is love" (1 Corinthians 13:13).

Exactly, I thought. If we put anything else before this, it would be like putting the cart before the horse. Understanding the Father's love is important in receiving healing and His blessings as well as being able to minister to others. If you are unable to accept His love, you are essentially rejecting it.

I have found that this is one of the foundational keys to receiving healing. If you were to take a survey and ask people if they believe God heals today, many would say yes. But if you were to ask if they thought that He would heal *them*, this is where people start to doubt.

We must understand that He loves us. When we can accept this truth and open our hearts to receive His love, all rejection leaves. You may even be able to receive healing without this truth, but if the enemy comes to put sickness back on you, and you don't understand the depth of His love for you and the price that He paid, you'll have a hard time keeping the healing. Knowing the written Word is not the same as knowing the Living Word—Jesus. We must have both!

Think about this: Which comes first—intimacy in marriage or babies? Intimacy, of course. Babies are the fruit of that intimacy. So if we want to birth some things for God and be fruitful for Him, then we must first get to know Him. And there's no greater place than to be alone in His presence.

Use Me Lord

One day when I was crying out to the Lord, I said, "God, use me to pour out your love and healing in the earth." Instantly I felt the Lord's dissatisfaction with my asking Him to use me. "I don't want to *use you*," He said. "Would you ask Dennis to use you to have his babies?" I thought about that for a minute. The answer is no! I don't want Dennis to use me to have his babies, and he wouldn't want to use me either. Our children are our fruit that came naturally out of our intimacy. Yes, of course we wanted to reproduce children, but that's not why we were intimate. So our intimacy with God shouldn't be *in order* to bear fruit, but out of a desire for being together. He will pour through us, but He doesn't want to just use us. As we spend time in His presence, the fruit will come naturally out of our love relationship.

> **Intimacy with our Creator is so important**
> **that we cannot bear fruit**
> **without it, for fruitfulness flows out of intimacy.**

A couple of years ago, I read an article Patricia King wrote about the battle for intimacy. She writes, "Recently, I had a talk with a good friend who just returned from Mozambique where she spent some time with Heidi Baker. Heidi told her, 'You have no idea the battle I have fought to maintain intimacy and to fight distraction.'

Intimacy—this is the battlefield. This is what the enemy desires to steal more than anything! If he can steal our intimacy with the Lord, he gets everything. Intimacy is the most important factor in our Christian experience, and when you understand the importance of something, you are willing to fight for it."[3]

In John 15, Jesus explains that He is the vine, His Father is the vinedresser, and we are the branches. If we don't bear fruit, He'll take us away. If we bear fruit, however, He'll prune us so we can bear more fruit. Just as a vine has to stay connected in order to bear fruit, we must abide in Him because we can't bear fruit by ourselves. If we abide in Him and His words abide in us, we can ask whatever we desire and it will be done for us. Our Heavenly Father is glorified when we bear fruit because it points back to Him (John 15:1-8).

We need to follow Jesus' example. No matter how busy He was, He always pulled away from the crowd to be alone with His Father. If Jesus needed to do this, how much more do we need to? We're told that He went away to pray. To some people prayer seems kind of boring, and that could be true if your time with God is only one-sided. If all it means to you is to read off a checklist of things that you desire, that *would* be boring. But prayer is much more than that, it's communication with the lover of our soul. We are to come into the presence of God by thanking Him and praising Him for all He has done. Then as we enter into worship, we can enter into the Holy Place with Him where He lives. In this place, He will fill us with His love, for this is the fuel we need. This is where He pours into us what will flow out of us.

The Mystery of the Lean

My friend Dana Hanson of Lord Warmington Studio painted the picture at the beginning of the chapter for this book. She did a great job showing the bride of Christ leaning into Jesus in order to battle. It shows that we get our strength from leaning into Him. I once heard Steve Mitchell talk about the *mystery of the lean* at a conference where he was leading worship. His nuggets have helped me in my life.

In Song of Solomon 8:5 it says "who is this coming up from her wilderness leaning on her beloved?" This seems to imply she really couldn't come up and out until she learned to lean as opposed to trusting in her self. That is so true isn't it?

The second thing is that His strength is made perfect in our weakness, for when we are weak then He is strong (2 Corinthians 12:10). There is an inward leaning that looks like weakness on the outside but is really a strength. Part of the reason it is mysterious is because it's so opposite of what the world teaches, as most things in the kingdom are. Paul actually rejoiced in his weaknesses or his inabilities so that the "power of Christ" would rest on him.

Keys to the Mind of Christ

If your prayer time with God is dry, maybe you need to get into the river of His presence. It's in the place of soaking in God's presence that He pours Himself into us. We become one with Him in that place, and we take on the mind of Christ. Out of knowing and experiencing Him, we're able to move and have our being in Him.

When you're in love with someone, you like to spend a lot of time with that person, right? Pretty soon you start to think and speak like that person. Many married couples actually start to look like each other. This is what happens when we spend time with Jesus; we begin to look like Him, sound like Him, think like Him, and say the things He says.

This will be one of our keys to victory in the end times. We must be overcome with love for Jesus. As we sit in His presence, we will be filled with the essence of who He is. It's out of that place of knowing and experiencing Him that we can know the plans He has for these last days. So often we ask Him a question and then we move ahead feeling as if it is His will for us to do things when it isn't His plan at all. We must not move until He says move. We must get His strategies out of the secret place. His glory is falling on those who have positioned themselves to receive Him—not just something from Him, but to be with Him just because they love Him.

Those who seek His face and are operating in the Spirit will receive the mind of Christ. Bill Johnson says that as we get heaven on our minds, we will be able to release heaven upon the earth because our minds are the gatekeepers! We will be filled with His essence, and His glory will flood the earth through ordinary believers who are passionately in love with Him. It's not about our ability, but our availability. As you avail yourself to Him, He will visit you too with His glory.

Father God is revealing His end-time plans to those who are humble, passionate lovers of His Son. It's time to awake and arise! You are a spirit inside a human body, and God who is Spirit is offering you the opportunity of a lifetime to join with Him to advance the kingdom of heaven upon the earth. Surely His kingdom is coming in power for those who will make themselves ready and available to the Spirit of God. Start today! Don't wait any longer.

There's a war over our minds right now to get us to give in to busyness. Some of this busyness is even doing things for God. But instead of constantly "doing," we need to come into His presence to just rest and receive from Him. As you do this, He will show you what's on His agenda for you.

Intimacy with God begins when we radically pursue Him with our whole heart. Gary Oates teaches about this in his article, "Soaking: The Key to Intimacy."[4] King David wrote, "When You said, 'Seek My face,' my heart said to You, 'Your face, O Lord, I shall seek'" (Psalm 27:8). God invites us in James 4:8 to "draw near to God and He will draw near to you."

God is saying to us, "Seek my face! Come near to me and you will find me!" In our hearts we are crying out, "*Yes*, Lord, we desire you!" But our flesh is screaming "*No*, I have other things to do!" The enemy will always remind us of things to do, even godly things, to keep us from intimacy with God. And because our flesh is used to being busy, it usually wins. We must resist it, however, and follow the leading of our heart. The problem is that when you've been out of the presence of God for a while, you forget how wonderful His presence really is and how desperately you need it.

Encounter with Jesus

After praying for people at a conference in 2000, I had a very real experience with Jesus. I asked one of the leaders to agree with me for my sister to receive healing because cancer was attacking her body. He said, "Angela from the first time I saw you, I knew that you didn't know the Father's love." In my heart I was thinking, *What are you talking about? I'm getting ready to teach on the Father's love at a women's meeting!*

You see, before I was saved, I actually thought God hated me. My own father was unable to show me love because he hadn't received it himself. He was filled with anger and rage and he screamed a lot. I transferred that to Father God, assuming He felt the same way about me. Then after receiving the Lord, I only had head knowledge of His love as something I had read in the Bible or heard others speak of. But how can any of us really show love unless we've first experienced it ourselves?

At the time of the conference, however, I had two children, and God had revealed His love to me through them. When my daughter, Moriah, was an infant, she cried all the time. I felt deep pain and agony as she suffered from colic and screamed for hours daily. But when she was quiet, I would just hold her in my arms and rub my fingers over her face while singing love songs to her. I remember one night being so filled with love for her that I felt like I could explode. I noticed every detail of her face and how very beautiful she was. I adored her cute little button nose and her long, beautiful eyelashes and her porcelain skin. I remember thinking, *This is love. I so love her that I even love and care about every hair on her head.* Then I remembered the scripture passage about how even the hairs on our heads are numbered. I thought, *Wow, God loves me like this!*

During special moments like this with Moriah and Israel, I felt the love of God for me personally. When Israel was born, he was my "joy boy." I even joked with my friends that I misnamed him—that his name should have been Joy. I was able to experience the joy of having a baby who was happy. I was (and still am) so in love with my children that I experience the love of God through them daily.

But at the conference, this leader had just told me I didn't know the Father's love. As I looked at him, it was as if Jesus came down, got into his body and was looking at me through his eyes. The love I saw still causes intense joy to spring up from the depths of my heart today. It was unlike any love I'd ever seen, felt, or experienced. It was fiery, but liquid and penetrating—more passionate than I had ever seen. I knew he could see right through me.

The only way I can describe that experience is to compare it to the day I married Dennis and to remember the passionate love we had for each other. As abundant as this love is, the awesome, eternal love of our Savior far surpasses the deepest, most fulfilling love between husband and wife. It is like a mighty mountain compared to a grain of sand. There was so much love in Jesus' eyes for me that I thought I would burst. It was so deep that it felt as if I could get lost in it. This leader would speak with passion to me and say, "Angela, He loves you so much!" Oh, how I wanted to hear that; and oh, how I wanted to see those eyes!

I knew that I needed that love. God created me to experience this depth of passionate love, but it was so intense that I felt like screaming, "Who, *me?* You love me *that* much?" I had never desired anything more than this love, but it was hard to receive so much of it. It was all-forgiving and passionate. Though He holds the whole world in His hand, it felt as if He desired to be with me more than anyone or anything else in the universe. Friends, we were created to have this kind of love experience with God on a daily basis, this side of eternity. But this was more than I could receive. Even though there was no condemnation whatsoever, this passion was so intense I frequently had to look away.

Whew, He loves me! I thought. *He knows my name and is actually passionately in love with me!* I felt like a young girl with her first love, and I wanted to scream. He knew me! He knew everything about me, and yet He still desired me. He continued to speak of His great love for me, and it broke me—in a good way. This probably went on for only a short time, but it felt like an eternity before I fell to the floor and cried deeply.

When I returned home, all I could do for the next two weeks was to sit on the floor and worship Him. If you've ever been a newlywed, do you remember how you dropped your friends for a while? All you wanted was to be alone with your lover. When my friend Kris called me that week, I remember telling her that I couldn't leave His presence. She said, "That's okay, you can just take Him with you." I said, "No, you don't understand. He and I are in a really deep place, and I need to be alone with Him."

I was so captivated by the Lord's love, all I could think about was the way He said my name and the way He looked into my eyes with such amazing passion. I knew that I was His focus and that there was nothing He didn't know about me—or anything that I was concerned about that didn't also concern Him. I knew He had felt all the pain I'd ever felt. He knew the ways I had sinned, and yet He loved me so unconditionally. It was the most amazing feeling in the world!

As I asked the Lord what happened, He told me to go to Ephesians in my New Living Translation Bible. I read that our roots will grow down into God's love and that we would have the power to understand how wide, how long, how high, and how deep His love really is. It then went on to say that we are to experience the love of Christ, though it is too great to fully understand (Ephesians 3:16-19).

This was it. I had experienced the love of Christ for myself! Nothing in my life came even close to measuring up to this. I hadn't even known this was possible. Why hadn't anyone ever told me that I could have this? I decided that this was one part of my testimony that I needed to share with as many people as I could.

After this encounter, my deepest desire was for God to pour His love through me so that others would be able to experience it here on the earth. Friends, we don't have to wait until we pass through the pearly gates to know His great love for us. It's more than words, and He wants you to experience it for yourself now, even today. So what are you waiting for? Get hungry and thirsty for an encounter with Him! If you seek Him and cry out to Him, He will fill you because He always feeds the hungry.

A few years earlier, I had an encounter with God in which the Holy Spirit came upon me like a thousand volts of electricity. It started at my feet and went up and down my legs for a few minutes. Then up and down my back over and over again, then up and down my head, and then down my arms with electricity flowing out my hands. Dennis and I had been birthed into revival right after getting saved and had experienced the tangible power of the Lord. But this was *way* stronger, and, to be honest, it scared me! But I'd learned something when I first got saved. If something unfamiliar happened, I would ask God to give me liquid peace if it was Him. So when I asked Him about this experience, all the fear subsided — it felt as if a bottle of liquid peace had been poured out on me.

Ever since that earlier experience over 12 years ago, I feel the anointing of God like electricity pouring out of my hands when I'm in His presence or when I pray for people. But after this experience with Jesus and His passionate love, the power that shot out my hands was intensified and now felt like flames of fire. In Ephesians 3:19, it says that you will experience the love of Christ, and then you will be made complete with all the fullness of life and power that comes from God. From this I understood that my experience with the love of Christ filled me with the fullness of God's life and His power, and this was what was shooting out of my hands.

Do you remember the old song, "More love, more power, more of you in my life?" Well, that's it exactly. If you want more love, spend time with Jesus because He *is* love. If you want more power, spend time with Jesus because power comes out of His love. Whatever you need, it's all found in *Him, who is love!*

In Psalm 46:10, it says we are to be still and know that He is God. Gary Oates teaches us that, "be still" literally means to cease from striving. It means to let go and relax, to turn down the volume of the world and listen to the quiet whisper of God. It's getting still and coming into a place of rest — soaking in His Presence. The result is that you will know He is God.

The word "know" — *yada* in Hebrew — is literally an experiential knowledge of God. We aren't told to be still and know *about* God. It's being still and knowing God experientially. The highest level of *yada* is in "direct, intimate contact." This refers to life-giving intimacy, as in marriage. Applied spiritually, it suggests intimacy with God in prayer that conceives and births blessings and victories. Bible reading and prayer are not enough. We must take time alone with Him, not asking for anything but more of Him and His presence in our everyday lives.

You Will Experience the Presence of God

Several years ago, the Lord taught me that He would direct my path after I got into His presence in close intimate contact each day. He tells us to trust in Him with all our hearts and to lean not on our own understanding. In all our ways we are to acknowledge Him and He shall direct our paths (Proverbs 3:5-6). The word "acknowledge" here is also the word *yada*. I've learned that if I get into His presence the first part of each day, He fills me with His desires and directs me along the right path.

Psalm 37:4 says to delight ourselves in the Lord and He will give us the desires of our hearts. Here's how that works. As we spend time in the secret place with God, we become impregnated with His heart and His desires. Then those things become our desires, and He will give them to us. Remember, it's all about wanting to be with Him because we love Him, not to get something from Him. We must seek His face and not His hand.

I've read a book that tells about this—*Journal of the Unknown Prophet* by Wendy Alec. She had been visited by Jesus for 10 days, and He spoke to her about the prerequisites to the healings, miracles, and power of the end-time age:

> And as I watch them only worship Me—not for my power or My anointing, but for the wonder of communing in My presence—then I shall move My mighty hand and I shall pour out a portion of My Spirit upon these precious ones.

> And this is the great outpouring that shall come from My Sovereign hand upon those who truly love Me, upon those beloved ones who seek only My face. For surely they are the ones who hold my Person and My presence dearer than their ministry, for they want to be with Me more than they want to be used by Me. These are My beloved, these are My trusted ones. And so I shall release them into the four corners of the Earth with passion and with power, with might and with fire.[5]

So if we truly want to be used in this great outpouring of God we must put first things first. Intimacy with God is the priority.

Mary and Martha are an example of this (Luke 10:38-42). Most of us are familiar with this story, but let's look at it again. Mary sat at Jesus' feet while Martha was distracted with much serving. She was so upset with Mary that she told Jesus about it. She asked Jesus if He didn't care that Mary had left her to serve them all alone and told Him to tell her to help. But Jesus told her she was worried and troubled about many things and that Mary had chosen the good part, which wouldn't be taken away from her.

He was saying, "Martha, keep the main thing the main thing! Don't fret over getting everything done and trying to make everything perfect, but first and foremost spend time at My feet." It's from this place of intimacy—abiding and resting in Him—that we are to live and move.

God acts for the one who waits for Him (Isaiah 64:4). The Amplified version puts it this way: "God . . . who works and shows Himself active on behalf of him who earnestly waits for Him." Saints, He desires that we wait on Him, just as a passionate bridegroom awaits the arrival of his new bride.

God has shown me over the years how to be a Mary-Marth—first to sit at His feet to receive His love and His essence, and then after that to get to work. Some just want to sit at the feet of Jesus, and that isn't what He had in mind at all. James 2 tells us over and over that faith without works is dead.

Spending Time Soaking in His Presence

At a "Healing the Brokenhearted" conference with Gary and Kathi Oates, Gary shared about soaking in the presence of the Lord. He emphasized how important it is to spend time alone in the presence of God. If we have areas in which we still need to be healed, it's good to soak in His presence. Gary compared it to soaking a casserole dish. If food was stuck to a dish you used to bake a casserole, you could remove it in one of two ways. You could either try to scrape off the food with a knife, or you could put it in the sink to soak. It's easier to just soak the pan and then come back and dump it out later. All the food would rinse out easily. I don't know about you, but I'd much rather soak and allow God's love and presence to cause the junk in my life to fall out instead of scraping at it with a knife!

After the conference, I decided to increase my intimate time with the Lord. So even though I'm extremely busy, I started soaking one hour in the morning and one hour before going to bed. Even if I felt that my soaking time had been unproductive, I decided to press in because there's a cumulative effect with spending time in the Lord's Presence. God was making an ongoing deposit into my innermost being. As I began to pour out, that anointing flowed out of the deposit He had been making all along.

During this time, I began having the most amazing dreams I've ever had. Also, my sensitivity to hear Him was much stronger. I had been under an extremely large amount of stress. The picture God gave me as I continued to spend time soaking in His presence was that I was like a live wire, but His presence came and surrounded me like insulation. As we soak in His presence, we extract more of His fullness, and it will pour into those places where we are barren. The cumulative effect of spending time with the Lord will produce an increased anointing in your life, which will serve as a springboard to a life of miracles.

The apostle John made a mind-boggling statement: ". . . as He is, so also are we in this world" (1 John 4:17 NAS). The implication of this verse is clear: believers should be like Him. That means we need to do what He does. We know He only did what He saw His Father doing, so He spent quality time in the Father's manifest presence. This is the only way we will ever understand His compassionate heart for His children—by spending time soaking in His presence.

Conclusion

Intimacy with God is how we come to know and experience His passionate love for us personally. Spending time soaking in His presence is a discipline we must have in order to access the kingdom of God. It's a transition from the flesh into the spirit, where He lives. God's timing for the saints to take their place and do the greater works that Jesus promised to His believers is now upon us.

One day I was crying out to God for answers. I so wanted to understand how to get more of His power so we could see everyone healed from sickness and diseases. As I cried out, I said, "God, there have to be some basic things that we need? What is the yeast that will cause it to grow and to multiply?"

This is what I heard: "It's the anointing that comes out of intimacy. This is the core ingredient. This is the yeast, and you get it from the river of My presence. It is there that one is filled and receives an increase in the anointing." As believers, this is what we give out—His liquid presence!

But then I heard, "You must teach them to go to the river daily." Just as the children of Israel had to get fresh manna every day, so we must get fresh manna and fresh water from the river of life and teach others how to go to the river for themselves daily. This is how we live supernatural lives naturally.

So choose to be consumed with a passionate love for your God. Rest in His presence regardless of the pressures and deadlines that are calling your name. Cast your burdens upon Him because He cares for you. His burden is light and His yoke is easy (Matthew 11:30).

I heard a preacher once say that while revival costs in the here and now, the absence of revival will cost throughout all eternity. God is calling His army of believers, the lovers of His heart, to join together and hear the clarion call. What is the clarion call? It is an urgent call to action. So come up higher, and receive your marching orders!

Remember, there's no greater reward than receiving His love in His presence. He wants you to experience His passionate love today. He chose you to bear fruit, and as you abide in Him, you will. Remember, all fruitfulness is birthed out of intimacy—so arise and take your place with Him, face to face!

CHAPTER 5: The Commission and Assignment

I've heard many ministers ask: "Are you in full-time ministry?" It isn't a trick question, but your answer may reveal how you view reality. God's Word declares that every believer is a minister. Our contemporary mindset considers ministry a full- or part-time job, but scripturally, it simply means fulfilling what the Word of God commands. So yes — you're in full-time ministry.

For many years the Lord spoke to me over and over that my job was to equip the saints to do the work of the ministry through healing the sick, displaying His power and leading others to Him. Not every believer is expected to engage in a healing or deliverance ministry as a full- or part-time vocation, but every believer is called, according to God's Word, to engage in the "work of the ministry" (Ephesians 4:11). That's what this book is about: calling each believer into the knowledge that we are Kingdom ambassadors and are on the job 24/7. Whether you are a successful business executive on Wall Street, an engineer, a school teacher or a stay-at-home mom or dad, God wants you to take your place by releasing His kingdom upon the earth.

It's time that this message of taking our place gets into our churches. Each person is called to be a light and to be the hands and the feet of Jesus outside the four walls of our church buildings, where the harvest is. Doug Spada, founder of the nonprofit venture His Church at Work (*www.HisChurchAtWork.org*) describes this new paradigm in churches as "converting cruise ships to aircraft carriers." He goes on to say that most churches have become like cruise ships. Those who attend are passengers. They're brought to the ship to be entertained and fed, and then they return to their everyday lives. Instead of cruise ships, churches can aspire to become like aircraft carriers. The congregation isn't there for the program, they're on board to be taught, equipped, and refueled for a mission. The important work is done off of the aircraft carrier, as fighter planes (individual believers) do battle wherever they're sent—*taking their place*!

Kingdom Ambassadors

We know that Jesus commissioned us as His ambassadors to do business until He returns, but exactly what are we to do? We are to *re*-present Him. Jesus said, "As the Father has sent me, I am sending you" (John 20:21 NIV). Once we are in His kingdom, He calls us to go out into the world in the same way the Father sent Him into the world. In other words, we are to show people what God is like. Just as an ambassador is sent to a foreign nation to represent a king, so we are sent to represent Jesus and take care of kingdom business on His behalf. We don't go in our own name and with our own opinions: "Well, *I* think..." No, we say, "*Jesus* said..." We call on *His* Name. When we do that, God will stand behind His Word.

This means that we are to do what Jesus did while He was on earth. What comes to mind when you think of Jesus' work? I think about a loving Savior who humbled Himself and gave up everything to show us how to bring heaven to earth. He only did and said what His Father told Him (John 5:19). He was full of the love and compassion of His Father and poured it out on everyone who would receive it. Even when His disciples tried to keep the children away from Him, He told them not to hinder them because the Kingdom of Heaven belongs to those who are like children (Matthew 19:14).

Jesus walked in the Father's love and gave it away. This is what fueled Him to sacrifice everything, even to the point of pain, betrayal, and death. He taught us about the Kingdom of God and gave us a tangible example of what His Father was like. Jesus said, "He who has seen Me has seen the Father" (John 14:9). He also said, "As You sent me into the world, I also have sent them into the world" (John 17:18).

This chapter is about taking your place by doing what Jesus has commissioned you to do. You've probably read that when Jesus walked on the earth, He went through all the towns and villages, teaching in their synagogues, preaching the good news of the kingdom and healing every sickness and disease. When he saw the crowds, he had compassion on them because they were harassed and helpless like sheep without a shepherd (Matthew 9:35-36). Jesus couldn't reach all the people, but He healed everyone who came to Him.

I find it interesting that even though He couldn't get to everyone everywhere, He didn't seem anxious at all about it. Did He have a burden for people? Yes, but this is why He raised up His disciples to do the works that He did. Notice also that He didn't call the Pharisees and Sadducees to follow Him. He called four fishermen, a tax collector, and plain old ordinary people from different walks of life. God isn't looking for how good we are; He's looking for hearts that are turned toward Him for Him to pour through.

The Workers Are Few

Jesus told His disciples that the harvest was plentiful but the workers were few. He then told them to ask the Lord of the harvest to send out workers into His harvest field (Matthew 9:37-38). As someone who wants to see the world saved and healed, I have often carried the heavy burden of this feeling. I felt that I was responsible to lead everyone everywhere to the Lord and get them healed. Then one day Elizabeth, my friend and pastor, said, "Angela, you can't care about it more than He does. It's not your responsibility, and you can't heal the whole world."

It is this and so many other things He has taught me along the way that have allowed me to do the works of Jesus from a place of rest and leaning on Him. Truly the harvest is great and the workers are few. But this is why He has commissioned me to write this book; it's to show you what God has called each one of us to do. We all need to do our part by shining our light from the high place. As we take our place by doing the works of Jesus, our Father will be glorified. Jesus said that His yoke is easy and His burden is light. As long as we are abiding in Him, He will do the work through us. All we have to do is show up, get filled with His glory, and He will pour through us.

Jesus Commissions His Disciples

In order to multiply Himself, Jesus first commissioned His twelve disciples. He started by giving them power and authority over all demons and diseases. He sent them to preach the kingdom of God and to heal the sick (Luke 9:1).

The kingdom of God is simply His presence. He is no longer just "out there." Jesus opened the way for Him now to live within us. When asked by the Pharisees when the kingdom of God would come, Jesus said it doesn't come with observation because the kingdom of God is within you (Luke 17:20-21). In other words, the kingdom is not observable, but it is righteousness, peace, and joy in the Holy Spirit (Romans 14:17).

As believers, we are to release God's kingdom on the earth. The presence of God was once in the temple behind the veil, but it is now living within us. When we understand this—that He actually lives within us—we can move in power. People who base everything on what they see or hear have a hard time with this, but Jesus was trying to get them to understand that this was a spiritual kingdom. In order to operate in this realm, we must engage it with our spirit and by using our spiritual senses.

Everywhere Jesus went, He healed the sick and preached the kingdom of God. Then He appointed 70 others and sent them two-by-two into every city where He Himself was about to go (Luke 10:1). As a side note, my experience has been that whenever possible, it's best to take at least one other person with you. It's especially important to go with another person if you're going to pray for someone at a hospital or nursing home, or if you're trying to raise someone from the dead at a morgue. However, being alone shouldn't stop you if you are at the grocery store, the office, or even in a hospital. You don't have to have another person to agree in prayer with you. I know this is true, as I've prayed for many people on my own and have seen instant miracles. It's just more powerful when you have more people in agreement.

Jesus said that if two people agree on earth concerning anything they ask, it would be done for them (Matthew 18:19). In the Healing Rooms, we pray with three people on each ministry team. As the scriptures say, one can put 1,000 enemies to flight, and two can put 10,000 enemies to flight. Being a former financial planner, I love numbers, so if you're like me and you've done the math, then you can see that three could put 100,000 enemies to flight. Pretty cool, huh? In the Healing Rooms, we are really seeing as much power in the agreement of three people as a healing evangelist would operate in. But you don't have to be a part of the Healing Rooms to see God work. He loves to show His power in the marketplace, especially among unbelievers and new converts. Remember that healing is a sign to the unbeliever! Just step out and watch Him perform miracles in front of your eyes. Then as they get healed, teach them to pray for others right away and they too will see people healed.

Jesus told His disciples to heal the sick and proclaim that the kingdom of God had come near them (Luke 10:9). We need to do the same thing. We can teach people about the realities of a loving God who gave everything He had so we could be free from sin, sickness, disease, and pain, and that He has given us abundant life instead. When the 70 followers went out, they became extremely excited when they found that the demons obeyed them. However, Jesus told them not to rejoice over that, but over the fact that their names were written in heaven. He told them that He had given them authority over serpents and scorpions and over all the power of the enemy so that nothing could hurt them (Luke 10:17-20). The devil is subject to you because he lost heaven as his home and inherited hell. You received Jesus' authority and have inherited heaven as your eternal dwelling place and can access the kingdom of God even while you're here on the earth. It's time to start living like that's true. You are a child of the King of kings and the Lord of all lords! He has given everything to you because you are a co-heir with Jesus.

Childlike Faith

Jesus thanked His Father for hiding spiritual things from the wise and prudent and revealing them to babes. The word for *babes* is often translated as *childlike*. In the Jewish New Testament it says that

God concealed these things from the sophisticated and the educated, yet revealed them to ordinary people (Luke 10:21). Jesus is trying to point out that the work of the kingdom is not about our ability. As we exercise the simple faith of a child, we can and *will* do all this. When we rely upon Him to do the work, miracles happen.

Jesus said that unless we are converted and become as little children, we will not enter the kingdom of heaven (Matthew 18:3). God is indeed revealing the kingdom of heaven in our time, and ordinary people around the globe are doing the works of Jesus.

Last Words of Jesus — Our Commission

Have you ever been with anyone right before they've "passed away"? Their last words and instructions are the most important things on their heart because they know they are going away and that they won't be able to speak with you again.

The last words Jesus spoke to His followers are known as the Great Commission. These words are meant for us today if we are truly following Him. There's a reason we don't call them the Great Suggestion. His commission was an authoritative order, not a piece of advice. It's something He has commanded us to do, not just something that would be nice to do if we felt like it. In other words, this is our assignment while on the earth.

> And He (Jesus) said to them, "Go into all the world and preach the gospel to every creature. He who believes and is baptized will be saved; but he who does not believe will be condemned. And these signs will follow those who believe: In My name they will cast out demons; they will speak with new tongues; they will take up serpents; and if they drink anything deadly, it will by no means hurt them; they will lay hands on the sick, and they will recover" (Mark 16:15-18).

Here are a few very important details that I'd like to point out to you. We are all called to go into the world and proclaim the good news of the kingdom, for this is the gospel. To many people they think that this means going to other countries and that is why we send so many missionaries to Africa and China. This is partly true,

110

but what about your world and where you live? I believe that this commission is to each of us to share the good news of our testimony in our own worlds. As each of us reach out to share the love of God with others this will happen. I think of the movie, Pollyanna and how one little girl changed a whole town by releasing hope, love and happiness. We can be like that and see our world change right before our eyes. I know because I witness it everywhere I go.

While in a hotel recently I reached out with God's love to one of the hotel clerks. She needed prayer but was extremely busy checking others in, so I invited her to the Healing service where I was going to preach. She came and brought her family. Her two daughters got saved, one of them got healed and all of them received the baptism of the Holy Spirit. I had the opportunity to reach out and love on another hotel clerk and her 17 year old son. The Lord showed me some things about the son and I prophesied over him. This caused him to realize that God not only knew him, but loved him and I had the privilege of praying with them to receive the Lord. At breakfast we loved on the lady who was working and were able to encourage her and to pray for her as she needed a change in her life. We got to love and bless the lady who cleaned our room and were able to encourage her faith. Everywhere you go you can be used to impact your world.

What is your world? I can bet your world could use a little ray of "Son-shine". My friend Kelly says that her world is like a hamster wheel where she travels in the same pattern week after week covering about 9 square miles. For you this could include going to your job, going to the grocery store, the barber or beauty shop, the workout gym, the post office, sporting events, restaurants and even Starbucks. Wherever your world takes you, you should display the love of God to those around you, for this is your world.

Maybe you don't feel that this pertains to you because you think you can't preach. The word "preach" comes from the word *kerusso*, which means to publish or to openly proclaim something that has been done. The word gospel comes from *euaggelion*, which means glad tidings (good news). So maybe you can't preach, but do you speak? Can you share things? Of course you can! Did you know that there isn't a testimony without a test? So all you need to do is tell of your test and how God helped you pass through the fire without getting burned. As you share what God did for you, it will be an opportunity for others to get in on the blessing. Jesus said that the signs would follow those who believed, not just those who were in the five-fold ministry. It's true, ordinary believers around the world are doing exactly as Jesus said they would do. They are taking their place by healing the sick, speaking in tongues and casting out demons.

Jesus said, "Heal the sick, cleanse the lepers, raise the dead, cast out demons. *Freely you have received, freely give*" (Matthew 10:8).

I have found that people are frequently anointed to bring healing to others who have the conditions they used to be bound in. For example, since God healed my back and neck, when I pray for those who need healing in that area I usually see people healed instantly. This is one of the ways that what the enemy means for evil God turns around for good (Romans 8:28). Not just that, but if the enemy steals anything from us, he must give back seven times (Proverbs 6:30-31).

Healing for Today

At a conference recently a young family came up and asked me to pray for their son who had back and ear pain. They told me he didn't believe that he would be healed because they had been praying for a long time and hadn't seen an answer. I asked him if he wanted to believe and he said yes. I told him that he needed to base his faith on the Word of God and not on his experience. I explained Isaiah 53:4-6 to him as well as 1 Peter 2:24 where it said Jesus took sickness upon His own body and that by His stripes we were healed. I told him that he needed to let go of what he hadn't seen because that was keeping him in unbelief and asked him if he was ready to believe God's Word. He agreed, so we prayed for him and he was healed. I had him check it by moving around a lot because we wanted to make sure that he received all of the healing. After running around the building there wasn't any pain, so I had him go and tell a few people at the conference. As he did this he prayed for a woman who had back pain and she was healed. Friends, this is what it's about. As we get healed, we need to reach out and pray for others to be healed because *freely we have received, and freely we should give it away.*

Billboards

I've prayed and cried out to God for years to give us billboards all over Atlanta that tell how Jesus is healing the sick. I want *everyone* to know that He still heals today and that His power is available to us all.

A couple of years ago, I'd been teaching a Healing School when one of my students emailed to tell me that her friend Patsy was in a coma. She asked if I would call Patsy's husband, Ron, and pray with him. I did and then mailed him the "Healing Confession Sheet." I told him to read these confessions of healing scriptures over her at least three times a day. She was in another state, so I continued to pray with Ron over the phone for her healing and to encourage him in the midst of the battle. During this time many around the United States heard what happened and the body of Christ joined us in prayer. Ron spoke these healing confessions over her every day and believed that God was faithful to fulfill His Word. Within a few months, he called to tell me that she was getting better. He said that when the Lord completely healed her that he wanted to put up a billboard giving God all the glory. When he asked me what it should say, I told him that he needed to make it clear that Jesus healed his wife as a testimony to people from other religions.

Ron eventually put up many billboards to proclaim that Jesus healed Patsy and to direct people to their website address where they could read the whole story: *www.patsysmiracle.com.* He currently has six of them in Georgia. When I saw the billboard last summer, God told me to call Ron about having a link to our Healing Rooms on his website so people would know where to go for Jesus to heal them. But even before I could, he called a mutual friend and said he wanted to talk to me as soon as possible. When I shared what the Lord told me He said he would love to put a link on their web site, and he also posted an article of mine called "Forget Not All of God's Benefits."

TV News Special

Shortly after Ron put the Healing Rooms link on his website, a local TV station contacted him and Patsy to film their story. Ron told them that God healed Patsy and that the Healing Rooms helped by praying for her and showing him how to pray over her every day. He called me excitedly to say they wanted to come and film us at the Healing Rooms. I was excited too because I want the testimony of Jesus to spread all over Atlanta. What better way than through a major TV station?

As it turns out, the station wanted to film a private prayer session, and I couldn't allow that. I told them we would be glad to meet with them, and they could feel free to film what God is doing in the Healing Rooms, but that we couldn't allow the prayer session to be on TV. These sessions are private, not for the public eye. Though I believe we are called to utilize media to get the truth out about our awesome healing God, news media can sometimes put a negative spin on things. Recently God told me that I am to tell His children that they all need to be billboards. As you go out and share the good news of how Jesus is healing the sick, you too will be His walking, talking billboard.

Clerk Saved

Most of the time, I'm armed and ready, looking for a way I can pour out God's love and power. Sometimes, however, the opportunities come when I'm in a hurry and not looking for one. Once I was standing in the checkout line at Walmart when a young lady came up to me and said, "Ma'am, I can take you down here." Boy, was I relieved—I always try to avoid long checkout lanes.

"Do you remember me?" this young lady asked. "I'm the one who asked you about your children last week." Focused on getting in and out of the store as quickly as possible, I wasn't ready for what was about to happen. "Oh yeah," I said. "Now I remember. Do you remember what I told you?"

"Yes, you told me that your son and daughter weren't twins, but were 17 months apart."

Wow, she had been paying attention! "Do you want to hear about a miracle?" I asked. "God made my son Israel as smart as his sister, and they both are in fourth grade together."

"Really?"

I usually don't ask this next question because it can shut doors quickly, but the words just came out of my mouth without thinking. "Do you have a church?"

"No, but I need one."

I could tell she wasn't very happy, so I continued. "If you were to die today, do you know where you would spend eternity?"

"I don't want to know," she said in a scared voice.

"What I meant to say," I explained, "was that if you were to die today would you like to know that you were going to heaven?"

"YES!" she shouted. I then told her about Jesus and how He took all her sins so she would be forgiven and to give her an abundant life. I told her that He came to turn her life around if she would repent and receive Him.

"Hold on," she said, "I have to go get someone." So she left the register and got another lady who was working at the front desk area. She returned with her friend and said, "Here, this lady is going to pray for us so we can make sure we are going to heaven." She stopped and bowed her head waiting for me to lead her to Jesus. I had her repeat after me.

When she had completed a couple of sentences, she stopped me and said to her friend, "Hey, wait, you need to pray this too!"

"I already received Jesus and I know I'm going to heaven," her friend told her. This made her happy, so she asked me to continue. As we were praying, the manager came up behind her and was trying to ask her a question. She put her hand up as if to say "not now" and wouldn't stop our prayer time. By the time I got to the end of the prayer, she was crying. Now, that's God! I wasn't even looking for an opportunity to be a light for Jesus. I hadn't even been very loving like I normally try to be because I was in such a hurry.

Since then, I realized that it doesn't matter where you are or what your circumstances are. If Jesus is in you, others will notice it and want to draw on the anointing inside you. Even when it's not convenient we need to take time to slow down and to love those around us because we just never know if there is a divine appointment in the making. We need to be available, even if we have other plans. A friend of mine has a saying: If you want to make God laugh, tell Him your plans! It's funny, but it's true. God is good—He'll use you even when you aren't ready if you'll just be available to respond to the gentle nudges of Holy Spirit.

One thing I always do when I lead people to the Lord is to have them ask for the Holy Spirit to baptize them as well. Had I not been in a checkout lane at Walmart, I would have taken more time to minister to this woman. I would have given her an opportunity to ask questions and asked her if she felt anything when we were praying. If we will have people ask the Holy Spirit to baptize them when we lead them to the Lord, many times we'll find that they feel His tangible presence in the form of heat or electricity. It's also good to explain that the Spirit now lives inside of them and makes power gifts available to them so they can pray for the sick and get words of knowledge for other people. I would also explain that one of the evidences of the Holy Spirit is the ability to pray in a heavenly language. This enables us to pray perfect prayers as the Holy Spirit prays through us to Father God. Then I would encourage them to give it a try by giving voice to it.

Take It to the World

We can take the light of Jesus to the world whether it's on the job, in a health club, to the beauty shop, or anywhere else we go. God's kingdom power will flow out of us in the form of His love and His supernatural ability to meet people's needs wherever we are, because His kingdom is within us. The good news isn't just that people can be freed from their sins, but that an abundant life in the kingdom is available to them today. We're supposed to be emptying out the drug houses and restoring people to wholeness in the name of Jesus. We have something that will turn them in another direction and satisfy them so that they never need to take another drug. As someone who was instantly delivered from addiction to alcohol, I know God can do in one minute what Alcoholics Anonymous takes months or even years to do.

How hard is it to lay hands on people and release God's power? It's very easy because He's the One who heals. We see even small children do this. All it takes is simple faith and a willingness to step out, speak God's Word and lay hands on people to see them healed. I started doing this shortly after I got saved, even before I'd ever read the Bible. I learned a couple of healing scriptures, and as I would step out and lay hands on people they would get healed.

As I have grown in the Lord, I've realized that I don't even need to lay hands on everyone. I can simply speak the Word, and they will be healed. Many people get healed as I pray for them over the phone. So don't limit yourself to laying hands on the sick—just speak the Word, and you'll see people healed. Healing is only hard when we think that we have something to do with it. We can't heal anyone. We just need to be available for Him to pour through us. If you step out in faith, you will see instant miracles. Don't think about it, just go do it!

Out of the Pew and Into the Harvest
A couple of years ago, the Lord told me that I was going to start preaching in churches in order to mobilize the saints out of the pews and into the harvest. We must believe the Word of God, receive our marching orders, get out of the pew, and focus on advancing the kingdom of heaven on earth. We aren't called to just go sit at church every week. That's not our destination. Cal Pierce says if we stay in the pew long enough, we'll smell that way! We must give out because the more we pour out, the more God will fill us. We're to be filled with truth and His presence and then give it away.

We need to stop waiting for revival. Revival isn't out there some-where waiting to take place. It's inside *you!* It will happen as each person takes their place. Just go and release His power through you today. As the saints receive the fire of God for themselves and take their place, they will spark revival fires everywhere they go. The enemy won't be able to stop this fire. The truth is that Holy Spirit is already moving mightily in revival throughout the earth today. He is awakening the bride of Christ from a deep sleep and stirring up hearts to receive the revelation of "Christ in you, the hope of glory" (Colossians 1:27). His primary purpose is to reach the ends of the earth with the gospel of Jesus Christ. Will you rise up, "take your place," and do what He has commanded you to do?

Whether you decide to stand up and take your place or not, you are in the battle. You can either lie there and take the assault of the enemy or rise up in your God-given authority and take back everything the enemy has stolen from you—*and* show others what's available to them.

Time is running out—many are dying without knowing Jesus. If one of your children were missing, wouldn't you do everything in your power to find them and bring them home? God is asking you to help bring His children home. When we believe that we are who He says we are and really understand that He lives in us, we will live like this and not just hope we can do it. We don't have to look for signs and wonders—we can just do them. They will be a sign for many to find their way back home. If Holy Spirit truly lives in you, it's all of Him, not just part of Him. If He's living in you, then 100 percent of His power is inside you and revival is about to happen!

Nehemiah

Nehemiah had a very big vision. He wanted to see a wall built around his city, but he didn't have enough time, people, or resources (sounds like us, doesn't it?). But each person committed to build the stone wall in front of their own house, and it was done in record time.

If each of us would just commit to do what's before us, the impossible will become possible. We must all take our place and build the wall in front of our own house. God needs you—really. He wants to flow through you. Remember, it's not your ability that He's looking for but your availability. This means that you stand and do warfare for your family. If they get sick, you pray for them to be healed—not simply with a weak request to God, but with the authority He gave you. You can command sickness to go and release healing virtue into their bodies. If you get sick you do the same for yourself.

You should also pray for people at the grocery store, at your job and everywhere else you go. It's time for Christians to stop walking past the sick and hurting without releasing the kingdom of heaven into their lives. God wants us to stop concentrating so much on our own lives and take time for the people all around us. I'm not talking about doing this in a pushy, bulldog kind of way, of course. I know from experience that this doesn't work well. Let's use Jesus as our example. He loved people and reached out to them with the compassion of our Father. Remember, you can release His love and be the mailbox to deliver a message to them from Him.

Fluorescent Bulbs

God is calling each of us to take our place by being a light in the world. Some Christians are a bright light that startles other people, causing them to run in the opposite direction. It's not that we should hide our light, but we need to have discernment to know how much light they can take. As we wear love, it softens the light that we carry so others can receive the light. I've found that it's better to be like the new fluorescent bulbs. They start out dim and brighten over time. For those who are in darkness soft light is much easier on the eyes. Then as time goes on, your light can brighten up more and more as quickly as they can handle it.

After one of my "Take Your Place" weekends, I took a group of people to the mall so they could use their gifts and see God heal the sick in the marketplace. Surprisingly, we had a hard time finding people who looked physically sick to pray for. We split up into groups of three, and I encouraged the ladies on my team that we needed to just have fun and watch God bring people to us. And He did! The first was a lady at a makeup counter in Macy's. She approached us; we expressed God's love and kindness, and then asked if she needed to be healed. As we prayed for her she felt His presence, but would need a test to see if she had received her healing.

When our time at the mall was almost up, I sensed the Lord say it was okay to go to a store where I needed to get something. As we walked into the store, I saw an empty massage chair. I had been standing most of the day and was physically tired. So I thought, *Now this is what I'm talking about! God loves me so much, I bet He'll give me a divine appointment as I sit and get massaged.* And guess what—He did! I didn't even have to try. The guy who worked there sat beside me and started talking to me. I learned a little about his life, and God gave me His love for this young man. He didn't have a physical healing need, but he had a much bigger need, he needed Jesus! He was drawn to the Christ in me. I learned that he just started going to a Catholic church, and from there I explained the gospel in such an easy way that he wanted to receive the Lord. He said it made so much sense and that he had never heard it that way before. He immediately said yes to receive the Lord. After prayer, he hugged me and asked me to come back for a visit. Recently I went back to the store with Den and the kids and he remembered me. He told me that after we had prayed before, that he received a promotion and was now the Assistant Manager of the store. He believed that it had to do with our praying, and so do I. That is a "Go Jesus!"

When I go get pedicures, God always gives me divine appointments. I've prayed for so many people in nail salons and seen them healed and then led them to the Lord. I hardly even need to look for divine appointments anymore; they just seem to fall into my lap, as they will for you. We just need to have our eyes open to see them!

The Lord has called you to do this also. Did you know that most people come to the Lord and into the fullness of the Spirit through a friend or family member, not through huge evangelistic crusades? That's why each of us must take our place by being a light to those around us. He loves every one of them with an everlasting love. He wants to pour His love through you to touch those you come across on a daily basis. It may be a word of encouragement, as we all need that from time to time. Maybe they need healing or a prophetic word, or perhaps they've never received Jesus. You get to be the vessel to deliver His love on the earth. This will show others who He is and what He is like, enabling them to come up higher so they might shine His light in the earth.

Take the Seven Mountains

As I mentioned in the introduction, I shared the vision that the Lord gave me about writing this book with our church staff about a week after God gave it to me. That night my pastor, Johnny Enlow, said he was also writing a book called *The Seven Mountain Prophecy*. It is about the "Elijah Revolution" that is now being released in the earth, which must precede the second coming of Christ. Johnny writes:

"There are seven manifestations of Elijah. One of them is the practitioner of the supernatural. Elijah comes as the antidote to the religious spirit—that which has a form of godliness but no power (2 Timothy 3:5). Religion has a spiritual look but no substance or power. The Elijah Revolution will usher in a major healing revival everywhere it goes and will demonstrate the power of our God. Elijah revolutionaries will walk in unprecedented power and presence of the Lord. Through their words alone, they will cancel droughts, plagues, and adverse weather. Supernatural experiences will be their 'bread,' and they will demonstrate the truth that 'greater is He that is in me than he that is in the world' (1 John 4:4)."

This book is yet another picture of how we are to be a light for Jesus on the high places—the seven mountains, that is. Johnny explains in his book that our assignment in the world is to take dominion over the seven key structures of society:

1. Media
2. Government
3. Education
4. Economy
5. Religion
6. Celebration and Arts
7. Family

What I find interesting is that God gave both of us a vision of how we as the children of God are to be lights for Him that are set upon a hill. This book is about how we can walk in the power and the presence of the Lord to release the supernatural everywhere we go, whereas Johnny's book is about how to apply our faith as we learn to take the mountain God has called each one of us to. Johnny's book is a must read for all Christians in order to disciple the nations. We need to do both.

Power of the Testimony

Many years ago, my first mentor, Herb Mjorud, told me that it wasn't my responsibility to lead everyone to the Lord. He said it *was* my responsibility, however, to share the testimony of what God had done in my life with those around me. As I mentioned, when I met Herb and Thelma, they were in their 80s and were taking appointments in their home to pray for people to be healed, delivered, and filled with the baptism of the Holy Spirit. After Herb found out what a person needed, he would tell them a testimony of someone who had been healed or delivered from that and about the great things he had seen God do around the world. Then he would explain what the Bible says about healing and how it's part of our inheritance. By the time he was ready to pray for them, they were *ready!* They couldn't wait for him to lay his hands on them in order for them to receive their healing.

In Psalm 78, the children of Israel were told to make known to their children the testimonies of what God had done. Since they forgot to tell of His testimonies, the miracles were forgotten. Future generations therefore didn't know they served a miracle-working God! God promised David longevity for his dynasty for generations to come *if* they kept His covenant and His testimony. We need to do the same by being watchful and preserving the testimony.

When Jesus told His disciples that He was sending them out as the Father had sent Him, they took the baton and passed it to the next generation. But several generations later, believers dropped the baton and forgot to tell the testimonies of God's power and how they were to do the works of Jesus. Let me tell you, saints, a generation is rising that is ready to pick up the baton again, realizing we are here to destroy the works of the devil.

How many people in our country today know that our God is still healing those who are in pain, sick and diseased? Not many. What about those in most churches? Still the same answer, right? That may surprise you, but I know that it is true. I have been in the healing ministry for over 10 years, and I'm surprised by the number of Christians who think I'm in a cult or something because I teach the Word of God on healing and see Him do miracles.

Now what about Spirit-filled churches? How many of them know not only that God heals the sick but that everyone should be operating in the power of the Spirit and doing the same things that Jesus did? Sadly, the answer doesn't get much better. It's still not many. It isn't that Spirit-filled Christians doubt God's ability to do miracles; it's just that too many of God's precious children haven't experienced His miracles personally. Why is this the case? Perhaps this sounds too simplistic, but I believe it's because the testimonies of Jesus aren't told enough.

Healing is supposed to be a sign to the unbeliever that our God is all-powerful, but it's also a sign to many unbelieving believers. It's time for all Christians to learn the truth and to take their place in the Great Commission. As we take our place the next generation will be able to walk in a greater measure of God's power than we do today. But we must keep telling of the miraculous works of the Lord. Let's use our mouths to start proclaiming the good news of the kingdom of God and the great things He is doing today! Revelation 19:10 declares that the testimony of Jesus is the Spirit of prophecy. So let's start prophesying all over our cities that Jesus is the Healer!

Sharing Testimonies Brings Miracles

Bill Johnson of Bethel Church in Redding, California, tells testimonies in his healing services more than any other minister I've ever seen. I've actually seen others get healed instantaneously just by hearing that God healed someone else of the same condition. I think this is partly because it shows them that God doesn't have favorites (Romans 2:11). When people hear a testimony, it sparks the hope that He will do it for them also.

Bill has the most powerful teaching on this subject that I have ever heard. I once heard him say that our testimony is the part of yesterday that has been redeemed and the only thing we can bring from our past. My past was dark and depressing before I was saved. I wouldn't want to go through it again for anything in the world because it was so traumatic. But I now have an anointing to help others get healed and delivered from the same painful things I went through. I'm sure you've been through some things in your life and have a testimony of being healed, delivered, or experiencing victory also. You must share your testimony with those who are still in bondage to pain, sickness, depression, alcohol, and more, because they need what you have. Freely you have received, freely give it away.

Grab Hold of a Testimony

When you hear a story, your imagination can actually visualize it, right? You can do that with God's miracles too. You have access to *all* of His miracles, so go ahead and dream about them. If there's anything you need, you can go to the Word of God. If He has done it for someone else, He can do it for you. It's part of your inheritance, so grab hold of it. You can pull it out of the spiritual realm into the natural realm. God calls those things that are not as though they are, and we can do the same (Romans 4:17). Why? Because it's already done in the Spirit realm and is accessible to us today, we just can't see it yet.

Honestly share your testimony

Bill recommends that if you pray for someone out of fear, you shouldn't edit that out of the testimony. Believe it or not, it will help others. The testimony of our Awesome God is that He heals people even when we don't fully expect or believe that He will. Our report must be honest. We must not embellish or take away from it; it reveals the nature of God and His covenant with man. If we get into fear or doubt, it's only because we forgot the record. That starts when we stop talking about what God has done. Let's keep our eyes, ears, and minds focused on the truth of His testimony.

The followers of Jesus did miracles, and today there are many Christians who believe the Bible and are doing them also. Now it's your turn to step out of the boat and fulfill the Great Commission of loving others and sharing what God has done for you. Our message is that with Jesus, all things are possible. Miracles are normal. We want people to have an excitement and anticipation to meet Him because He is the message. So *re*-present Him to people around you. To many you are the only Jesus they will ever know, so make sure to represent Him the way He really is. Step out with the simple faith of a child, laying hands on the sick, commanding the sickness to leave and God's power to be released to bring restoration. Remember Jesus said that these signs will follow those who believe. You can expect that the signs will follow you as you speak about Jesus and how he heals the sick. If you don't take risks, you won't have the miracles. But if you do, you'll see sickness and disease bow their knee to the name of Jesus, and see people healed in *no time!*

Have Them Share Their Testimony

After people receive their healing, it's important for them to tell others what God did for them. This is one way of sealing the healing. We overcome the enemy by the blood of the Lamb and the word of our testimony (Revelation 12:11). The word of our testimony releases the power. When Paul and Peter got into trouble, they would go back over their time of visitation. So let's keep rehearsing God's testimonies and keep them forever in our mouths and our minds.

In my experience, when I am faithful to step out and pray for people, I usually see God heal them instantly. I wish it were always true, but we're not seeing everyone receive their healing like when Jesus walked on the planet. However we must continue to do as He says, regardless of what we see. We must be as tenacious as a bulldog, though, and not give up. Bill Johnson has said that we are to pray for each person as if everyone we ever prayed for received their healing.

I love reading about others who have stepped out in faith and how God worked through them. John Wimber was a man of persistence and faith whom God used mightily to heal the sick. Sit back and read this excerpt and be encouraged.

John Wimber — A Pioneer

Here is the account of John Wimber:

"The actual process of learning to pray for the sick was accompanied by God purging me of pride and self-sufficiency. For the first ten months I prayed for the sick, for ten months I failed. During this time I was ridiculed and slandered, but still I chose to pray for the sick."

For six months, "almost every sermon I preached was about divine healing. Only a few weeks into this period, God spoke to me about having an altar call after every sermon to pray for the sick. I did not want to have altar calls, but in obedience to God the next Sunday I called the sick forward and we prayed for them. At the first altar call no one was healed. . . . I repeated the altar call the following Sunday and thereafter for eight or nine weeks—but still not one person was healed. As the barren weeks rolled on, I became despondent."

Wimber tells how he finally became so angry with God he declared he would not teach about healing anymore. Then God spoke to him clearly and said, "Either preach my word or get out." The Lord told John, "Preach My Word, not your experience."

Wimber goes on to say, "So I continued to teach about Christ's example of praying for the sick and the need that we continue to do as he did. . . . But after ten months of unsuccessful prayer, I had my greatest defeat. . . . On this occasion several men and I prayed for another man (I cannot remember what his condition was). We prayed for two hours, praying every prayer that we knew, desperate to see the man healed. Finally, in despair, we stopped." Wimber threw himself on the floor and cried out to God. He was brokenhearted. Finally he limped home and went to bed wondering what the future would hold. The next day he received a call from a new church member asking for prayer for his wife who was sick with a fever. John went over to their home and prayed for her and relates how he, "mumbled a faithless prayer, and then turned around and began explaining to her husband why some people do not get healed—a talk I had perfected during the previous ten months." What happened next was that the wife got up healed and asked John if he wanted to stay for breakfast! "The healing ministry was born in me, at the moment I least suspected it would be."[6]

CHAPTER 6: Holy Spirit

When I was a young Christian I was intrigued by something one of my friends in the ministry used to say as she ministered. She said she always knew if it was Father God, Jesus, or Holy Spirit who was speaking to her. I knew Jesus; He's my Savior, and through Him I had learned to get to know my Father in Heaven. But I didn't know or understand Holy Spirit, even though I knew He was a person—the third person of the Godhead with all the personality of God. Many of us think about Him as being a Spirit that fills us and empowers us. But a person? That was hard to understand.

Because Holy Spirit's job is to point people to Jesus, we don't often think about Him and who He is. He doesn't speak on His own authority but only what He hears from Jesus or Father God (John 16:13-15). He's like the servant of Abraham who went to find a bride for Isaac. Abraham, as a picture of Father God, entrusted his servant with the task of looking for a bride to marry Isaac, a picture of Jesus (Genesis 24). In the Genesis account, the name of the servant is never known, just as the Spirit is often behind the scenes. His mission was to find the bride who was chosen by God and bring her to the son.

Another "snapshot" of the role of Holy Spirit can be seen in the story of Queen Esther and the servant of King Ahasuerus. Esther needed to know how to please the king, so she relied on the eunuch Hegai to teach her and give her wisdom about how to gain the king's favor—just as we can rely on Holy Spirit to teach us about our King.

Not long ago as I spent time with the Lord in worship, I started crying out again to know Holy Spirit. I was somewhat surprised when He said, "I am the One who speaks to you. I am the One who encourages you and gives you the grace to do what you are called to do. I am the One who comforts you. I am the One who gives you the mind and thoughts of Christ. I am the One who reminds you of the words of Jesus. I am the One who teaches you and gives you wisdom, knowledge, and revelation. I am the One who lives inside of you and is your constant companion, and I am the One who will never leave you."

I never thought about it like this, but He's right. He's all this and more! He is always with me, He never leaves me, and He enables me to do everything I need to do. He's always waiting for me to turn to Him and ask for direction. He loves me and wants me to know Him more deeply. He always forgives me and wants me to commit to find time alone in His presence so He can teach me the ways of my Father. It's just that I usually think of Father God or Jesus doing these things, not Him!

I quickly repented and told Him I never really thought about Him being a person who lives inside of us. Not just part of Him, but all of Him! He's the exact representation of Jesus and the Father, just as Jesus was the exact representation of His Father. They are three persons, yet are all one. Holy Spirit never points people to Himself, but He points people to Jesus, and Jesus points people to our Father. I believe that this is why so many people live their lives without much thought of Holy Spirit, because no one is pointing to Him. In this chapter, I'd like to do just that!

Here's what I've learned about Him. Just as Father and Jesus are love, so is Holy Spirit. He's passionate and always waiting for us to turn our attention toward God. He always has an answer for whatever we're asking. He lives inside of us and knows us better than anyone else in the world does. He's a constant companion and my best friend. No matter what, He never turns His back on me, even though in the natural I deserve it sometimes. He has been described as having the Mother heart of God, and this makes sense because Jesus calls Him "the Comforter."

When I'm going through a hard time, I've learned to turn to Holy Spirit first rather than to anyone else. What's so wonderful is that because He lives inside us, He's always available any time of the day or night. He sticks closer than a brother and is my greatest cheerleader—next to my husband, that is. He's always giving me a "high five" in the spirit when I pass the tests and trials I find on my journey in life. As I make myself available to Him, He gives me the mind of Christ and fills me with all wisdom and knowledge. The truth is that I've been seated in heavenly places and have been blessed with every spiritual blessing, and He is my Great Reward. Did you know that? *He* is our Great Reward this side of eternity!

We daydream about what it's going to be like in heaven one day when we're with Jesus and our Heavenly Father. But you know what, friends? Holy Spirit is just like them, and He lives inside of us today. Do you remember what Jesus said about His relationship with the Father? "If you've seen me, you've seen my Father." The Holy Spirit could just as well say, "If you've seen Jesus, you've seen me." What Jesus said about Himself and our Father pertains to Holy Spirit as well. He's our Great Reward, and we can experience the love and presence of God through fellowship with Him today.

The Person of the Holy Spirit

Recently one of my friends told me that many people don't believe that Holy Spirit is a person. I had no idea people thought that because I've always been taught that He's the third person of the Godhead. "There are three that bear witness in heaven: the Father, the Word, and the Holy Spirit; and these three are one" (1 John 5:7). Since Father and Jesus are indeed persons, so is Holy Spirit. It's that simple!

Important Facts about Holy Spirit

- Holy Spirit is the One who gives us revelation (Luke 2:26).

- Holy Spirit is described in the New Testament as coming in the form of a dove. The dove symbolizes peace, innocence, and purity throughout scripture.

- We don't need to worry about what to say beforehand in a situation because, as we lean into Holy Spirit, He will give us the words (Mark 13:11).

- If faulty human parents will meet the real needs of their children instead of deceiving them with harmful gifts, how much more can we expect our Heavenly Father to bless us with the best gift, Holy Spirit, as well as lesser gifts (Luke 11:13). Our primary needs are spiritual, and a proper relationship with God through Holy Spirit is the ground of assurance that He will provide both our spiritual and material needs.

Baptisms

The first time the Holy Spirit is talked about in the New Testament is when John the Baptist declares that though he baptized people in water, Jesus would baptize people in the Holy Spirit and fire (Matthew 3:11). These are described as two separate experiences. Water baptism can be performed by individuals, but Jesus is the one who baptizes us in the Holy Spirit and fire.

The word *baptism* means to dip repeatedly, to immerse, or to submerge. In water baptism, John submerged people into the river, but the Holy Spirit filled them. The baptism of the Holy Spirit is available to everyone who desires to receive it. Jesus' role was not only as the sacrificial Lamb but our empowering Lord—the Baptizer with the Spirit. He saves us, but then He wants to fill us continually with an ongoing flow of His life and power. He pours His Holy Spirit upon His redeemed, enabling us to declare and demonstrate the power of the living Savior wherever we go until He comes again.

John Baptizes Jesus

When Jesus had been baptized, He came up out of the water, the heavens were opened, and He saw the Spirit of God descending on Him like a dove. Suddenly, a voice came from heaven, saying, "This is My beloved Son, in whom I am well pleased" (Matthew 3:15-17). Immediately after this, the Spirit led Him into the wilderness (Luke 4:1).

Jesus' ministry did not begin until He received His anointing as Messiah. He received the empowering when the Holy Spirit descended upon Him. Though conceived and born by the Spirit (Luke 1:35) and sinless throughout His whole life (John 8:46), He did not attempt ministry until He had been baptized in the Spirit's power.

The Ministry of the Kingdom

After Jesus received the baptism of the Spirit, He started His earthly ministry declaring the presence of God's kingdom followed by miracles, signs, and wonders (Luke 4:14-15; Matthew 4:23-25). If Jesus couldn't do ministry without Holy Spirit, we can't either. We must have His power to advance kingdom ministry through us, His church. People should receive the baptism of the Holy Spirit immediately after receiving Jesus as Savior or when they are water baptized. We should not try to do ministry without first being filled with Holy Spirit. Unfortunately many people have not been taught this, and they attempt to live the Christian life without the full release of power that only the Holy Spirit can provide.

In order to truly take our place, we must get into the flow of Holy Spirit's power. We must be filled by Him continually because we can't pour out what we don't have. God is a Spirit, and His kingdom is a spiritual kingdom. In order to function in His kingdom, we must focus on getting into the flow of His Spirit.

The kingdom remains a mystery to people who don't really want it. But people who have a heart for God, who want to know Him and serve Him, will see something that the world can't see. "We have received, not the spirit of the world, but the Spirit who is from God, that we might know the things that have been freely given to us by God" (1 Corinthians 2:12).

The only one who can teach us is Holy Spirit, and we only understand His teaching as we lean into Him. "The natural man does not receive the things of the Spirit of God, for they are foolishness to him; nor can he know them, because they are spiritually discerned" (1 Corinthians 2:14). What more needs to be said? Let each of us personally hear His command: "Receive the Holy Spirit!" (John 20:22).

Indwelling of the Father and the Son

Jesus told His disciples that it was better for them that He was going to heaven so that the Helper, the Holy Spirit, would come (see John 16:5-15). He also said that Holy Spirit would:

- convict the world of sin because they don't believe in Him;

- convict the world of righteousness because He was going to His Father;
- convict the world of judgment because the devil is judged;
- guide us into all truth;
- speak not on His own authority, but say whatever He hears from Father;
- tell us of things to come;
- glorify Him by taking the things He said and declaring them to us.

Before Jesus left to return to heaven, He met with His disciples. He told them that He was sending them just as the Father had sent Him. He then breathed on them and said, "Receive the Holy Spirit" (John 20:21-22). But this was not the baptism of the Holy Spirit, for in Acts 1, He told His disciples that they were to wait for the promise of the Father and that they would be baptized with the Holy Spirit. These are two separate experiences.

Coming of the Holy Spirit

When the Day of Pentecost arrived, the disciples were all together in unity. A sound like a mighty, rushing wind suddenly came from heaven, and it filled the house. "Then there appeared to them divided tongues, as of fire, and one sat upon each of them. And they were all filled with the Holy Spirit and began to speak with other tongues, as the Spirit gave them utterance" (Acts 2:3-4). People had come to Jerusalem from all over for the feast, and when they heard these Galileans speaking everyone else's languages, they were amazed and perplexed (Acts 2:5-13).

Peter's Sermon

Do you remember how, just a few chapters earlier, Peter denied knowing Jesus three times? After having received the baptism in the power of the Holy Spirit, this same disciple was able to stand up and preach a powerful sermon. Peter explained that the people were witnessing the fulfillment of Joel's prophecy about God pouring out His Spirit on all flesh. Did you notice that Peter was no longer double-minded when Holy Spirit filled him? This is a clue for us. If we're double-minded, we need more of Holy Spirit's power in our life. And you, my friend, are the one who determines how much you get by how much time you spend with Him.

Remember, the flow of Holy Spirit's power comes upon those who love God and seek His face. It comes upon those who want to be with Him more than they want to be used by Him. God responds to our hunger and our thirst for Him. So the next time you feel that you're being attacked with lies and start wavering in your faith, step into Holy Spirit and start receiving from Him. We must operate out of our spirits and not our flesh.

The infilling of the Spirit will give us boldness to do things we couldn't ordinarily do in our own flesh. I know some people in ministry who are naturally very quiet and shy but very bold in the Spirit. It seems hard to believe, but it's true.

Again we see in Acts that the baptism of the Holy Spirit is a separate experience from water baptism. When the apostles who were in Jerusalem heard that those in Samaria had received the Word of God, they sent Peter and John to pray for them so they could receive the Holy Spirit too because, as yet, He hadn't fallen upon them. They had only been baptized in the name of the Lord. But when the disciples laid hands on these new believers, they received the Holy Spirit (Acts 8:14-17).

The Holy Spirit Falls on People

One time when Peter was speaking to the Gentiles, the Holy Spirit fell upon all those who heard the Word. The believers who had been circumcised were astonished because the gift of the Holy Spirit had been poured out on the Gentiles too. They then heard them speak with tongues and magnify God (Acts 10:44-46).

When Paul was visiting Ephesus, he asked a group of believers if they had received the Holy Spirit when they believed. They said they hadn't heard of Holy Spirit and that they were baptized into John's baptism. When Paul laid his hands on them, the Holy Spirit came upon them, and they spoke with tongues and prophesied (Acts 19:1-6).

We need to recover the dynamic power of the Holy Spirit, which transformed and empowered the early Christians. The Bible unequivocally declares, "Be filled with the Spirit" (Ephesians 5:18). Scripture reveals that the person of the Holy Spirit has been the primary agent in the ministry of the Word throughout the centuries. It states clearly that the triune Godhead operates co-equally and eternally as one unit. Yet each of them has a different function: the executive is the Father, the architect is the Son, and the contractor is the Holy Spirit.

Roles of the Holy Spirit

The scriptures tell how the Holy Spirit is uniquely and distinctly at work. According to numerous biblical references, He was the author of both the Old and New Testaments, and He was the anointer of kings, priests, and prophets throughout both testaments. Specifically, the Holy Spirit anointed the prophet Joel to prophesy of the day when He would be poured out and when His gifts would be exercised in the church throughout the whole age (Joel 2:28-32; Acts 2:17-21).

In every respect, Holy Spirit operates in the church as a definite personality—a person given as a gift to the church to assure that the continued ministry of the resurrected Christ is expressed and verified. He has all the characteristics of a person. He has a mind, will, and emotions; He has relationships with human beings; He engages in a variety of activities; and He shares all the attributes of both the Father and the Son.

Acts provides five accounts of people receiving the fullness or baptism in the Holy Spirit (Acts 2:4; 8:14-25; 9:17-20; 10:44-48; 19:1-7). Several common manifestations show up in each of these accounts. In all of them, there was an overwhelming sense of God's presence; lives were transformed, and the church grew, strengthened, and increased its activity. Three of these events involved immediate speaking in tongues. And the general result of the baptism events was an increase in spiritual attitudes of thankfulness, joy, humility, and zeal.

Even though the Holy Spirit operates in every believer and in the many ministries of the church, every believer must still answer the question of Acts 19:2: "Have you received the Holy Spirit since you believed?" Many Christians today don't understand that the baptism of the Spirit is for all believers today just as it was 2,000 years ago. We must have His empowerment if we are to do any of the works that Jesus did.

Spiritual Gifts

There are three kinds of gifts we call spiritual gifts. Paul described these categories of gifts in 1 Corinthians 12:4-6:

1. There are different kinds of gifts, but the same Spirit.
2. There are different kinds of service, but the same Lord.
3. There are different kinds of working, but the same God works all of them in all men.

I once heard someone say that these three kinds of gifts are associated with a different member of the Trinity, yet each is a manifestation of the life of Jesus through His people.

Motivational Gifts

Different kinds of working. These are different approaches to meeting human needs which we call motivational gifts. The Father places within each of us a motivation to minister in a particular way. These are expressions of the heart of Jesus and are listed in Romans 12:6-8 as prophecy, serving, teaching, encouraging, giving, leading, and mercy. Each believer will have one of these basic motivations as the primary driving force behind his or her ministry.

I once heard a helpful illustration of how these gifts operate. Suppose you are sitting down for a meal at a large table with several other Christians, each with a different motivational gift. Suddenly one of the children stands up and knocks over a glass of juice.

- The teacher will try to give instruction. He will tell the child that if he puts the glass farther from the edge that it probably won't happen again.

- The prophet will give correction and point out that the child should have paid better attention to what he was doing.

- The giver will run to get the child another glass of juice because he sees a need and wants to meet it.

- The person with the gift of serving will clean up the mess and see if anyone else needs anything.

- The person who has the gift of mercy will start hugging the child and comforting him so he doesn't feel sad.

That's how the motivational gifts function. They are all found in Jesus and express an important facet of His character in the believer. When a person is saved they receive at least one of these gifts.

Ministry Gifts

Different kinds of gifts. The Greek word for "gifts," *charisma*, refers to a miraculous faculty given by God. These are produced by Holy Spirit and are called ministry gifts. Through the operation of these gifts, Jesus continues His ministry of healing the sick, casting out demons, and revealing the compassion of the Father to His children. They are listed in 1 Corinthians 12:7-10 as manifestations of the power of God released to His people to equip them for service: words of wisdom, words of knowledge, faith, gifts of healing, working of miracles, prophecy, discerning of spirits, different kinds of tongues, and interpretation of tongues.

All these gifts are available to every Christian as they are needed. In the Healing Rooms, our team members operate in all of these gifts "as the Spirit wills" to heal the sick and bring them to a place of wholeness. Paul was a good example of this. He was an apostle, but he quite frequently taught the Word of God, cast out demons, healed the sick, prophesied, received words of knowledge, and spoke in tongues. He strongly exhorted Christians to seek to operate in all the gifts and to pray for additional gifts.

But when God calls a Christian to function in one of these gifts on a regular basis, that becomes known as "their ministry" or "their gifting." I know several women and men who have an ongoing ministry of healing, others of prophesying, and so on. 1 Corinthians 12:27-31 tells us that no one ministry will be given to all Christians—for example, not all will be apostles, teachers, or prophets; but all the gifts are available to each of us to flow in as Holy Spirit determines.

Leadership Gifts

Different kinds of service. The Greek word translated here as "service" is *diakonia* and refers to an office or a position of service within the body. These leadership roles are established by Jesus to equip His church for healthy functioning. A church will be hindered in its ministry if all of these offices are not in place. In Ephesians 4:11-13, expressions of the authority of Jesus are seen in what is often referred to as the "five-fold" ministry: apostles, prophets, evangelists, pastors, and teachers. Though every believer benefits from the presence of these offices, only a handful of Christians are called to occupy them. However, their job is to *equip you*, a saint of God so you can take your place and do the works of the ministry!

Operation in the Gifts

Many Christians think they either have spiritual gifts or they don't, and that God is the one who chooses to pour them out. This is true to an extent, but we're also told to desire and pursue them. These gifts are not for us, but for helping encourage and strengthen the body of Christ and to bring others to the Lord. The Bible describes the functioning of the gifts as a process by which we grow. We are to stir up and exercise the ones that we do have and to pray for and seek additional gifts. As we're faithful with what He gives us, He'll entrust more to us. We can actually receive an impartation of spiritual gifts from others. As we grow in our gifts, we can become more like Jesus.

Receiving Holy Spirit and His Baptism

When you asked God to forgive you and invited Jesus into your heart, do you think He did? Of course! But why do you believe this? Not only because the Bible says so, but also because you've heard it taught so many times. Remember, faith comes by hearing the Word of God. The reason many people have such a hard time believing they will receive the fullness and power of the Spirit is because they either don't know the scripture or because they haven't heard it taught very much. But just as we believe Jesus will come into our hearts when we ask Him to, so will He baptize us with the Holy Spirit when we ask and believe.

As I mentioned in chapter 1, Den and I went through a couple of classes on the baptism of the Holy Spirit at our Lutheran Church a few months after we received the Lord. It's so good to know what the Word of God says about this so you can stand firm when the enemy tries to convince you it isn't really for you. Just as the enemy comes to try and steal a person's healing after they've been healed, so he will come to try to convince you that you didn't receive this gift and that you're making it up. That's why this chapter is so important; we must know what the Bible says in order to understand this wonderful part of our inheritance.

I'm so thankful for Herb and Thelma Mjorud, who helped me believe the Bible and not be stopped by fear, doubt, and unbelief. Herb came to the Lord as an atheist attorney and then became a pastor in the Lutheran Church. He preached the born-again message and brought many into a relationship with God. Then the Lord led him into the fullness of the gospel by revealing the power that was available to him.

Miracles for Today

Herb told me about a man in his church who was very sick with a terminal condition. One day, this man came to Herb and asked him if James 5:14-15 was true.

> "Is anyone among you sick? Let him call for the elders of the church, and let them pray over him, anointing him with oil in the name of the Lord. And the prayer of faith will save the sick, and the Lord will raise him up. And if he has committed sins, he will be forgiven."

Herb told the man that if he was asking if the Bible was true, the answer was yes. Then the man said, "Okay, then call the elders of the church because I want to be healed." This was not very common in the 1960s; actually, Herb didn't think that God still healed the sick. Needless to say, Herb didn't have faith for this man's healing. But the man wanted the elders to pray, so Herb called them together hoping that someone would have faith. Herb remembered that they would pour a lot of oil over the person being anointed in the Old Testament. So as they gathered together, he quoted James 5:14-15 and poured a whole bottle of olive oil over the man's head. When they were done, the sick man stood up and, to everyone's amazement—especially Herb's—he was healed!

The word got out, and many people came to be anointed and prayed for. Even though God was healing the sick, the baptism of the Holy Spirit and speaking in tongues were still foreign ideas that Herb didn't really believe in—that is, until he had another encounter. One day as he was preparing to preach a service, Holy Spirit fell on him and he began to speak in tongues. From Herb's experience and that of so many others, I've learned that people are really just "one encounter away from a new theology."

Herb later became an evangelist and traveled around the world holding healing services and seeing the power of God heal many kinds of sickness and disease. Blind eyes opened, deaf ears were healed, creative miracles occurred, and a man who died during a service was raised from the dead as Herb prayed for him.

The baptism of the Holy Spirit opens the door for us as believers to walk in the power of God and begin doing the works that Jesus did—and even greater works. As we use our prayer language, Holy Spirit prays God's perfect will through us, and we're also built up in our faith (Romans 8:26; Jude 20). Just as Herb did, we will begin to see signs, wonders, and miracles released as we obey what Holy Spirit shows us.

Herb and his wife, Thelma, took me in as a daughter in the Lord and taught me all they had learned about healing. Herb went home to glory five years later in his mid 80s. Thelma is still one of my dearest friends and is 95 years young. She is still praying for people and is one of my greatest intercessors.

Be Like the Bereans

Maybe you want to receive the baptism of the Holy Spirit but have been told it isn't for today or that tongues is demonic. Be like the Bereans (Acts 17:10-11) and search the scriptures yourself. Choose to believe God's Word and let go of anything that anyone has told you that's contrary to the Word of God. Receive God's promise—His Holy Spirit and His fullness—today! Don't wait any longer. The enemy has been stealing from all of us for way too long. It's time we receive the fullness of God's power and take our place of dominion in the earth again.

CHAPTER 7: Understanding Your Identity

One of the most important ways I can help you "take your place" is to help you understand your identity and who you are in Christ. The more you can understand who you are from His perspective, the more abundantly you will live. You need to see yourself from His heavenly viewpoint—as a redeemed saint who was bought with the blood of Jesus, the most costly, precious thing in all the world to our Father. He did this so you would know the depths of His extravagant love toward you. You need to know you are a child of God and a co-heir with Jesus. Everything that belongs to Him now belongs to you, and you have free access to it all. You must know that you are not just someone who was once a slave who is now free. You are an ambassador of God's kingdom, and you now hold the keys to set others free and bring them into the abundant life in God's kingdom on the earth. What could be more exciting than that?

From Slavery to the Palace

As you know, we were born into sin and became its slaves. But Jesus came to redeem us and set us free—not just for freedom's sake, but to adopt us into His royal family as princes and princesses. Maybe no one ever told you that you are of the royal bloodline, but you are. You have the DNA of God Himself and were fashioned into His likeness and image. You are no longer a bondservant, but you are an heir of the King of kings and the Lord of lords.

The problem is that many of us still live as if we're in slavery and don't have a choice. But we do! We don't have to live like chickens scratching in the dirt when we were created to live like eagles flying in the heavenlies! You have the choice to become all you were meant to be. The key is to know you have a choice and that it's up to you to take hold of it.

God gave us free will and lets us choose the kind of life that we want to live. It's sad, but many Christians live like they are blind, poor, sick, depressed, and hungry slaves. All the while, they have been given the keys into the royal kingdom and could have gone there anytime day or night to eat, drink, and be merry. Everything they need is available to them. Many of God's children didn't get their needs met or were abused when they were young, and have a hard time understanding kingdom living. If that's you, allow the truths shared in this book to help you understand your inheritance and how to enjoy "all His benefits".

There's More than Enough

Kris Vallotton and Bill Johnson wrote a wonderful book on our rights and privileges as sons and daughters of God called *The Supernatural Ways of Royalty*.[7] In Chapter 2, Kris writes about how the enemy tries to convince people that poverty is their portion in life. They believe that there will never be enough for them, that the glass is always half empty rather than half full. They live in fear, thinking that their resources are limited and their well is going to dry up. These people have a hard time rejoicing when other people are blessed because they feel that someone else's blessing means less for them. This is a lie! God has more than enough; His well will never dry up. If He needed to, He could put money in the mouth of a fish to get it to you! A poverty mentality will keep people in a miserable life. The truth is that everything we need has already been provided for us.

The prodigal son in Luke 15 shows us this point more clearly. Having wasted his inheritance, the younger son came home to beg for forgiveness. He figured that being a servant in his father's house would be better than having nothing. But his father, who had been waiting for his return, saw him yet a long way off and ran to meet him. He threw his arms around his son and cried tears of joy. This son, whom he thought was dead, was alive! The father had the fattened calf killed for a great celebration.

Everyone came to the party except for the older brother, who stayed outside because he was angry and felt slighted. "Why aren't you coming to the celebration?" the father asked the older brother. This son was madder than a hornet: "You gave him the fattened calf, but you didn't even give me a goat." Stunned by this attitude, yet filled with great love and compassion, the father turned to him and said, "I gave him the fattened calf, but you own the entire farm."[8]

Why would this older brother have been so upset just because he didn't get a goat when he really owned the whole farm? It's because he didn't realize that he was indeed a son and not a servant. It's sad, but so many of us get caught believing this lie like the older brother did. The fact is that we aren't just workers in the kingdom. We must not see ourselves as merely servants, but as sons and daughters of the King. We're princes and princesses. Our Daddy has more than enough, and He desires to bless us more than we even want to be blessed. He wants to lead us more than we want to be led. Just believe!

Ambassadors of the Kingdom

As we saw in an earlier chapter, we serve Jesus as kingdom ambassadors, not as slaves. He no longer calls us servants/slaves, but He calls us friends. The word *ambassador* is the English translation of the Greek word *presbeuo*, which has the root meaning of being a senior representative possessing power and authority. An ambassador represents the government that appointed him. His power and authority are delegated. When he speaks in his official capacity as ambassador, his voice is the voice of the government he represents.

In the same way, we represent God's government—His Kingdom— as His ambassadors here on earth. He has delegated His power and authority to us for that purpose. If we are His ambassadors, we have authority to act in His name and on His behalf. In fact, this power and authority are actively at work in us right now. And we are more than ambassadors; we're His friends. Jesus said, "No longer do I call you servants, for a servant does not know what his master is doing; but I have called you friends, for all things that I heard from My Father I have made known to you" (John 15:15). God never designed us to live a life of poverty in any area of our lives. We are to be more than conquerors. All the silver, the gold, and the cattle on a thousand hills belong to us because they belong to Him. We are joint heirs with Him now and in the age to come. Remember to just KISS—Keep It Simple Saint! Don't complicate it; even children can understand God's way in His kingdom. Actually, the more childlike we become, the easier it will be for us to understand the ways of His spiritual kingdom and to receive from our Father in heaven.

Eagles in Scripture

God's creation reveals everything necessary for people to know there's a God. It shows us He is a God of love and perfection while leaving no reason for men to ignore or deny Him. Jesus often used a natural situation to explain a spiritual truth, as when teaching about the parable of the sower in Mark 4. And throughout the Bible, God likens Himself and His children to eagles. He never compared Himself or His children to a turkey. Unfortunately, many of us would have to be categorized as a crow, turkey, buzzard, or even a chicken, rather than an eagle. But it's time for you to take your place as an eagle Christian.

God uses the eagle in all its majesty, kingship, and sovereignty of the air to describe the Christian, who is made in the image of almighty God. The eagle is the King of all the birds of the air and is symbolic of Jesus, who is the King of kings. Christians should live as children of the King!

Lessons from the Lives of Eagles

Over the years I have heard a lot of sermons and read a lot of articles about the lives of eagles. One teacher who has some great things to say about the eagle is Glen Clifton. He describes two types of eagles: the imperial eagle and the golden eagle. The imperial eagle (also called "bald" or "American" eagle) represents sovereignty and kingship. Jesus has made us "kings and priests": according to Revelation 1:6. The apostle Paul declares that in Jesus we have power always to triumph (2 Corinthians 2:14) and that through Him we can do all things (Philippians 4:13). As a part of His royal family, we should walk in a way that reflects the fact that we reign in this life through Him (Romans 5:17).

Since gold is a symbol of deity in the Bible, the golden eagle represents God's nature. Since we have been bought with the blood of Jesus, we now have a new nature. We have been cleansed and purified by the blood of Jesus, and all things have become new (2 Corinthians 5:17). We can partake of His divine nature because He lives within us (2 Peter 1:4). Now you and I can be as He is and rise up and learn to fly with Him in the heavenlies.[9]

Another great teacher on the subject is Jimmy Oentoro. He believes we can learn a lot by studying the life of an eagle.[10] As Christians, we were born to fly with God, just as eagles belong to the sky. Eagles don't belong in cages, and neither do we. Just as the eagle keeps his gaze on the sun, we need to focus our gaze on God and the things of heaven. We do that by setting our minds on the things above and not on the things on the earth (Colossians 3:1-2). As the heavens are higher than the earth, so God's ways are higher than our ways and His thoughts higher than our thoughts (Isaiah 55:9). We must therefore get the mind of Christ in order to be free and to fly with Him. Our limited perception will always cause us to fly lower than we ought to.

"While other birds hide in their nest," Jimmy says, "the eagle flies toward the storm. The special anatomy of her wings causes her to be lifted up higher during the storm than during a clear day. She flies toward the sun, and she is not disturbed by the dark clouds, the flash, nor the sound of the storm because she focuses her eye toward the last place she saw the sun. The eagle speaks about people who have the ability to live beyond their situation, even when the storms of life hit them, because they focus their eyes on the Son."

Birds generally don't like storms and would rather hide from them. But eagles fly toward them knowing that a storm will enable them to fly higher. Like the eagle, God has given us the ability to be lifted up higher during the storm as we draw near to Him. And honestly, Dennis and I have found that to be true. It has been during our difficult, trying times that the Lord has seemed closest to us. But it's really we who came closer to Him, as He's always there for us.

It's just that we lean more heavily upon Him during difficult times. I believe that when we get to heaven, we will thank Him for the difficulties we experienced during our lifetime because they kept us close to Him. And there's nothing more important than that.

It's interesting that eagles always seem to have a purpose for their actions. They either fly toward the sun or dart down toward the ground to catch their prey. Chickens, on the other hand, will follow those who are moving in a certain direction without even knowing where they're going. Many people follow the crowd and succumb to peer pressure. But we're called to be like eagles; as we stop following the majority around us and look to the Son of God, we too will fly with certainty as our spirits engage with Him.

Many Christians act more like turkeys than eagles. Turkeys are birds of fear. This keeps them chained to the ground and the lower, base things of this life; fear always brings bondage. We should never be chained to the things of this world. My friend Marc Buchheit says we're to be free radicals. The word *free* means released from captivity, enjoying liberty, not bound, confirmed, not hampered or restricted. The word *radical* means "on the cutting edge" or pushing the limits of the natural limitations and going into the supernatural lifestyle.

The eagle likes to fly high in the bright sunshine with freedom in her wings. The eagle Christian wants to soar in the spirit and is not held in bondage to fear because of the things of this world. They are free to experience the finer things Father God has so abundantly provided for them.

The Dwelling Place of the Christian

Eagles build their nests in a high place, typically on a rock. Christians also should position their lives in the secret place on the rock, Jesus:

"He who dwells in the secret place of the Most High shall abide under the shadow of the Almighty. I will say of the Lord: 'He is my refuge and my fortress; My God, in Him I will trust'" (Psalm 91:1-2).

146

God is our help in time of need and will be a refuge and fortress for us to run into. Just as an eagle loves to sit all alone basking in the presence of the sun, so we need to sit all alone in the presence of Jesus and allow His presence to saturate us. And just as baby eaglets are born with their mouths open and are always hungry, so we should be as well. God is a good Dad and always feeds the hungry. Are you hungry for the food of His Word that He feeds His children? If so, great! If not ask Him to increase your hunger so you desire more of Him.

It's Time to Fly

As eaglets grow, mama eagles begin removing the comfort from their nest to pressure them to fly. In some ways, that's what God does with us. We want to stay in our comfortable nest and would love for God to spoon-feed us for the rest of our lives. But we must grow up.

When we're new Christians, it seems that God supplies anything we need without our even needing to work for it. But the day comes when we must move out of the nest and begin to fly ourselves. Just as Peter needed to use his faith to step out of the boat and walk on water, so we need to step out of our nests and believe that we can fly with Him. As we learn to hear the voice of God and to cooperate with Holy Spirit, we will be able to navigate on the winds of the Spirit. God loves us too much to leave us as baby Christians forever. We must learn that tests are only markers to check our progress and for us to move from one level to another.

Paul tells us that God is able to do exceedingly abundantly above all that we ask or think according to the power that works within us (Ephesians 3:20). Saints, we need to think about that! Let's read it again. He can do exceedingly abundantly *above* all that we can ask or think. And here's the key—*it's according to the power that works within us.* He is in us, so of course we can learn to fly. We have to learn how to use God's power and release it in our lives.

Are you having your nest stirred right now? I can promise that God loves you and knows what is best for you. He pushes His people out of the nest sometimes, and He always has a good reason. He has places He wants you to go and experiences He wants you to be involved in that are beyond anything you can imagine. But to enter into these things, you need to come with Him. You need to leave your comfort zone and reach out in faith.

Before the mama eagle teaches her eaglets how to fly, she first must ensure that their wings have grown in properly. Sometimes they have to wait, and they never like that. We can relate to that, can't we? Many of us find ourselves in that situation from time to time. We want to move on to the next part of our destiny, but we aren't ready yet. We feel that we are, of course, but like the mama eagle, God knows best. God makes sure you can fly before He will have you give it a try. He's the best teacher and will make sure you can pass the test before He gives it to you. One of the things I've learned about God is that He will always give us more opportunities to pass, no matter how many times it takes us. Like a good mother or father, He continues to say, "Get up, you can do it, try again!" Our Father knows that truly all things are possible and will continue to encourage us. We just need to make sure that we are stopping to listen to Him.

The mama eagle picks up her eaglet and takes him out of the nest. The eaglet is ecstatic. He feels the breeze rush over his wings and his adrenaline rises. He feels that he too can fly and wants to give it a try. As the mama eagle turns for home, she drops the eaglet and he starts to plummet toward the ground at a fast and furious speed. He cries out to the sky hoping that his mama will come and rescue him. As he is falling, the eaglet's life must pass before his eyes! Certainly this was a mistake, he thinks to himself. But he feels the comfort of his mama's wings catch him and carry him back up towards the comfort of his nest. Then once they get 500 feet from the nest, the mama eagle drops her baby again. Frantically trying to save himself, he starts to flap his wings. This couldn't be happening again. It must have been a mistake! His mother just saved him from death, so how could he be falling again? Plummeting to his death, he thinks back to the old nest. Sure it was getting uncomfortable, but anything beats this.

Little did this young eagle know that his mama was trying to show him that he could fly all by himself and that he needed to build up his muscles in order to do it. There were many things he needed to learn. In addition to building muscles, he would eventually learn how to wait upon the wind current and to catch it in order to soar. As he was tumbling fast toward the ground, he daydreamed about how comfortable the nest had been when he was a baby eaglet and just wished he could go back. Thankfully, again he feels the comfort of his mama's wings come under him to soften the fall as she carries him high toward the heavens again.

After several falls, I'm sure the young eaglet might be wondering if his mom is crazy or if she is trying to teach him something. He again remembers the great love that she has for him and knows that she always has his best interest at heart. This causes him to question his attitude and his response rather than her actions. The next time he's dropped, it's different. His heart is settled that this is a learning experience, not a murder attempt. He refuses to fear. Instead, in complete confidence in his mother's love, he sticks out his wings a little more purposefully and finds out that this time he can maneuver. It may be kind of awkward, but this time he realizes that the wind currents will take him up and cause him to soar just like his mama does.

I have found that when the feeling of fear tries to crush me, I can trust the Lord. When we can't see His hand or feel His wings beneath us, we can always trust His heart. We can know that this is a growing experience for us and that He wants us to prosper in every area. When trials and troubles come your way, you may want to rebuke the devil. However, I've learned that we need to be careful because we may be talking to the wrong person. Sometimes we don't understand things because of our limited perspective and blame the devil for things that God is causing to help us to move out of one chapter in our lives into another. I know the devil comes after us sometimes, but he isn't the source of everything that befalls us. Sometimes our discomfort comes from God Himself. Let me clarify something for you though. I'm not speaking of sickness, this is always from the enemy. I'm talking about life experiences and learning to fly.

Have you ever noticed that God uses refining fires in order to remove our impurities? Job said, "He knows the way I take; when He has tested me, I shall come forth as gold" (Job 23:10). Like the mother eagle, God may be orchestrating certain events in our lives out of love in order to teach us the mysteries of the air currents of His Spirit. "As an eagle stirs up its nest, hovers over its young, spreading out its wings, taking them up, carrying them on its wings, so the Lord alone led him" (Deuteronomy 32:11-12).

The Blame Game

About seven years ago, Den's department at work was being eliminated. He looked everywhere for a job and couldn't find one. We were doing what we knew to do. We were rebuking the devil and calling forth a new job for him, but no job came. In order for him to find work, it looked like we were going to have to move away from Minnesota. I know the weather isn't fun, but our family and friends were there. I had been ministering quite a bit, and we'd found the perfect church. Chuck and Robin Rinke were the pastors and later became two of our closest friends. We didn't want to leave, but we were like eaglets getting pushed out of the nest!

I decided that we needed back-up prayer, so I called up my friend, Pastor Ramona Rickard, director of Heart for the Nations Bible School where I'd graduated. When I told Ramona what was going on, she laughed at me and said, "Angela, that's not the devil, that's God! You're on fire, and God is going to move you somewhere to bring revival." She went on to tell me that this was happening to quite a few people they knew and that they too had been rebuking the enemy. After telling Den about my conversation with Ramona, we asked God to forgive us for rebuking the devil if He was the one who was trying to move us. We submitted our hearts to God and told Him that if this was His desire, He had the right to change our hearts into His desires. By the end of the week, we knew He wanted us to move to Atlanta to start Healing Rooms there.

Only God could have changed our hearts because we became so excited about this. Many years later, we now see that this seemingly bad situation has turned out to be good. We opened the first Healing Room in Georgia in October, 2003. I'm now the state director for Georgia, the South Carolina state advisor, and the regional director to help oversee the birthing of Healing Rooms in North Carolina and Tennessee also. I get the privilege of helping raise up many in the body of Christ to do the works of Jesus by healing the sick and setting the captives free. We're so glad God moved us to Georgia. We tell people now that if God wanted us to go back, we would have to hear Him say so audibly!

So let me encourage you. When things aren't turning out as you'd planned, give the Lord your heart to fill with His desires, and pray in tongues. He'll put His desires in you, and you'll be praying perfect prayers.

He Carries Us on Eagles' Wings

Before Moses gave God's children the Ten Commandments, God told him to remind them that He bore them on eagles' wings and brought them to Himself (Exodus 19:4). He wanted them to know that like a mother eagle, He was always there to save them and take care of them. He wanted to remind them of His love and His goodness so they would understand that the Ten Commandments were not to harm them but to protect them so they'd have a wonderful life.

There are times when you may feel that your comfortable nest has been destroyed. My recommendation is to keep your eyes on God and keep advancing. Refuse to look back. God wants us to be eagle Christians who will advance His army forward in order to bring in the final harvest. We can do this as we put our complete trust in Him, knowing that if we fall, He will be there to catch us.

Maybe like the baby eaglet you're questioning why something is happening in your life and feel that God has dropped you. Remember that when you can't see His hand, you can *always* trust His heart. Step out of the comfortable nest and jump into a victorious experience with Him. The walk or flight of faith is always risky, but it has great rewards. When you think you're at your end, that's the time when God carries you.

I can tell you from personal experience that it's the difficulties we go through that turn us into eagle Christians. So don't just look at the pain—look at your progress. The process God has us go through is so important and is strengthening us so we can fly with Him for all eternity!

You are growing up and learning to fly, even if you lose altitude, hit a little turbulence, and have a few crash landings. There are things that bother you now that won't bother you as time goes by. Why? Because as you stay close to God, He is strengthening you to handle difficulties. Just as the eagle reaches its full potential by learning how to handle adversity, so can you. As he discerns the thermal currents of the coming storm, you can learn to discern the empowering flow of God's Spirit and yield to Him.

The next time a storm comes your way, get close to God and wait on Him. He'll help you see yourself as He sees you—as more than a conqueror. As you see your weaknesses and surrender them to God, His strength will come and lift you higher. He'll give you the courage to declare out loud, "I can do everything God asks me to do as I lean into Jesus. Thank You, Lord, for putting this difficulty in my path so that I can see my weakness and surrender it to You. I believe You are strengthening me, changing me, and working this situation out for my good."

Father's Love Will Take You Higher

It has been my experience that not only can storms cause you to fly higher, but so can the Father's love. As I mentioned in chapter 1, I was abused, and prior to receiving the Lord I felt that my own father hated me. This was not true: he just didn't know how to express love.

My encounter with Jesus caused me to experience the awesome love of God for myself. But when God gave me Cal Pierce as a human example of a father, and I felt his love, acceptance, and encouragement, it caused me to soar. I honestly feel that I can do anything now because he cheers for me. We all need other humans to express the love of God to us. God is calling you and me to reach out with His love and to love those around us. To me, Cal has been a human picture of my true Father's love, which gives me the acceptance and encouragement that I really needed. It's amazing how the gift of encouragement and love helps others to blossom. Try pouring it out on those around you and you will see their lives changed.

Just as Cal cheers for me, encourages me, and says, "Angela you can do it," I know now that my Daddy in heaven does so as well. No matter what I go through, I can see his smile and the love in his eyes and feel his big hug that encourages me. This love has made me feel complete. With my heavenly Papa's love, I feel as if I can truly do anything; and with His love, so can you.

We are living in an increasingly fatherless society. If you haven't received the love or blessing from your natural father, I'd highly recommend asking God to give you a great spiritual father like Cal has been for me. A spiritual father will be able to stand in your natural father's place, bless you, and tell you how proud he is of you. Father God so desires for each of us to be fathers and mothers for others who have been unloved and not cheered for so that everyone might know Him and His love.

Renewed Like an Eagle

The eagle is the most majestic bird in the sky. But an eagle molts at least once in its life. This is a wilderness time for an eagle and can cause great depression. They begin to lose their feathers around the age of 30, and their beak and claws begin to alter as well. During this time, an eagle begins to walk like a turkey because it doesn't have the strength to fly. It loses its ability to see and can no longer hold its head up. This is discouraging and very traumatic to such a proud, majestic bird.

Some have observed older eagles delivering food to the ones going through this molting stage. It seems that only the older birds understand what it's like to go through this experience. During molting, eagles grow weaker and weaker, and since they only eat meat, they need help from others around them. They understand that they will die if they don't renew themselves.

Christians are to encourage others who seem to find themselves in the valley of the shadow of death. Have you been near death yourself, or been close to anyone who has? If so, you know how hard it can be and how desperately you relied on those around you to help encourage you, and even feed you at times. During these times it can feel as if all hell has come against you. This is when we need our brothers and sisters to remind us of the great love of our God and of our inheritance. That's why each of us need to take our place by allowing the love and compassion of Jesus to flow out of us to them. You truly can be a lifeline to those around you. You don't have to look far to find people who are fighting for their life. Like the older eagles, you can drop nourishment and encouragement to them.

Reaching Out to a Prostitute

On the way to the Healing Rooms one night with Cal and Michelle Pierce in Spokane, we saw a young woman who was calling out to us for help as we passed by—or at least that's how I saw it. When I asked Cal and Michelle what she wanted, they told me she was a prostitute. I was shocked—I'd never seen a prostitute before. After dropping Cal off, I felt the compassion of Jesus for this young woman and wanted Michelle to go back there with me so we could help her. We had to drive around the block a few times before we found her, but by this time she was with a friend, so the lifeline went out this night to two young women instead of one. We told them that God loved them and had a plan for their life. One of the young women said she had been calling around that day for help because she wanted to go to a treatment center to get free from drugs. She was discouraged because she hadn't found the help she needed. I told her that we were God's answer and that He wanted her to be free. I asked her if I could pray for them. By the time I got to the end of the prayer, she said she didn't feel like working anymore that night and asked if we would give them a ride home.

I ministered to these girls the whole way home, explaining that God wanted them to know how very much He loved them. I found out that they both came from broken homes where they weren't loved and cared for. They both had a lot of unforgiveness, so I shared my testimony with them. They both forgave those who had hurt them and released all the pain and bitterness that night. It seemed as if time stopped in the short drive home that night so we could bring them in closer to the Lord's heart and presence. Michelle recently told me that she and Cal haven't seen these two ladies on the streets since. I believe that God completely set them free that night.

After Michelle and I shared this story later at a Healing Rooms conference, a lady came up and said she was encouraged by our testimony because her daughter was a stripper and hadn't talked to her in a year and a half. We prayed for her and asked God to release the angels to send someone to her daughter. That night on the way home from the conference, her daughter called for the first time in one and a half years. Go Jesus! It's as each of us take our place that we can be the mailbox that the Lord will deliver His message through to those who are hurting and in great need.

Encouragement Needed During the Wilderness

During an eagle's time in the wilderness, she can remember when she used to fly high in the sky. This encourages her to make the hard and painful trip back to the top of a rock in order to be renewed. It can be a 36-hour walk to reach the top, where she pulls out her feathers one by one and then continues to bang her beak and claws on the rock. She then sits on the rock and focuses her eyes toward the sun, basking in its presence and allowing its warmth to heal her. After 40 days, she's ready to dive into the air and catch the wind current and begin to soar once more. With purpose in her heart, she flies toward the sun with new strength. This time she flies to a height she has never been able to reach before. This is what happens for those who wait upon the Lord in order to be renewed.

"Do you not know? Have you not heard? The LORD is the everlasting God, the Creator of the ends of the earth. He will not grow tired or weary, and his understanding no one can fathom. He gives strength to the weary and increases the power of the weak. Even youths grow tired and weary, and young men stumble and fall; but those who hope in the LORD will renew their strength. They will soar on wings like eagles; they will run and not grow weary, they will walk and not be faint" (Isaiah 40:28-31 NIV).

Are you ready to begin this next part of your journey with Him? Maybe it's a bit more of an adventure than you're used to, but remember that there's a guarantee: if you can keep your trust in Him, you will fly above and over the storm and soar higher than you ever have. You will grow from strength to greater strength, from faith to greater faith and from glory to greater glory!

Spread Your Wings and Fly

Now it's your turn. You need to learn to spread your wings and fly. You need to learn to stand on the promises of God regardless of the severity of the storm you're facing. We need to move from praying to proclaiming and then step out and start to fly. As you surrender to the person of the Holy Spirit, He will carry you supernaturally through all the trials.

I experienced this when my sister was about to leave this world and cross over into eternity. The presence of the Lord helped me through it as I kept my heart and mind focused on worshipping the King of kings, my sweet Jesus. You can either scream and get into fear like the turkey, or wait for the movement of the wind (Holy Spirit) like the eagle. As you enter into the gulf stream of His presence He will take you above the storm. He desires that you run into His arms so that His love, joy, and peace will protect you and fulfill your deepest needs and desires. This is available to you today; you don't have to wait any longer.

In Christ Jesus, we have been called to be eagle Christians—to share in God's majesty, not robbing Him of His glory, but as eagles to reveal the glory of God to men from the high place. We must show other eaglets how easy it is to fly with Him as we continue to fly into the Son. Let us always give glory and honor to the master eagle Himself who has mothered us, fed us, thrown us out of the nest, borne us on His wings, and taught us how to fly. Let us give glory to the Author and Finisher of our flight lessons! Won't you come and take your place as we learn to fly with Him?

CHAPTER 8: The Authority of the Believer

S everal years ago I heard that God told some modern-day prophets to quit asking Him to stop the bird flu because He had delegated that authority to them. They needed to take their place and command the bird flu to die and make declarations that it wasn't coming to their state. Remember, God gave us responsibility; it's what we allow that is allowed. If sickness comes on you or your family members you must command it to leave. He has given us all authority and all power in the earth, and at the name of Jesus, every knee must bow and every tongue confess that He is Lord (Philippians 2:10-11).

In order to take dominion in the earth, it's very important as a child of the King to understand that you've been given all authority. The strategies of hell are designed to distract and derail you from receiving God's abundant life. The enemy tries to stop us with his accusations and intimidation. We must not only defend ourselves but also focus on advancing forward like those in the armed forces. I've found that having an intimate walk with the Lord will help insulate you from the destructive attempts of the devil. There really is a shelter under His wing which we can come into and be safe.

Jesus gave us the authority to destroy the works of the devil and his cohorts and to enforce obedience in His name (Mark 16:15-18). We receive His delegated authority when we receive Him as our Savior, but having authority doesn't do us any good if we don't use it. I've also learned that our authority is only as good as our submission to Him. Jesus said, "If you love Me, keep My commandments" (John 14:15). Then in the next chapter, He said, "If you obey my commands, you will remain in my love, just as I have obeyed my Father's commands and remain in his love" (John 15:10).

No Discrimination

The bottom line is that Holy Spirit works through yielded vessels. Galatians 3:28 says there is neither Jew nor Greek, neither slave nor free, and neither male nor female. We're all one in Christ Jesus. He created us all, and He is the same Holy Spirit in every believer!

When God moved us to Georgia, I had no idea that there would be people who wouldn't want to have me minister in their church because I'm a woman. I had never heard of such a thing. In Minnesota, I was never looked down upon because I was a woman. I had a lot of female role models in the ministry, and this allowed me to see that the Holy Spirit was the same whether flowing through a woman or a man. God is looking for yielded, empty vessels that He can move through. He doesn't care what our ethnic origin or gender is, because we're all one in Christ. He wants people to see Him through His vessels. It's not about us.

I go out and minister with the support and prayer backing of my wonderful husband. He really is my greatest encourager. My pastors encourage me too. I'm grateful to Johnny and Elizabeth Enlow for opening the door to me as a woman to use their church to start the first Healing Room in Georgia. It was a divine set-up! Johnny is a man who totally believes that women should take their place in ministry in order for the body of Christ to see the fuller expression of God in the earth. His CDs on "Women in Ministry" are the best teaching I've ever heard on the subject.

I believe in submitting to the Lord and those He has placed over me. I fully submit to Cal and Michelle Pierce and those in the International Association of Healing Rooms. I'm submitted to Johnny and Elizabeth as well as my husband Dennis. If Den thinks I shouldn't do something and I feel that I should, we pray and ask for God's perfect will to be revealed to us because we want to be in agreement with Holy Spirit. But if we still can't agree, then I'll submit to him. By submitting to those who are in authority over me, I have the protection of God. There are too many people in the body of Christ who, because they have been controlled by others, refuse to submit to those who are in authority. This only opens the door to the enemy so he can continue his job on the earth of stealing, killing, and destroying.

If you can't find a pastor who exhibits healthy leadership, keep looking. They're out there. We've been so blessed by Johnny and Elizabeth. They truly understand what being a pastor is all about. They have a kingdom outpost mentality; they realize that the Lord sends people into the church to be trained up in order to be sent out. They hold people loosely yet lovingly, knowing that His children can hear His voice and will know where they are to be positioned. If someone leaves, they bless them to go where God is leading them next. They always extend an open invitation to people to come back any time they want. True spiritual leadership isn't threatened by the ways God moves people in and out.

Walk as Jesus Walked

In order to walk in our authority, it's important to see how Jesus walked in His. He didn't go around acting rough, tough, and militant. He walked in the love of His Father, for He too was love, and He extended the love and mercy of God everywhere He went. Likewise, we must walk in His love, and as we obey His commands, His authority will also work mightily through us.

How much power do we have over the enemy? *All* power! Jesus transferred power and authority to the church so nothing could injure us (Luke 10:19). Now it's up to us to use it to stop and reverse the work of the devil. Since Jesus lives inside us, and the enemy is under His feet, then the enemy is also under our feet. And if he's under our feet, how big could he be?

God placed all things under Jesus' feet and appointed Him to be head over everything for the church (Ephesians 1:22). That means He gave *all* power to the church. There's no greater power than *all* power! Remember, when Jesus stomped on the devil's head? He took back the keys of the kingdom and gave them to us, so we are now the ones who are in charge and in control. He said that whatever we bind on earth will be bound in heaven, and whatever we loose on earth will be loosed in heaven (Matthew 16:18-19). He also said we could tread on the enemy (Luke 10:19 NAS).

Tread means:
1. to step, walk, or trample so as to press, crush, oppress or injure something;
2. to treat with disdainful harshness or cruelty;
3. to perform by walking or dancing.

Therefore, brothers and sisters, we are to crush the enemy with harshness and cruelty. And we can do it by walking or dancing. If this is true, why do we bow down to the enemy and accept whatever he gives us? Because we believe his lies and forget who's in charge. The last time I read the Bible, it said that Jesus gave us the keys to the Kingdom. This means you're in charge and that you have authority over the enemy and his works.

You Are Not a Victim

We can count on the fact that there are unseen evil forces that have been assigned to steal, kill, and destroy everything good in our lives. The Bible clearly teaches that these demonic forces band together to commit acts of aggression against us. We have every right to take authority over the enemy because Jesus stripped Satan of his power *once and for all*. "And having spoiled principalities and powers, He made a show of them openly, triumphing over them in it" (Colossians 2:15). Therefore the forces of hell are already defeated and there's no reason for us to feel victimized by the devil's attacks. The death and resurrection of Jesus gave us all the victory we need.

Rick Renner wrote a wonderful article on the Elijah List that describes just how decisively and openly Jesus defeated principalities and powers.[11] His triumph was complete, and it humiliated the enemy. When we look at ourselves in the mirror, we are looking at a victor, not a victim.

Understanding Your Enemy

Soldiers try to understand how the enemy thinks and attacks so they can protect themselves. They also are taught how to fight well so they can win. If they ran around thinking that they had to take whatever their enemy said or did to them, our country and world would be in very sad shape. We can learn a lot from these great men and women who serve our country.

Let's take a look at how Satan and his cohorts operate and how they came to attack Jesus. After Jesus was baptized in the Jordan River by Holy Spirit, He went into the wilderness to fast and pray in preparation for His ministry. Let me ask you, what day did the devil decide to tempt Jesus? No, it wasn't on the first or even the tenth day. He saved his attack until the end of the 40 days when Jesus was very hot, very tired, very hungry, and extremely thirsty. This is also what the devil and his cohorts do to us. They strike their hardest when we are in a weakened condition. I always recommend to my friends and those I teach to make sure that they are taking care of themselves physically by getting enough rest and eating well; otherwise they may fall for some of the enemy's lies. It seems that the enemy attacks us when we are really hungry, tired, having a bad day, having a fight with our spouse, or when our kids are pitching a fit.

Another thing I have learned is that we must prioritize our families. Sure sometimes we will need to be away from them, but having a strong marriage and strong relationships with our children is so very important! If we don't prioritize them the enemy will, and we can't allow the enemy to have them. Amen!

When Jesus was attacked, He didn't fight with the enemy or yell at him. He simply stated, "It is written." It's extremely important to know the Word of God because this is the only sword that can defeat the devil. "The word of God is living and active. Sharper than any double-edged sword, it penetrates even to dividing soul and spirit, joints and marrow; it judges the thoughts and attitudes of the heart" (Hebrews 4:12 NIV).

If you feel beaten up, quickly realize that you've fallen for the lies of the devil and stand up and take your place. His battle plan is to throw fiery darts at us and knock us down. Then when we're down, he kicks us some more and bombards us with every attack he can muster. He tries to get us to focus on the things he is doing to us, as if those things were the truth. Then he tries to get us to believe we have to take whatever he serves us. The bottom line is that he's trying to make us feel as if we're victims and that there's nothing we can do.

So if a doctor tries to tell you that you or someone you love has a disease, don't sign for it. It may be a fact, but it isn't truth! The truth is that you have the authority to rebuke the sickness and command it to leave. Then you can release the creative power of God to heal your body. I call this a divine reversal. What the devil meant for evil, God is now going to turn around for your good. He'll turn your mess into your message and as you share your testimony it will point people to Jesus.

When the storms of life come your way, be like the eagle. Keep your face looking at the Son and fly into Him. His Spirit will allow you to ride above the storm because you are an overcomer. Greater is He that is in you than he who is in the world (1 John 4:4). When the devil tries to get you to take whatever he throws at you, lift up your head and keep your eyes upon the promises of God. Remember your position of being seated in heavenly places is far above all demonic forces.

A year ago, a friend came to a training I did, and the Lord showed me she was struggling with feeling defeated. This had sucked the life out of her so her light couldn't shine brightly anymore. The Lord gave me this song for her in the middle of the night. I sing it quite often now, and believe it or not, it has set many people free in spite of its foolishness. The melody and a few of the words go to a song that Whoopi Goldberg sang in a *Sister Act* movie many years ago.

Here's how it goes:

You Gotta Get Up Offa That Thang!

When the enemy comes against you and bombards you with
fear,
you know what you've got to do, you've gotta get up offa your
rear.

You gotta get up offa that thang! Jump up and you'll feel better.
You gotta get up offa that thang, shake it off, shake it off, shake
it off, yeah!

Take your place, army of God, take your place, do an about
    face,
Take your place and run the race!

When the storms of life try to take you down, get Jesus on
    your mind,
Turn your back on the devil and get up offa your behind.

You gotta get up offa that thang! Jump up and you'll feel better.
You gotta get up offa that thang, shake it off, shake it off, shake
    it off, yeah!

Take your place army of God, take your place, do an about
    face,
Take your place and run the race!

So the next time you fall and feel like you can't get up, remember
this song and get up offa that thang! If you feel too weak to get up
on your own, call a friend to help. Remember, you were created to
soar with Him in heaven, not to lay down and scratch in the dirt like
a chicken.

The Whole Armor of God

Paul admonishes us to put on the whole armor of God in order
to stand against the forces of hell. It's clear that our warfare isn't
against physical forces, but against invisible forces that have well
defined levels of authority in a real sphere of activity. Paul not only
warns us of a clear structure in the unseen realm, he instructs us
to take up the whole armor of God in order to maintain a "battle
stance" against this structure. All of this armor is not just a passive
protection in facing the enemy; it's to be used offensively against
these satanic forces (see Ephesians 6:10-18).

Shield of Faith

Roman soldiers were the best trained and best equipped fighting
force in the world. We can learn a lot from them. They knew they
were going to win—as long as they kept their shields up. As Paul

saw the kind of attack Satan unleashed against God's people, he perceived that the physical warfare of the Roman army was an analogy of the spiritual warfare of Christians.

In ancient warfare, it was common for armies to use a storm of arrows to terrify their enemies. If we were soldiers, and thousands of flaming arrows began to strike all around us, the number one thing in our mind would be getting out of there! That's how we often feel when Satan attacks us. But the Roman army had a piece of armor that provided a solid defense against this kind of attack. In many cases it was the secret weapon that brought the army victory. This piece of armor was the battle shield.

The shield used by Roman soldiers was not like the round metal discs we often see in movies. It was a large, metal rectangle — about five feet high and three feet wide — that could shield the entire length of a man's body. Soldiers marched shoulder-to-shoulder, linking their shields together to form an impenetrable wall like an armored tank. Then a line of soldiers behind them raised their shields in order to cover them from the top. This fortress of shields stopped the fiery darts from hitting them. As the enemy got even closer, the Romans would slip their swords through the narrow slits between the shields to strike their opponents.

When Paul thought about our struggle against Satan, he realized that God has given us a shield like that — a shield of faith. When the body of Christ comes together and links shields, we will be able to cause our enemy to retreat. But we must learn what our shields really are and how to use them. God has provided a perfect sacrifice for sin through His Son, Jesus, who was stretched out and nailed to a wooden cross. His purpose was to receive upon Himself all the afflictions that Satan intended for us. Therefore, our shield is Jesus!

Note Paul's final directive: we are to be "praying always with all prayer and supplication in the Spirit" (v. 18). Thus, prayer is not so much a weapon or even a part of the armor as it is the means by which we engage in the battle itself and the purpose for which we're armed. To put on the armor of God is to prepare for battle. Prayer is the battle itself, with God's Word being the chief weapon we employ against Satan during our struggle.

We use God's Word as our sword to defeat the enemy. It's the most powerful weapon we have. Sometimes people say things like, "All we can do is pray." Listen, if you're praying God's Word and using the authority He has given you, prayer is the most powerful thing to use in all the world! It isn't a last resort. But you must understand the power of His armor in order to use it.

What Holds Us Back

I'm sure you've heard it said that the battlefield is in the mind. We've already talked about feeling like a victim, but I do want to talk to you about how to position yourself to win. Several years ago I was preparing to preach a message on how to receive our inheritance, when God spoke to me. "Angela, tell them that in order for them to receive their inheritance and to keep it, they must learn to gain mastery over their minds."

What exactly is that? Since the battlefield is in the mind, we must use the weapons of our warfare in order to pull down strongholds. We cast down arguments and anything that would exalt itself against the knowledge of God. Since strongholds are first established in our minds, we are to take every thought captive (2 Corinthians 10:4-5).

How do we do that? Behind every stronghold is a lie, and behind that is a fear. These fears become more real and more powerful than God's Word. We must not fail to trust in the provision of God that is ours through Jesus Christ. Some of the weapons that pull down these strongholds are: God's Word (Hebrews 4:12-13), the blood of the cross (Revelation 12:11), and the name of Jesus (Mark 16:17). Spiritual weapons pull down these strongholds and break our bondage (see Ephesians 6:13-18).

Over the years, I have heard Bill Johnson share on the mind and how we need to have it renewed in order to release the reality of the kingdom of God on the earth. The mind is a powerful instrument of the Spirit of God. When our minds are renewed God can use us to do His will. Many of us live our lives believing the lies of the enemy and this will stop God's kingdom from being advanced in the earth. We must think the way God thinks in order to release His kingdom of abundance to those around us. Living with unrenewed minds allows the kingdom of darkness to be advanced. So you have to decide: Who is going to drive your boat—the truth of the Spirit of God, or the lies of the enemy? We must have the mind of Christ in order to be effective in the kingdom—that is, to think the thoughts that He thinks. Fill yourself with the Word of God so you can think what He thinks. John Paul Jackson has a wonderful CD called "I AM: 365 Names of God" that has helped me with understanding who He is.

If what we allow our minds to think and focus on determines how we live our lives, then we must take this very seriously. Every thought and action in your life speaks in some way of allegiance to God or to Satan. Both are empowered by your agreement. Renewing your mind means learning to recognize what comes from hell and what comes from heaven, and then agreeing with heaven. If a delivery person comes to your door and wants you to sign for a package, but you hear a hissing rattlesnake in it, don't sign for it. The problem we have is that it sounds so familiar that we go ahead and sign for it. We think, *when it rains, it pours*; and then we receive it as if we don't have a choice. We agree with packages sent from hell far too often.

The fact is that *you have a choice*. Don't receive that package! You're in charge, so decide what you will allow. Don't allow your condition to determine your position. If you've fallen, you don't have to stay there. *Get Up Offa That Thang!* No matter how we feel or what is going on in our life, we must not forget that our position is that we are seated in heavenly places and that the enemy is under our feet. Since our minds are the gatekeeper, it can be used for God or the enemy. We can be a gate to release the devil's power to kill, steal, and destroy in our own lives and the lives of those around us, or we can be a gate to release the kingdom of God to bring about restoration with His abundant life.

Walk in love, forgive, and do not speak evil about anyone. If you don't forgive or if you speak evil, you're being used by the enemy. The enemy comes in through our hurts and is able to get us to believe lies about them. Hurts cause us to see life through wrong-colored glasses. If you allow yourself to become offended, you can open the door to the enemy through unforgiveness. So walk in love and go to those who have hurt you so you can work it out.

Communication and walking in grace and forgiveness are some of the most powerful weapons we can use against the enemy. Otherwise he will try to get us to believe something that isn't true. Our goal is to agree with heaven all the time so that we speak God's words. As we speak His Word His angels ascend and descend freely on assignment from God.

Captives vs. Prisoners

Isaiah said we were anointed to proclaim "liberty to the captives" and "freedom to prisoners" (61:1). Kris Vallotton gives insight on captives and prisoners in *The Supernatural Ways of Royalty,* which he co-wrote with Bill Johnson. He believes this shows two different kinds of situations people may find themselves in. A prisoner is someone who has opened the door to the jailers (tormentors) through sin or unforgiveness. Therefore they have to forgive those who have hurt them in order to get free. In the game of life, there isn't a "get out of jail free" card. In order to get free, you must set those free who have hurt you by releasing them to God. And when you do, you can watch God perform a miracle in your life too.

As long as we live on this earth, we will have opportunities to become offended. Just *refuse*, no matter what anyone does to you. This is the bait of Satan, and he's just trying to get you to play his game. I know personally how hard it is to forgive, but believe me, it is the key to getting free, healed, and walking in the love and abundance of God. Honestly, it's one of the biggest keys to freedom I've ever seen. I was once bound up as a prisoner too, but I'm free now because I chose to forgive! Remember it's a choice, not a feeling!

The other type of person is a captive. These are people who have been captured in battle and are held as prisoners of war. As ambassadors, we're like the special ops team in the military that goes in and saves those who have been held captive. These people do not have unforgiveness, but they are held by the enemy because of the lies they've believed. As we've seen, the enemy drives our boats too often by getting us to believe his lies. This is why it is so important to renew our minds. In actuality, we give the enemy permission to punish us because we believe his lies are true.

Recently a friend of mine and I didn't see things eye to eye because of a lie that was believed. I explained that it was a lie, and this person said, "No, it isn't; I see this as truth." What I realized was that we both saw the situation differently. We had to go to the root to discover the lie. Because we all believe lies at times, we desperately need Holy Spirit to help us discern truth. And when a lie is exposed, we need Him to help us get to the root of where it came in.

I always recommend that people have someone in their life they can be completely honest and open with—someone with whom you can share things that make you feel fearful or make you want to run or quit. This may or may not be your spouse. I have several people in my life I can trust to help me with this. The enemy always comes in familiar ways so that we don't recognize him or his lies. Especially because of my past, the enemy really tries to get me with the familiar lies I grew up believing. Most of the time I'm able to grab hold of them, cast them out of my mind, and speak the truth. If I start feeling sad, anxious, or fearful, though, I'll tell someone else so they can help me with it. One of the ways the enemy gains an advantage with many Christians is through our reluctance to be honest and admit our struggle. If he can keep it in the dark, he wins. If we will share our struggles with someone and bring them into the light, Satan's lies are exposed and he will be defeated.

The enemy starts young. He deceives small children to establish strongholds in their thoughts so they see everything from a wrong viewpoint. My children are so very different, just like Den and I are. I'm vocal, and you always know what I'm thinking. Israel is just like that. Sometimes when he's being disciplined, he will yell out, "Mom, I feel like you don't love me." I'm so grateful for his honesty! I'm not glad he feels that way, but because he's open and tells me the lies the enemy is feeding him. When he says things like that, I'm able to ask him if he really believes it. He always says he knows it isn't true but that he feels that way. The enemy has tried so hard to get my son to have a stronghold of rejection and a feeling of being unloved in hopes that he'll see things from a skewed viewpoint. But as we're open to discuss his thoughts, he's able to say, "Devil, that's a lie. The truth is that my Mom loves me and is disciplining me because she loves me."

Now my daughter, Moriah, is less expressive, like her dad. When she's upset, she runs off to her room. When I go talk to her, she's eventually able to tell me the lie she has believed, and we're then able to walk through it like I do with Israel. This is *so* powerful. Try it with those around you to help them be able to understand that not all of the thoughts they have are from God, or are even their own. Sometimes their thoughts are the lies of the enemy. These lies will bind them to keep them from walking in their abundant inheritance.

You'll need to take all thoughts captive and discern where they are from. If they are bad, whether they are from you or from the devil, get rid of them. Say to yourself, "I fall out of agreement with the lie that _____ and declare the truth that _____." Sometimes we just have "stinking thinking" and need our minds renewed to think God's thoughts.

Here's a little thing God has taught me: If you eat a piece of bad fruit, you'll get a stomach ache, right? So if you start feeling sad, depressed, anxious, fearful, or anything else that isn't good, realize that you've swallowed some bad fruit. Since the battlefield is in the mind, the thoughts you entertain are the fruit, and if you chew on the fruit (thought) long enough you will swallow it. So if you start feeling bad, back up and ask God what lie you believed that made you feel that way. Maybe you felt rejected or unloved by someone around you. Do you know that most of the time when you fall for this lie, it isn't even based on reality? It was just a lie you believed and received through wrong-colored glasses. For example, if I felt rejected, I would see things through purple glasses and you would see things through clear glasses. We could talk about this until the cows come home and would never agree, because I see things purple and you see things as they really are. Did you also know that people who suffer from a spirit of rejection actually project rejection onto other people and it causes people to not want to be around them?

If you will use these tools, you'll get free from the lies of the enemy and stay free. Then you can help other people learn how to do battle and gain victory over their thoughts. This is where we win or lose the battle *every day.* In order to live in the liberty that Jesus died for us to inherit, we must walk out of the captivity the enemy tries to keep us in. The more you can get free in your thoughts, the more you will be free to receive the joy of the Lord.

Our Tongues

The other thing that holds us back is our tongue. Life and death are in the power of the tongue (Proverbs 18:21). In James 3, we learn about how untamable our tongue really is. We can bridle the whole body with it. As small as it is, the tongue can be compared to the rudder of a ship. Even though ships are large and can be driven by fierce winds, they can be turned by a small rudder. In the same way, the tongue is a little member and boasts great things. It can start a huge fire and defile the whole body. The Bible declares that every kind of beast and bird has been tamed by mankind, but "no man can tame the tongue. It is a restless evil, full of deadly poison. With the tongue we praise our Lord and Father, and with it we curse men, who have been made in God's likeness. Out of the same mouth come praise and cursing. My brothers, this should not be" (James 3:8-12 NIV).

Since what we speak determines our harvest, let's make good choices in what we decree. We must stop praying like widows and take our place as the bride of Christ who is seated in heavenly places with her Bridegroom. We don't need to ask God for things He has already given us; we simply need to start declaring and calling forth our inheritance. Confessing the Word of God will cause things to change as well as strengthen your spirit. Thankfully, the days of begging are over; we are literally coming as the bride of Christ by proclaiming and declaring God's Word. As a bride, we face God, and when we resist the enemy, he must flee. So get your Bible out and start declaring His Word, for His Word is sharper than a two-edged sword.

If we're ever going to get out of the pews and advance to the front line, we must stand up and start moving. And our job is not just to get to the front line but to advance the army of God and take dominion in the earth. We cannot allow the enemy to continue to control our future. Remember you're in charge, not him. The King and His kingdom live within you. But if it just stays in you, how good is it? We don't want to be like the Dead Sea. It only receives water and it doesn't give out so it is dead. If we just come to church to occupy a pew, continually receiving but never giving out what we receive, we too become like the Dead Sea. But the more we pour out, the more He pours in.

Taking the Kingdom by Force

Jesus lived the Kingdom life and was our example of how to live as a Spirit-filled believer on the earth. Jesus demonstrated that the Kingdom of God rules over everything, and He taught us that the violent take the kingdom by force. "From the days of John the Baptist until the present time, the kingdom of heaven has endured violent assault, and violent men seize it by force [as a precious prize—a share in the heavenly kingdom is sought with most ardent zeal and intense exertion]" (Matthew 11:12 AMP).

This is violent spiritual warfare. If a robber came into your house and wanted to kidnap your daughter or son, would you just let him do that? Would you just nicely tell him to leave? No, you'd get violent! You'd knock him down, tie him up, and throw the sorry loser out. This is what we must do when the enemy comes to try to steal anything from us or those around us. We need to rise up in our authority and take charge, not just sit idly by.

The Son of God was manifested in order to destroy the works of the devil (1 John 3:8). When Jesus left this earth, He transmitted the job of destroying the works of the devil to us. If we allow the enemy to continue unchallenged in the earth, he will be able to continue to kill, steal, and destroy. Can you imagine what our world would be like without the police or our armies bringing forth justice? We must teach Christians the truth that God allows what we allow. In other words, you are like the sheriff on duty. You are to enforce God's rule by destroying the works of the devil and releasing the Kingdom of Heaven on the earth.

Think about how we react to a criminal:

1. If something is *stolen* from you, you call the police, who would pursue the thief in order to get it back. When they caught the thief, they would put him in handcuffs, haul him away, and throw him in jail.

2. If a person is *killed*, the police go after the murderer, put handcuffs on him, and throw him in jail.

3. If your property is vandalized or *destroyed*, you call the police, who again would put the vandal in handcuffs and take him to jail.

The work of the devil is like this, and as the spiritual police, we have the authority to do something about it. Jesus said in John 10:10 that the thief comes to steal, kill, and destroy. In the spirit, we see evidence of the devil's work in the lives of men, women, and children in the form of sickness, pain, disease, poverty, and depression. Yet it continues to go on, and only a few people in the body of Christ even do anything to stop it.

Remember, however, what the second half of John 10:10 says: "I have come to give them life and to give it more abundantly." When we make this our primary understanding of God's will and His kingdom and then preach and share it, everything else will fall into place. We must stop walking past those who are sick, hurt, or in pain and take our place to give them the restoration that Jesus came to give us all. Take back what God has given you to be a steward over. It doesn't belong to the enemy. Remember that Jesus has given you all power and authority over him. Therefore you are a *sheriff on duty* 24 hours a day, seven days a week.

Don't expect law-enforcement to be easy. The devil is like a bad tenant who has been evicted but refuses to leave. But you own the place, so you can go in and tell him to leave and take his dirty garbage with him. Then ask Holy Spirit to come and fill the home with His presence and fix what has been damaged. Instantly, the home is like new.

This is how it happens in life. When someone is sick, find out if there is a crack and where the door may have been opened. If there is sin, they need to ask God to forgive them for the sin. You have the authority as sheriff, and the blood of Jesus is your badge. Use your prayers and decrees as your gun, and tell the dirty scoundrel to leave in Jesus Name. Ask Holy Spirit to cleanse and restore everything that has been damaged. This is how divine reversal happens.

Everything that was bringing weakness and disease leaves and the abundant life of God is released to bring restoration.

This is a general rule. If you're trying to lead a person to the Lord, you can just pray and they'll be healed. This sign will show them who He is and they will want to repent and receive Him.

Time for Restoration

One night I was watching "Deserving Design" with Vern Yip on HGTV. It was about a young couple who had saved all their money to buy their first house. Along with their two small children, they moved into the house only to find it was a money pit. Shortly after moving in, the husband was walking through the living room and almost fell through the floor. After moving back the carpet, they found it was black and moldy. In fact, the entire house was full of mold, and their dream had now turned into a nightmare. They had to gut the house and start all over. They lost most of their furniture and needless to say they were devastated and heartbroken. Unwilling to face foreclosure, this young couple knew they had no other choice but to work hard to fix up their home. So they got busy and started rebuilding. As I watched this moving story, I began to cry. Israel was sitting next to me and saw that I was crying. He too was sad, so we cried together and talked about how thankful we are for everything the Lord has given us. But wouldn't you feel heartbroken if this happened to you? Well, many people in your own church, neighborhood, and even family have a "house" in *desperate* need of repair—their body is sick and in pain—and they need Holy Spirit to help them.

By the time Vern, the designer and show host, came into the picture, this couple was very tired and worn out. They took Vern to the kitchen to show him what they had. There was a working refrigerator and small table that held their plates, cups, and silverware—all plastic because they didn't even have running water. I don't think they even had a stove. In the living room was an old couch, a TV on a little stand and a few kids' toys. That's all. The walls were incomplete. The floors in both the kitchen and living room were just plywood. They were tired and broke and desperate for help. They were so thankful that Vern was willing to come and do one of the rooms. Vern thought about it and didn't know which room he wanted to do, but he decided on the kitchen because they at least needed to be able to cook for their family. And they were ecstatic! They would now have running water and a stove that worked.

Vern took them shopping, and like kids in a candy store, they picked out new dishes and glasses. Vern gave them a beautiful, completely new, working kitchen with a stove, three sinks, a dishwasher, new flooring, and gorgeous cabinets. To top it off, he knocked down a wall and made it an eat-in kitchen with a new table. Then he decorated it all with the finest accessories. As if that wasn't enough, he had compassion on this young couple and did the living room as well. The beautiful wood floors extended from the entryway through the living room and into the kitchen. They painted the wall with new, textured paint, gave them all new furniture, a built-in entertainment center, framed artwork, and lovely accessories around the room. Their house looked like a million bucks! I couldn't wait for the couple to come home to see it.

As they walked into their house, they screamed. The man held his hands over his mouth in unbelief at the beauty of what he was seeing and started to cry. The looks on their faces made it worth all the work and money that was spent. "Not only did you do our kitchen, but you gave us a living room to be able to enjoy with our children," they exclaimed. Vern could hardly hold back his excitement and ushered the couple into their new kitchen. As they walked through their living room to the kitchen, they were in complete awe. They couldn't believe what they were seeing. Like a kid on Christmas morning, the wife ran to the oven to open it and looked inside. "Wow" she exclaimed. "And it even works!" She ran to the sinks and put her hand under the running water and screamed, "Wow, running water!" They looked in every cabinet and drawer as if they had just been given a billion dollars and wanted to see every one of them. They cried as they thanked Vern and his team again and again!

Of course by now, as you can imagine, Israel and I were crying even harder. I thought, "Wow, I'd love to be able to help people like that."

Resurrection Power

You know what, saints? *We can* help people like that! We have resurrection power living inside of us because Holy Spirit indwells us believers and we've been given a commission from Jesus to use it. How many of us take for granted some of our most simple blessings? What about the fact that we feel great, we can see, hear, walk, speak, work, and have food to eat? To many people, these things are a luxury they don't have. Yet we have the power and authority to be like Vern and give it to them freely. Jesus has commissioned each of us to take our place by telling people about the kingdom of God that is here in our midst. He lives in us and we can freely give to others what He has freely given to us.

Do you see the picture? The young man had to clean out all the rotten parts of the house, and then Vern went in and was able to give them a wonderful new home. When there is mold and death in a house, we can go in and command the enemy to leave and take his work of death and destruction with him. Then we can release the presence of God through our hands and call forth their inheritance. That's the minimum of what we should be doing. If each saint really understood his or her place and did that, think of what the earth would look like. We could clean out hospitals - and one day I believe we will! We then can teach people that they can do the same thing we've done. That's how we reproduce Jesus, not ourselves, in the world.

Remember, greater is He who lives in us than he who lives in the world (1 John 4:4). So don't fear what the enemy does—he's under your feet. Remind him that the Creator of the universe lives inside you and rebuke him in the name of Jesus. As God says in Isaiah 54:17, "No weapon formed against you shall prosper, and every tongue which rises against you in judgment you shall condemn. This is the heritage of the servants of the LORD, and their righteousness is from Me."

Come my friend and take your place of authority in the earth as you step into a life of miracles!

CHAPTER 9: The Anointing

Hundreds of years ago, Zerubbabel, governor of Judah, was given the enormous task of rebuilding Jerusalem's temple, which had been destroyed years before by the Babylonians. In the middle of organizing and laboring for this task, he had a vision that changed the way he thought. He saw a lampstand of solid gold with a bowl on top of it. On the stand, he saw seven lamps with seven pipes, and these lamps were connected to a pair of olive trees with one on the right and one on the left. When he asked the angel what these were for, the angel answered him and said: "'Not by might nor by power, but by My Spirit,' says the LORD of hosts" (Zechariah 4:6).

The word "might" in the Hebrew is *chayil,* which means strength or force, especially military strength. This spoke directly to Zerubbabel's situation because he thought it was up to him and the strength of his workers to accomplish the task. God was trying to show him that the temple would not be accomplished primarily through the force of an army nor through the muscular power or physical stamina of the workmen. Rather, it would be accomplished by the empowering of the Spirit of God.

This is a good lesson for us all to learn and re-learn. Human nature causes us to try and do things in our own strength. But the bride of Christ is called to lean into the arms of Jesus and receive her strength from Him. We see this illustrated beautifully in the picture at the beginning of chapter 4. It's His anointing, His empowerment. We try to do things independently of Him and in our own abilities and resources. But when the job gets too big and we realize we can't do it, He is right there to help when we cry out to Him. We need to learn just to give it up and let Him do it through us. Zerubbabel was forbidden to trust the resources of man to accomplish his task of rebuilding the temple. So we too must be built and sustained not by wealth or our own strength, but by God's Spirit.

If something is too big for you to finish, then it's more than likely a "God project," and you'll need Him and His supernatural ability to accomplish it. If something is easy for you to do, then what do you need the Lord for? Get excited when you see things that are impossible, for with God all things are possible! Many times it's not until we recognize our weakness and surrender it to Him that He can move in our situation. That's when our impossibilities are going to bow their knee to the name of Jesus.

Zerubbabel saw two olive trees next to the bowls in his vision. This speaks of God's unending supply of oil that comes through Holy Spirit. To save you a lot of grief and hard work, tap into Holy Spirit and His enabling power to achieve the tasks in front of you. Otherwise, you can quickly become burned out and frustrated. I know from personal experience. But when you tap into His unending supply, He makes it seem so easy—and it's fun. As you spend time in His presence, He fills you in order to pour His blessings and anointing through you.

Learn from my mistake—take the shortcut into productivity in the kingdom of God. Remember, it's about being a "Mary-Marth." You see, as His presence is poured into and over you, it changes you into His likeness. We desperately need to have Him smear His personality on us. Through Holy Spirit comes the empowerment for us to carry out the will of God in our lives. This my friend is what the anointing of God will do for you.

Jesus was here on the earth as Emmanuel (God with us) from the moment He was born. But it wasn't until he was 30 years old when He was baptized in water that the Holy Spirit also baptized Him. In other words, even though He was God, He needed Holy Spirit to anoint Him in order to cast out demons, heal the sick, and raise the dead, not to mention all of the other wonderful miracles He performed. If He couldn't do the works of the kingdom without Holy Spirit's anointing, how can we? If we'll just learn from Him, it will save us a lot of grief and we'll be more fruitful for Him. Remember, babies are born out of intimacy, not out of work!

It's not enough to know the Word of God or even to preach it if we don't have the Holy Spirit's anointing. Jesus knew the Word of God because He was the Word of God made flesh (John 1). If Jesus, being the Word of God, still couldn't do any miracles without the anointing, what makes us think we can? We must have both the Word of God *and* the Spirit of God.

There's an old saying that goes something like this: "All Word and you dry up, all Spirit and you blow up." We need both of them, and together they make an explosive and powerful force. By Jesus' example, we see that we must receive the baptism of the Holy Spirit and that we also must stay continually filled. Jesus did this by constant communion with God the Father and God the Holy Spirit. The scriptures reveal that He often went away to be alone and pray. So we too need to be alone and spend time with Him.

Jesus came to show us how a man who was anointed with Holy Spirit could bring the reality of the kingdom of heaven to earth. He said in John 14:12 that if we believed in Him, we would do even greater things than He did. This meant that the power and anointing of the Holy Spirit would come upon us so we could do the same works that He did. Only now this anointing wouldn't be confined in one man's body but would be in everyone who received it. That's why God wants each one of His children to rise up today and take their place as never before so that the whole earth can be filled with His glory.

We are called to be glory carriers everywhere we go. If we're going to become the pure and spotless bride, we need Holy Spirit to "smear" on us and fill us with His character, His power, and His love. His anointing will enable the end-time army to take the Word of God out of the four walls of the church and into the streets with power.

Christ, the Anointed One

The Hebrew word for *anoint* and *Messiah* is the same word, *mashach*. In the Greek it is *chrio*. So both "Messiah" and "Christ" mean "the Anointed One." Jesus Christ came as our Anointed One to do what God had purposed for mankind.

In Bible School I remember hearing that the name "Christian" was not something the early believers wanted to be called when it was first used. The word was originally meant to poke fun at Christians.

People saw the disciples of the Anointed One doing the things He had done, so they called them Christians, which literally means "like the Anointed One." It wasn't until the middle of the second century that those who followed Jesus actually started to find honor in the name "Christian."

I feel it is a great honor to be called a Christian and to have people look at my life and think that I am like the Anointed One. If people make fun of you because you're a Christian, don't let it bother you. After all, they ridiculed Jesus and the prophets. If they acknowledge that you are like Christ, they are recognizing His anointing, and that, my friend, is a *good thing*. People are supposed to be able to see that you are like Him. The name "Christian" today is more like a label for anyone who attends church regularly as well as those who believe in Jesus. Let's start showing people what being a true Christian really means.

Three Anointed Ministries

In his book *The Anointing*,[12] Ian Peters teaches that there are three ministries in the Old Testament that were recognized as having been anointed and appointed by God. First there were the prophets, as we see in 1 Kings 19:16; the priests as described in Exodus 30:30; and the kings as seen in 1 Samuel 10.

Jesus Christ is our Prophet, Priest, and King—the Anointed One in all three roles. The three anointed offices typified in the Old Testament are fulfilled in Him. But there's more: Christians—people who are like the Anointed One—have also received an anointing to serve and minister in these areas.

1. *Prophets.* We have been called to prophesy the Word of God to this generation. Paul says in 1 Corinthians 14:5 "I wish that all of you would prophesy." I believe that there is a call and an anointing on us to be a prophetic generation. Every Christian, everyone who is like the Anointed One, has been called to speak the word of God.
2. *Priests.* Priests offered up sacrifices to God. Like them, we have been called to be priests before God by offering up the sacrifices of praise and worship to Him. "Through Jesus, therefore, let us

continually offer to God a sacrifice of praise—the fruit of our lips that confess His Name" (Hebrews 13:15 NIV).
3. *Kings.* We have been called to be kings as well. The Bible makes it plain that we have been anointed by the power of God and by His Holy Spirit to rule and to reign—not just in the millennium, but also in this life. "How much more will those who receive God's abundant provision of grace and of the gift of righteousness reign in life through the one man, Jesus Christ" (Romans 5:17).

The anointing on these three offices, fulfilled in Christ (the Anointed One), is passed on to us as Christians (like the Anointed One) that we might reflect His nature, character, attitude, ability, and passion.

Protection of the Anointing

In ancient times, anointing oil was rubbed on sheep to protect them. This kept insects from attacking and bothering them. That's a great picture of what the anointing does for us. Since it's the power and presence of almighty God, nothing could be more protective. The more anointing you have, the more you will be free from things that have tormented you in the past. They will have to keep their distance from you. When the anointing comes, the presence and character of God comes with it, and demons are very uncomfortable around Him. As I've shared, I've been through a lot of torment and trauma in my life. But I've found that the more time I spend in the presence of God, the less I'm affected by things that used to upset me. I believe God's anointing is a protection that buffers me and causes the things of the enemy to not be able to attach to me.

Peter's Shadow

In the book of Acts, we read about how people brought the sick out into the streets and laid them on beds and couches so that at least Peter's shadow might fall on some of them as he passed by (Acts 5:14-15). Was it his physical shadow that healed people? I doubt it. It's God's tangible presence on and around us that will actually touch and heal people who are near us.

Just as the children of Israel had to get enough manna for their families, so we need to get enough anointing for those around us because we can't give out something we don't already have. We need to stop waiting until we are desperately in need before we get into the presence of God. We should get filled each day so we have more than enough for ourselves and for others too.

Wise and Foolish Virgins

This makes me think of Jesus' parable of the wise and foolish virgins. Ten virgins took their lamps and went out to meet the bridegroom. Half of them were wise, and half were foolish. Those who were foolish took their lamps but didn't bring oil with them. The wise took oil in their vessels with their lamps. But while the bridegroom was delayed, they all slept.

> "And at midnight a cry was heard: 'Behold, the bridegroom is coming; go out to meet him!' Then all those virgins arose and trimmed their lamps. And the foolish said to the wise, 'Give us some of your oil, for our lamps are going out.' But the wise answered, saying, 'No, lest there should not be enough for us and you; but go rather to those who sell, and buy for yourselves.' And while they went to buy, the bridegroom came, and those who were ready went in with him to the wedding; and the door was shut. Afterward the other virgins came also, saying, 'Lord, Lord, open to us!' But he answered and said, 'Assuredly, I say to you, I do not know you.' Watch therefore, for you know neither the day nor the hour in which the Son of Man is coming" (Matthew 25:1-13).

We don't want to be caught off guard. Let's get filled, stay filled, and release the aroma of heaven through everything we do. This will also encourage others to want to be arrayed with His sweet-smelling incense in order to be prepared for His return.

Jesus' Anointing

The best place to start in a discussion about the anointing is with Jesus. Acts 10:38 tells "how God anointed Jesus of Nazareth with the Holy Spirit and power, who went about doing good and healing all who were oppressed by the devil, for God was with Him." The Bible shows us very clearly that the anointing came upon Jesus at His baptism in the river Jordan when "the Spirit of God (descended) on Him like a dove" (Matthew 3:16).

After this, Jesus went into the wilderness where He was tempted by the devil. Luke records that not only did He go into the desert full of the Holy Spirit, but He returned from that experience "in the power of the Spirit" (Luke 4:14). His entire ministry was based on the fact that He was anointed by God.

Power of the Anointing

What do we do with the anointing? We can do whatever Jesus did. Let me take a minute to remind you that this is for you because He's in you, and if He's in you, it's His power that does the work.

Notice what Jesus said when He visited His hometown synagogue:

"So He came to Nazareth, where He had been brought up. And as His custom was, He went into the synagogue on the Sabbath day, and stood up to read. And He was handed the book of the prophet Isaiah. And when He had opened the book, He found the place where it was written:
"The Spirit of the LORD is upon Me,
Because He has anointed Me . . ." (Luke 4:16-19).

Jesus read this passage to the people that day to reveal that He was the fulfillment of this prophecy. Through this portion of scripture and throughout the Gospels, Jesus pointed out that the power of the anointing would be manifested in the following ways:

1. *"to preach the gospel to the poor..."*
Jesus' message was the good news that our Father loved us. "For He came not to condemn the world, but that the world through Him might be saved" (John 3:17).

Whatever your ministry or calling is, please be careful to minister out of the love of God and don't leave people feeling like they've been beaten up. Jesus loved sinners and showed them that He had made a way for them to receive life "more abundantly."

Recently a friend called to see if I would pray for her brother, a man in his 50s, who was addicted to drugs. He had been on drugs since he was 14 years old. When I met with him, I shared my testimony and just loved on him. I then sent him in to be ministered to by one of our teams at the Healing Rooms, and they too poured the love of God into him and prayed with him to be delivered. During the ministry time, he was able to forgive a lot of people—including Christians—who had condemned him because of his sin. This, of course, had left a sour taste in his mouth about God and Christians in general. The good news is that he left that night free from addiction and was baptized in the Holy Spirit. He called me when he got home to tell me how wonderful he felt and that he had spoken in tongues the whole way home. The good news that was ministered to him through a spirit of love set him free.

2. *"He has sent Me to heal the brokenhearted . . ."*

As we've discussed, Jesus came to bring wholeness, not just partial healing. He feels our pain and deeply desires to bring healing to our emotional wounds. This is part of the total package of salvation that He came to give.

3. *"to proclaim liberty to the captives . . ."*

He came to bring freedom to those who had been captured by the lies or strongholds of the enemy so they can soar with Him.

4. *"and recovery of sight to the blind . . ."*

Jesus was anointed to bring sight to the blind, hearing to the deaf, and abundant life into the bodies of those who were sick and diseased, healing them all.

5. *"to set at liberty those who are oppressed . . ."*

Jesus brought His anointing to set people free from all oppression.

6. *"to proclaim the acceptable year of the LORD . . ."*

The "acceptable year of the Lord" is also known in Leviticus 25 as the year of Jubilee, which occurred every 50 years. This was to proclaim liberty to those who were servants because of debt and to return lands to their former owners. Jesus was saying that because the Spirit of the Lord is upon Him, it is now the acceptable year of the Lord, and from here on out anything that has been stolen from us has to be returned and all debt forgiven. Now I don't know about you, but that is really good news because I've had a lot of things stolen from me and my family and have also owed a lot of debts!

Since you have Jesus living inside of you, the Spirit of the Lord God is upon you and He has anointed you to preach the good news to the poor, to heal the brokenhearted, to proclaim liberty to the captives and recovery of sight to the blind, to set free those who are oppressed, and to proclaim the year of the Lord's favor! So what are you waiting for? It's time you take your place and do what He did when He walked upon the earth!

We are to proclaim the acceptable year of the Lord. This includes *all* His benefits, not just some of them. We are to let other people know that Jesus took not only our sins, but all sickness, weakness, and disease so we could walk in divine health. We are to let others know of our inheritance—a treasure chest filled with good things. It only makes sense that if you have a treasure chest, you'd open it up to see what was inside, right?

Gravy Boats

My daughter Moriah drew this picture of a vision I received from the Lord many years ago. I was on my knees worshipping the Lord when I saw the glory of God being poured out of heaven as liquid gold. As it came down, it was poured into the back of an empty gravy boat and flowed out through the front spout. Having grown up in the Midwest; meat, potatoes and gravy are some of my favorite things to eat. God certainly knew how to speak my love language.

God showed me that I was an empty gravy boat and that I was to teach others that this is what He is looking for: empty, available "gravy boats." Our job is to get still in His presence so that He can fill us.

I have found that the amount of anointing we carry is determined by the amount of time we spend getting filled up. This of course goes back to our soaking in His presence. Have you ever tried to fill a moving gravy boat at Thanksgiving, or tried to saturate a sponge that wasn't in water? We must sit still in His presence to receive from Him. Of course, His anointing can come upon us when we're in action, but usually only in people who also know how to get filled up and stay that way. Remember, one of the keys Jesus showed us was His practice of often going away to be alone with His Father and Holy Spirit.

We must be yielded and empty gravy boats so that He can enlarge our hearts with His love so we can carry more of Him. The gravy boat is our heart and our spirit. "We have this treasure in earthen vessels, that the excellence of the power may be of God and not of us" (2 Corinthians 4:7).

God also wants our gravy boats to be clean. In the natural realm, pouring clean water into a bowl that is half filled with dirty water makes even the clean water dirty. The enemy comes to take our gravy boat by stealing our hearts and our affections. Therefore anything that is more important than God needs to go. We have to be careful not to put ourselves, anything or anyone else on the throne. Here are some things that we need to constantly take inventory of in order to keep ourselves pure.

- Self, having our own way, pride
- Rejection
- Selfish ambition
- Fear

These things will get our hearts and minds off of God. Then when we're trying to get filled, there isn't any room for Him! Let's put aside anything that would hinder us from the high call of being His vessels of salt and light in the world. We need to do everything as if what we do makes a difference—because it does, whether we see the immediate fruit of it or not. Remember that whatever we sow, that's what we will eventually reap.

The writer of Hebrews urges us to be single-minded toward God and our calling. "Since we are surrounded by so great a cloud of witnesses, let us lay aside every weight, and the sin which so easily ensnares us, and let us run with endurance the race that is set before us, looking unto Jesus, the author and finisher of our faith, who for the joy that was set before Him endured the cross, despising the shame, and has sat down at the right hand of the throne of God. For consider Him who endured such hostility from sinners against Himself, lest you become weary and discouraged in your souls" (Hebrews 12:1-3). Jesus endured the cross because *He saw your face*! So stay focused on Him and don't lose heart.

The enemy will do everything he can to distract us from focusing on Jesus. When you notice that your gaze is on others or on your own navel, quickly take them or yourself off the throne. Only Jesus should be your focus. Remember that offenses are the bait of Satan to bind us up and give him authority to wreak havoc in our lives. He can get us focused on ourselves with condemnation. So if you're offended with someone or if you feel condemned, realize that you have fallen into the trap of the enemy and he will try to use you to do his work in the world. If you fall for these things, he can use you to steal, kill, and destroy. Sound far-fetched? Maybe, but it's true.

Love Is the Foundation of the Kingdom

I heard a great teaching from Matt Sorger about how love is the foundation of God's kingdom. God will test our character, but when the tests come, will we be ready? We need to be glad for these tests because His glory will be revealed in our lives as we go through them. There's a great shaking taking place right now in the body of Christ. Anything that *can* be shaken *will* be shaken. So we need to take an inventory of our lives. We need to ask ourselves these two questions: "What am I building with?" and, "What am I building on?"

What are you building with? Look at your personal life, your family, and your ministry. It's extremely important to be "above board" in all areas. First of all, we need to be known by our love. Our marriages and our children are a picture to those around us of how we are doing. We can never get so busy with things in the kingdom that our families suffer.

Paul said if you build with gold and silver, it will stand the test when fire comes. But if you build with wood, hay, and stubble, it will be burned up when the fire hits it. So ask yourself—are you building with gold and silver or wood and hay?

Second, what are you building on? Paul said he built on the foundation of Jesus Christ. This is what the shaking is all about. As the fire comes, it brings to the surface things that are out of alignment. God reveals with fire the character of the work we're doing. This shows us what we are building with and upon. The foundation is Jesus, and He is what we need to build on, remembering that He is love.

This gospel that fulfilled the law and prophets was to love God with everything within you and to go love others with this same love. Jesus said, "You shall love the LORD your God with all your heart, with all your soul, and with all your mind" (Matthew 22:37). God is very concerned with the motives of our heart and our building on the right foundation. He will search our motives and test the quality of our lives. I remember hearing how the Lord emphasized the issue of love to one of His prophets. God told him that He was looking to see if this man had grown in love—not what he had done for the kingdom or how much he gave. Growth in love was God's measuring rod. The foundation of the kingdom and everything we do must be built on love.

Anything not built on love will be shaken down. 1 Corinthians 12:31 says to earnestly desire the best gifts and graces of God, but that there's still a more excellent way. What would be more excellent than seeing people walk out of wheelchairs, blind eyes open, demons cast out, and people healed of terminal illness? Love! If I can speak in tongues and prophesy but don't have love, I'm nothing. If I have the kind of faith that moves mountains but don't have love, I'm nothing. And if I give away everything I have to feed the poor and offer my body as a sacrifice but don't have love, it profits me nothing (1 Corinthians 13:1-3). The highest and best of all things is love, for God is love.

In other words, if you do anything that isn't built on the foundation of love, it's nothing in the eyes of God. You can't take credit for healing the sick, prophesying, or giving to the poor. You can't take credit for giving your body to be burned as a martyr. These are given to you by grace. What a shame it would be to serve the Lord all our lives but to have done it all with an impure motive! Can you imagine living your life like that, thinking that you had pleased God, only to find out in the end that your reward was burned up? Friends, let's take this area to the Lord and ask Him to *examine every motive* in our hearts to make sure that love is indeed the only foundation.

We need to make sure that we aren't doing anything to bring honor or glory to ourselves. We must wrap ourselves with the plain mantle of humility and learn to love everyone as the Lord does. If we try to take credit for what the Lord does, we will lose our rewards. God wants to love the world through us, if we will truly give Him our heart. This is where true power comes from.

Worship and Be Filled

Let's create an atmosphere of worship to our King and be filled with His love, keeping the atmosphere charged with His presence. It's in this place of intimacy that Holy Spirit will overshadow you and give you His personality. You'll receive His character and His power. This is why God can work through ordinary believers, not just those who have attended Bible school. Remember, God isn't looking for your ability, but your availability.

God chose the foolish things of the world to put to shame the wise, and He chose the weak things of the world to shame the things that are mighty (1 Corinthians 1:27). So He works through us not because we can do something good but because we know Someone good, and that is HIM! The more we spend time with Him, the more He will be able to pour through us.

I believe God uses people like me to proclaim this message because I'm weak and foolish. I'm an ordinary person like everyone else. I have weaknesses just like everyone else. Of course, all of us are very special in our Father's eyes, but there's nothing extraordinary about us except *Him!* That's why, when people give me compliments, I always point them to Him, saying, "GO JESUS!"

The only thing I've done is said yes to Him, but He's even the one who puts the "yes" in me. It's all about Him, and He gets all the praise, the honor, and the glory.

The truth is that if you will delight yourself in Him, He will give you the desires of your heart (Psalms 37:4). That's because He puts His desires, His love, and His power in you. You'll say "yes" to Him because you want to.

Ruth and Boaz

If you remember the story of Ruth and Boaz, you'll recall that Boaz told his servants to purposefully let grain fall from the bundles for Ruth to glean. After working in the field all day, she had one ephah of barley. Naomi, her mother-in-law, told her that Boaz was winnowing barley at the threshing floor and that she should prepare herself to go meet him. She instructed Ruth to wait until after he ate and was sleeping to uncover his feet, and then to sleep at his feet. When Boaz (a picture of Jesus) awoke he found her and gave her six ephahs of barley. What a picture! We can work all day for one ephah, or we can spend time resting in the presence of God and receive much more.

Desiring More Anointing

What do you have to do if you want more anointing? As we've discussed, the way to receive the anointing of God is to seek His face—not simply for the sake of His anointing, as that's just a by-product of intimacy. Most couples don't spend time together only so they can have a baby; they spend time together because they want to be with each other. So we don't just seek the face of our God for what we can get, but because we love Him. When you want to be with Him, then you will have more of Him to give to others. If you aren't passionate about being alone with Him, ask Him to give you that desire.

The enemy works really hard to keep us from prioritizing our alone time with God. The phone rings, you have deadlines for a project at work, the kids need our help or are fighting. Everything will pull on you to keep you from getting alone with God. But you have to just say, "No, I've got to be with Jesus." Nothing else matters! Make a commitment and follow through. It can't be optional; otherwise you'll find plenty of things screaming for your attention that will take priority over the gentle, sweet, drawing presence of the Lord.

I challenge you to carve out some time each morning, as soon as you get up, to spend time with Jesus. If you can only find 10 minutes, start with that. You can add more time soon. You'll find that He will awaken your heart to love Him more, and you will have such a hunger for His presence that you'll find yourself daydreaming about being with Him. If you miss it one day, don't give up. But do get right back to it. This will be your favorite part of each day.

On those days when you have more on your schedule than seems humanly possible to do, it's even more important to prioritize time with Jesus. If you will keep your alone time with Him, even if it's only 10 minutes sometimes, you'll see that you're able to get every-thing done in record time. It's really true—He makes everything so much easier. He wants us to understand that His will is to make things less burdensome for us. Always remember, you can bear more fruit in intimacy than you can by laboring.

As you do this, you'll get creative strategies, dreams, and visions, and the fruit in your life will be out of this world. Holy Spirit will rub off on you so much that you will even start smelling like a rose. Spending time with God is the greatest beauty plan in the world! He makes anyone look good because as you put on the One who is love, you'll start to radiate Him.

In all seriousness, I tell my girlfriends that putting on Jesus is the best and easiest beauty plan out there. Have you ever seen an ugly bride on her wedding day? No, it's not possible! Even someone who is not naturally beautiful will radiate beauty on her wedding day because she's in love—just as the One who loves us is so absolutely beautiful!

God wants to be anointed with our love and our worship. It should be "Lord, here I am, your servant. I pour out my life and my love upon you." As we take our place of pouring out our love on the Lord—His presence, His anointing and His glory will pour back on us.

CHAPTER 10: Faith

Faith is so important that without it you won't be able to step out and expect people to be healed. As I've shared, it's important to have our spiritual antennas up at all times so that we can reach out and touch people around us to meet their needs. I believe that if we're open and willing to do that, God will show us people who are crying out for Him, and we can bring His answer to their cry.

Recently I went to Spokane for the Healing Rooms' International Spiritual Hunger Conference. I love going places because God always gives me divine appointments, that is, if I'm asking for them and looking for them. One of those appointments came in the Salt Lake City airport on our way to Spokane, when a Muslim woman struck up a conversation with me. I responded in love towards her and found out that her friend needed healing. As I prayed for her she felt heat and electricity move through her body and realized that I had something she needed. This allowed me to lead her and her friend to the Lord. The next morning in Spokane, we had an opportunity to bless our waitress with God's love. She had recently given birth to a baby and had a lot of pain in her hip. As we prayed for her, joy seemed to come back as her face brightened, and the pain in her hip was totally gone. Go Jesus!

Later in the day, my friend and I had just stepped onto the elevator when a young man said, "I can tell you are Christians." When people open up like that, I believe that's a divine appointment in the making. So without thinking, the next thing that came out of my mouth was, "Yeah, do you need to get healed?" He said he needed healing in his knee. As I looked up and realized that we were already at our floor, I said, "Well, if you want to get healed, get off the elevator, and I'll pray for your knee." He and his friend got off the elevator with us. After asking what was wrong, I found out that he'd had surgery on his knee but still had pain. I had him place his hand on his knee while I placed my hand over his. I prayed a simple prayer commanding all the pain to go and then I called forth healing. Then I had him run down the hall to check it out. As he ran, he said it was getting better, so I had him return so I could pray again. I released the power of God into his knee once more and commanded it to be healed. Then I had him run down the hall again to check it out. He found out that it was even better, but not complete, so we prayed again. This time I told him that he didn't need to run down the hall, but to just lift his leg to see if it was complete. He said it felt better.

I decided to ask him what his name was and what he was doing in town. He told me that his name was Clarence and that he was the assistant to one of the conference speakers. It was as if a veil was removed and as I looked to his friend I realized that this indeed was one of the conference speakers for the Spiritual Hunger Conference. I'd never been in any of his meetings and had no clue who he was. As I introduced myself he confirmed that he was who I thought he was. Boy, was I embarrassed! If I could have crawled under the rug, I would have.

"Well, my knees need to be healed also," he said. "Will you pray for me?"

"Sure!" Turning to Clarence I said, "Clarence, this is what I teach people to do. The Bible says, 'Freely you have received, Freely give.' So I'm going to have you put your hands on his knees, and I will lay my hands over yours."

We prayed for this man of God, and he too was healed. This, my friend, is a "Go Jesus!"

Faith is so important that it's mentioned well over 300 times in the Bible. It's required for a Christian: "Without faith it is impossible to please God, because anyone who comes to him must believe that He exists and that He rewards those who earnestly seek him" (Hebrews 11:6 NIV).

So what is faith? "Faith is the substance of things hoped for and the evidence of things not seen. By faith we understand that the worlds were framed by the Word of God, so that the things which are seen today were not made of things which are visible, but invisible" (Hebrews 11:1-3). Therefore faith is believing even when you can't see it. It's being able to see in the spirit realm what your inheritance is, calling it forth, and then waiting for it to manifest. The things we see are actually made from things that aren't seen. So if you can see something in the spirit, you can have it—with eyes of faith.

Let's open the eyes of our heart and learn how to call forth those things that don't exist in the natural as if they did (Romans 4:17). Everything you need has already been provided for you, but you just can't see it right now because it's done in the unseen spiritual realm. God is a spirit. In order to receive things from His spiritual kingdom we need to learn to operate by using our spiritual senses, not our physical ones. That is why He tells us to walk by faith and not by sight (2 Corinthians 5:7).

Childlike Faith

Faith is simple—so simple, in fact, that Jesus said we ought to have the faith of a child. Only those who come to God in humble dependence and with the trust of little children will be able to enter into the kingdom of God (Mark 10:14-15). The kingdom belongs to the childlike, not because of something they have done, but because God chooses to give it to the humble and the apparently insignificant.

If you were to tell a child that you were going to take them out for ice cream after church on Sunday, they'd believe you, right? And if you forgot about it, you can bet they wouldn't. They would remind you until you took them. If you said you couldn't do it right after church, they'd keep on asking you until you could. Why? Because when you mentioned ice cream, they could see it in their mind's eye and were already looking forward to enjoying it. We need to see in our mind's eye whatever God says we can have, and then start imagining what it's going to be like to actually take possession of it—just like kids do with ice cream.

The truth is that God is raining down His multifaceted blessings everywhere. All we have to do is open up to receive them for ourselves. We need to be as hungry and thirsty as we'd be if we were in the middle of a desert. Those who hunger and thirst for His glory will be filled.

I find that many people try to put faith in their faith and feel that they aren't receiving from the Lord because they don't have enough of it. We must KISS—Keep It Simple Saint! As we continue to keep our faith in the simplicity of His Word, we will have what we are believing for. Jesus said if we have faith the size of a mustard seed, we would be able to say to a mountain to move from here to there, and it would move. With faith, he said, nothing would be impossible (Matthew 17:20). It's time we stop telling God how big our storm is and tell the storm how big our God is!

Lack of Faith

If you're struggling with lack of faith in an area of your life, ask yourself what lie you've believed that makes you think God isn't able to do that as well. Once you see what the lie is, ask God to forgive you for believing it, and put your trust in Him. For with God, all things are possible (Matthew 19:26).

Problem-centered people view their problems as being larger than their God. One of the tactics the enemy uses in this area is fear. I tell my children that the devil is only about as big as a flea, and all we have to do is stomp on him because he's under our feet. But the enemy has a very loud voice, and it seems that he screams through a megaphone. With fear, he causes people to see the trials and the apparent storms in their life as big as Mount Everest, which in turn shrinks their view of God.

A lady came into our Healing Rooms one day with a suitcase full of doctors' reports and medicines. She wanted to convince the team of how big her storm was and how impossible it was for her to be healed. The team had to help get her focus off what the doctor said and put it in the report of the Lord, which says she was healed by Jesus' stripes 2,000 years ago. She had to get her mind off of the problems and onto the Lord.

You see, we all have fear or faith—either in a positive way toward God or in a negative way toward the enemy and the difficulties he throws at us. Negative faith is called fear. It's never from God, for He has not given us a spirit of fear, but of power, of love, and a sound mind (2 Timothy 1:7). With God living inside of us, why should we fear? He loves us and is in control of the universe. In case you forgot, He holds the entire universe in the palm of His hand. There is no fear in love; but perfect love casts out fear, because fear involves torment (1 John 4:18). What helps me when I'm feeling anxious or fearful is to get everything into proper perspective. To do that, I get into His presence where His love and peace can calm my mind, my heart, and my spirit.

Focus on Jesus

I was on a local Christian TV station not long ago. I was feeling very nervous, so right in the middle of the interview I took a deep breath and focused on Jesus. As I did, His presence and love began to permeate me. The fear and nervousness subsided instantly, and His peace settled over me. At the end of the interview while still on the air, the host of the program said he saw the peace and gentleness of Kathryn Kuhlman upon me. Yeah, I thought, I may have reminded him of her because we both had Jesus!

If you will allow God to be God and put your trust in Him, you'll have peace in the midst of any storm or trial you face. If you abide in Him, the Bible says you abide in love (1 John 4:16). You've been adopted into the royal family (Romans 8:15). Remember, you are a prince or a princess, and the kingdom of heaven is your inheritance. Therefore you, not the enemy, are in control of your world.

If God is for you, who can be against you? The Lord is your helper and He is the maker of heaven and earth (Hebrews 13:6; Psalm 121:2). He only has good things for you, His precious child. As it is written: "Eye has not seen, nor ear heard, nor have entered into the heart of man the things which God has prepared for those who love Him" (1 Corinthians 2:9). But you can only receive them by faith.

We've talked about this truth in another chapter, but it also relates to this context of faith. The way we stay full of faith in God is by spending time alone in His presence and experiencing Him. Which is more real—the natural realm or the spiritual realm? The things we see are temporary and subject to change (2 Corinthians 4:18). As you spend time with Him, He puts things in their proper perspective.

Last Will and Testament

When someone dies, they leave a will—their last will and testament. Jesus left us the New Testament, or "new covenant," by which His blood paid for our sins and His stripes healed us. He has brought us into a new era. Our heavenly Father sent Jesus with the purpose of restoring relationship with Him and restoring everything that had been stolen from us, as seen in His declaration of "the acceptable year of the Lord" (Luke 4:19).

Let's say you got a call from an attorney representing Bill Gates, the billionaire who founded Microsoft Corporation. The attorney tells you Bill died, that you were his only living relative, and that he left everything he had to you. Now you might wonder if this was a hoax, but if you found out it was true, wouldn't you go to the reading of the will? Even if you still had some doubts, after you heard that you were truly named as the sole heir of his inheritance, you'd start believing really quick, right? And when they handed over the title deed to his yacht and his mansion on the beach in Hawaii and told you that 999 billion dollars that he had in his investment accounts were being transferred into your name, you'd start believing. I'd even bet you'd be jumping up and down! All it would take is having the title deed in hand. Though you hadn't seen the mansion or the actual money to be transferred into your account, you would still believe.

Why can we believe an earthly inheritance is ours when we've seen the signed will and have the title deed, yet have a hard time believing we'll receive our own heavenly Father's inheritance when we see the will of God written in the Bible? God's Word will not return to Him void, but will accomplish what He desires and achieve the purpose for which He sends it (Isaiah 55:11). As the Amplified Bible's translation of Hebrews 11:1 says: "Faith is the assurance (the confirmation, the title deed) of the things [we] hope for, being the proof of things [we] do not see *and* the conviction of their reality [faith perceiving as real fact what is not revealed to the senses]." Faith is our "title deed."

All of God's promises belong to each one of us. He doesn't show favoritism; what He did for one, He will do for all. In other words, He doesn't have favorites. These things are part of our inheritance. All of His promises are for us if we will receive them by faith and continue to believe until we receive them in our hands (2 Corinthians 1:20). The Bible clearly states what God's will is, and our redemption was signed with the blood of Jesus. Our inheritance is not just from any father but from our heavenly Father who made us and predestined us in His image and His likeness. Remember, you are in the royal family.

The problem is that too many of us don't know we're the King's kids and that everything that belongs to Him also belongs to us. The Bible declares that we're co-heirs with Jesus. Our problem comes because we can't grasp the things of the spirit realm. We live in the flesh and view things based on what we see and feel. But God is saying, "Come up here my sons and daughters and see what I have for you! It is seen through the eyes of the spirit, with eyes of faith."

Unclaimed Inheritance

I was a financial planner many years ago and specialized in retirement and estate planning. We had our clients fill out an estate-planning folder that would list all of their assets and who to contact upon death so the rightful heirs would receive all of their inheritance. We often find that when people die, they don't have their financial information together, and then their investments, annuities, and life insurance benefits go unclaimed. In other words, they remain unclaimed because their children don't know everything that is in their inheritance.

This happens to many of us in the body of Christ. People don't know what belongs to them, so they never do what's necessary to receive it. Even if they do see it, they may still fail to believe. Or perhaps they believe for a little while, but when they don't receive their inheritance right away they give up. With the title deed to Bill Gates' yacht and mansion in Hawaii, do you think you would possibly give up hope that it belongs to you and that one day you would receive it? No way! We need to have at least this much faith in the inheritance God has for us.

Unbelief in His Hometown

We read that even Jesus did not do many mighty works in His hometown, Nazareth, because of their unbelief (Matthew 13:58).

They didn't understand spiritual things and viewed Jesus only as the carpenter's son. They knew His mother Mary and didn't rightly discern the ways of God. If Jesus didn't do many mighty works because of their unbelief, what makes us believe we can receive anything from God if we don't believe?

Jesus said that if we can believe, all things will be possible for us (Mark 9:23). We need to speak forth God's Word and His will by faith! We shouldn't ever pray: "If it be your will, heal Suzy." This is admitting that we don't know His will and that we'll just leave it up to Him to see "if" He wants to heal her. That's a faith destroying prayer.

What if you went to the bank to get the money in Bill's checking account transferred into your account and said, "If it's in his will, I'd like all of his money transferred into my account." They would tell you, "I don't know if it's in his will or not." You would need to come with the title deed and say, "Here is my paperwork, and I'd like you to transfer all of the money from Bill's account into my account." Likewise, you can take your Bible out and say, "God, I see that healing is in your will, so with the faith of a child I command sickness to go, and I call for the healing virtue of Jesus to touch Suzy's body. I command her to be healed in Jesus' name!"

If you want something from God, you must first know what is in His will. God's perfect will is done in heaven, and He tells us to pray that His will be done on earth as it is done there (Matthew 6:10-11). So if something isn't allowed in heaven, we can know it isn't His will for us to accept it on earth. But if it *is* in heaven, then it belongs to you and you can call it forth through your declaration. I'm not talking about gold streets, but the provision that Jesus made for us in the Atonement. You don't need to ask Him if He will do it for you, it's already finished. Remember, we can do what Jesus did. He's our example, and He didn't ask God to heal people. He used His authority and commanded healing to come forth. In like manner, we should do the same.

When we know God's will and His promises, we can declare what He has already given us. In his book *These Walk on Water*,[13] Danny Steyne says servants beg, friends ask, but sons command. Since we are His children we command. We can stand on the promises written in His Word with confidence that we're staking a claim to something that's in our inheritance and according to His will. At other times, we may want something that is not clearly promised to us in the scriptures. Then we make supplication or requests of God, not knowing whether or not He will grant our requests—yet He tells us we may ask. The key is to know the promises God has already granted to us in His Word. For example, if I am a child in a family and I have my own bedroom, I can confidently go in and out of my room and sleep in the bed each night. But if I wanted to paint the walls a different color, I would have to ask permission from my parents. Some things are understood and known to be within the range of my privileges, and I do them without asking, while other things require additional asking and permission. God says that we are to believe in our heart and confess with our mouth and we will have what we say. So speak forth the Word of God and see your life blessed.

Wow Faith

My son, Israel, says we should have WOW faith—that is, Walking on Water faith! Like Israel, we all need to have the faith of a child. He is 9 years old and believes what God says simply because it's written in the Bible. He likes for us to pray for people everywhere we go and fully expects them to be healed.

One day recently, Israel wasn't feeling well, so I prayed for him. Then when I asked him how he was feeling, he said, "Good, Mom. You said that if two of us agree on anything, we will have it." Even if he isn't feeling totally well, Israel understands he will be healed as we continue to call it forth because healing is his inheritance. That's what God wants us to have: childlike, walking-on-water faith. Faith that absolutely believes despite what you feel.

You may remember the story of Jesus walking on water and Peter asking to walk on water too. That's faith. Peter knew Jesus had commissioned the disciples to do His works, so when he saw Jesus walking on water, he thought he'd like to give it a try. He was amazed as he stepped out of the boat because his faith caused the water to become substantial enough for him to actually walk on. But when he saw and heard the wind and the waves, he was gripped with fear and began to sink. Even in that moment, He knew that the Lord of all could rescue him, so he cried out, "Lord, save me!" And immediately Jesus stretched out His hand, caught him, and said, "O you of little faith, why did you doubt?" (Matthew 14:28-31).

We can learn a lot from Peter. He continued to walk as long as he kept his eyes on Jesus. But when he took his eyes off of Jesus and focused on the storm around him, he sank. No matter what storm comes your way, if you will keep Jesus as your focus, He will indeed keep you from falling.

How do we get WOW faith? Good question. The Bible says that faith comes by hearing, and hearing by the Word of God (Romans 10:17). As we spend time hearing the written Word of God and hearing the living Word Himself speak to us, faith will arise! For me, it was after spending a lot of time in His presence that I had radical, raw-power faith. One of the most powerful ways I have experienced this is when I have heard the Word of God spoken and then heard a testimony confirming that the Word is not only true but is still applies today. Regardless of the specific situation, faith comes by hearing. So as you share your testimony of how God has healed you, tell them they can believe for their healing as well because Jesus took all sickness in His body and that by His stripes, they have been healed.

Absolute Faith

A missionary friend was over for dinner one night and he shared about some of the different Spirit-filled churches he has been in on his journey. Surprisingly, many of them were filled with doubt. They believe God is good and generally know He wants to heal people, but he said they lacked *absolute faith*—faith that believes 100 percent that it's God's will for everyone to be healed here on earth.

How can we have 100 percent absolute faith for healing? It's easy when we see that this is part of the salvation package that Jesus already provided for us. Just as we can believe that we are saved and going to heaven one day, so we must believe for God's inheritance of healing for us also. We must let go of all doubt, even if it's only 1 percent. It's not enough for us to believe that God *can* heal, we must know that healing *absolutely* belongs to us. Again, let's go to the

Word of God, His will, to see what He says. "Bless the LORD, O my soul, and forget not all His benefits; who forgives all your iniquities, who heals *all* your diseases" (Psalm 103:2-3).

Since faith comes by hearing, it's important to be careful what you listen to. Remember the parable of the sower? We must be careful what we hear and how we hear. If anyone has taught you anything contrary to the Word of God, you must choose to believe His Word over what they have taught you.

However, if you've been listening to the Word of God, then I bet you're full of faith and ready to take on any challenge that comes your way. If you're struggling with fear or depression, you've probably been listening to the enemy. Remember, the devil is the father of lies, so it's important to grab hold of your thoughts.

Confidence

To have true mountain-moving faith is to have confidence. The Bible declares that "this is the confidence that we have in Him, that if we ask anything according to His will, He hears us. And if we know that He hears us, whatever we ask, we know that we have the petitions that we have asked of Him" (1 John 5:14-15). This is one of those passages you should commit to memory because it will help you KISS—Keep It Simple Saint. Simply hang on to your confidence.

Remember our example of receiving Bill Gates' inheritance? If you showed the bank your paperwork, otherwise known as the title deed (faith for Bible promises), you would tell them where to transfer the money and have confidence it would be done, right? The same is true of God's promises. You come to Him with the title deed (your faith in His written Word) and call forth what you want. You know He hears you and that you've obtained what you asked for. The Greek word for confidence in 1 John 5:14 means to be convinced and to have an inward certainty. The opposite of confidence is insecurity. If we are plagued by insecurity, we are agreeing with the voice of unbelief. Insecurity—which can also manifest itself as fear—is believing that God's promises will fail. Where there is true faith, there's no room for insecurity or fear.

Therefore you should thank Him, just as you would thank the bank teller and walk away, knowing that it's done and that you'll have the transfer as soon as the transaction is processed. The important thing is to remember that you made the transaction, so keep your confidence no matter how long the transfer takes. Just as transfers in the natural realm can take a while, sometimes it takes a while in the spiritual realm too.

This is where most people lose it. They give up! But we must not throw away our confidence because it has great reward. You need endurance so that after you've done the will of God you may receive the promise (Hebrews 10:35). You need to keep your confession of hope without wavering, remembering that God who promised these things is faithful (Hebrews 10:23). It's easy to keep believing if you keep your faith anchored in the One who is faithful and true!

Profiting from Trials

Did you know you can actually profit from trials? When we fall into various trials, we need to count it all joy because the testing of our faith produces patience. When our patience has done its perfect work, the Bible declares that we will be perfect and complete, lacking nothing (James 1:2-4). In case you missed that, let me say it again: If we will allow our patience to grow, we will come to know that trials are for our good. They are just tests that God knows we can pass so we can be promoted to the next level. Instead of getting upset about your troubles, get excited that you're in line for a promotion! During this time you get the opportunity to exercise your spiritual muscles in order for them to be developed. You'll have many opportunities in life to trust the Lord and have faith in Him. I've heard it said that faith works best in dung because dung is a great fertilizer! So it's when we go through difficult times that our faith actually has an opportunity to grow.

A Big Test

About three years ago, we had just one of these opportunities. Dennis got an amazing new job that would provide the finances for us to move closer to his work and to our church where the Healing Rooms are. On a trip to the lake one day, Den and the kids went off to hike, and I sat by the water to pray. I heard the Lord tell me to go to a specific area of town. I didn't know exactly where it was, but

God directed us. We loved the second neighborhood we drove into because it felt like home and the houses were very beautiful. We went to see a house in the neighborhood later that week and fell in love with it.

It would take several months of standing on our faith to receive this house because the owners had listed it much higher than we could afford, and it also took time for our house to sell. We had an opportunity for our patience to grow. We could have just said, "God, if it is your will for us to have this house then give it to us. If not, please find us a new house." However, since we had prayed and felt that this was our house, we decided to use our faith and stay in confidence that He wanted to give us our hearts' desires. After all, wouldn't I want to give my children "the bike" they desired rather than just the old model.

We finally sold our house and got the sellers of our desired house to come way down on the price all in the same weekend, which was a miracle all in itself. They also agreed to leave us several things in the house, a definite blessing from the Lord. We were so excited about the goodness of God, but then a *big* test came. One week before we were supposed to close on our house, Dennis was laid off from his job. Now what were we to do? We didn't have much savings and had no idea how we could possibly buy a new house without a job— especially when the new house was almost twice the price of our old one. It seemed that our dreams were being completely shattered.

Den and I went immediately into prayer as we needed God's wisdom concerning this. We told a few of our close friends and got differing opinions from them. Some thought this was God shutting the door to keep us from moving, but that didn't sound like God to us. We had been praying for months and felt that this was God's choice as well. If God didn't want us to move to that house, we wouldn't have felt so much peace and confirmation after praying about it. All the more reason to press into God and to hear from Him directly.

God gives us opportunities to trust Him, and accepting this turn of events as a "shut door" felt like retreating rather than advancing. A couple of our friends, including our pastors, encouraged us to move out in faith and watch the Lord work on our behalf. And while we knew it was important to seek godly counsel, we ultimately had to hear from the Lord ourselves. During this seemingly difficult time we had an opportunity to use our faith muscles in order to get larger ones.

So we drove down to the "new house" and prayed all the way, while praising God for His goodness! Now with our natural eyes, we didn't see God's blessing but still believed He was good despite what was happening. Having been through hard times in the past, we knew this was just another opportunity to trust Him more.

Many of the intersections in our city have a sign that says "Keep Moving." We really hadn't paid much attention to these signs before, but as we exited the freeway this day, it was as if the sign jumped out at us. That was sign number one. Then when we drove into the neighborhood, we noticed a vehicle called a Forerunner and sensed God saying we were forerunners. As we continued to drive in the neighborhood, we saw a Pathfinder and felt God was saying that we had found our path. We parked our car at the pool and walked down the very narrow sidewalk toward the house and again felt that God was saying that the path is narrow and few will find it. We saw gold flowers all over the sidewalk and felt that it was lined in gold just for us, His prince and princess. We then sat up at a park situated high on a hill that looked down into the backyard of our house. As we prayed, we felt we were like Joshua and Caleb spying out the land. It seemed that God was saying to us, "This is My promised land for you, but you must take it by faith. It's up to you if you will war for your new land."

Needless to say, the battle was on, and we were in the fight of a lifetime. We stayed in the presence of the Lord and in His Word. We prayed a lot and found out that He was right there with us. During this time, I heard Him speak to me more than ever before. He told me that He was the same God; He could do a miracle in the financial realm just as He could heal the sick. I could absolutely believe Him for doing miracles in people's bodies, but I hadn't been challenged to have faith in the area of finances before. God wanted to show us another aspect of who He is and prove that He is able to meet our needs no matter what the need was. I wasn't happy about having to go through this trial, but God proved Himself trustworthy. It's true what they say: without a test there isn't a testimony! We learned how to hold onto God tightly and to keep our faith in Him despite what we saw happening.

On the day that we closed on the house, we hoped and prayed they wouldn't ask us if Den was still employed at his job because we couldn't lie. But they never asked, and we received the house by faith. We signed the paperwork and took possession. After the closing, we grabbed some lunch at the local Subway. I was having a little pity party because the money that we were supposed to get at closing was next to nothing, and we had been counting on it to help us get by. I realized that I was putting my faith in the money and not in God, so I quickly repented and told God I trusted Him. After lunch, as I grabbed the car door to open it, I heard a voice say, "Dennis will have a job in one month." I immediately told him, and we rejoiced!

Of course, the enemy came to do his job of trying to steal our hope with the lie that this was only hopeful thinking. But instead of listening to the enemy, we again chose to put our trust in God. After all, He had always provided for us before, and He wants to lead us more than we want to be led. And as they say, the proof is in the pudding. God *had* actually spoken to me because within one month Den had a new job.

This is why it's so important to hang on to the confidence we have. We held on to what we knew God had told us even when it was extremely hard. We had to constantly watch our thoughts and gain victory over them because the thoughts of fear were bombarding us. As we continued in faith, we were able to watch Him move on our behalf. The key was that we stayed in prayer and in His presence and that enabled us to stand in order to receive the prize! If we had just sat back and not pressed in, I don't think we'd be living in our house today.

Stay Encouraged

To encourage us when we fall into trials, we need to recount all the times God has proven Himself faithful to us. Bill Johnson says he keeps himself encouraged by focusing on the miracles that God is doing now, not in focusing on what He is not doing. If you don't see God's miracles today or have a hard time remembering what He has done for you in the past, read about the biblical heroes of faith in Hebrews 11 and be encouraged. He's the same loving God and He wants to move in your life just like He did for them.

Faithful Abraham

By faith Abram obeyed God when he was called to go out of his own country and into Canaan, a land he didn't know. I once heard someone explain it this way: Imagine Abram saying to Sarai, "Hey, sweetheart, God spoke to me today and told me that we are to leave our country and our father's house to go to a land that He will show us. He said that He will bless those who bless us and curse those who curse us. He also said that through us, all the families of the earth shall be blessed." I can imagine Sarai might have been thinking, "Abram, you're off your rocker! You're 75, I'm barren, and we don't have any children. And you *think* God told you all this? How can I leave my family, my friends and my country to go ... Now where was that you said God told you we were going?"[14]

Once in Canaan, the Lord appeared to Abram and told him that He was giving this land to his descendants. Abram must have thought, "What descendents? I'm 75 and my wife is barren." Despite the facts, he decided to believe the Lord. Honestly, many times we just read the stories in the Bible thinking that people just loved doing what they did and had an easy time of it. It wasn't so! They had to go through tough times just like we do. They had to be patient in the desert times while waiting for the manifestation of the promises of God in their own lives. They went through many struggles in order to be called the heroes of faith. That's why it's so good to share honestly about when things were hard and how life wasn't a walk in the park, but that the Lord carried us through. That way, when others go through hard times, our testimonies will help encourage them.

Just as Abraham and Sarah had to wait for what God had promised them, so we too must wait for the promises of God to manifest in our lives. We say that we are a people of faith, but are we really? We wonder how Abraham could have possibly given up on God and gotten into human reasoning in order to assist God with the birth of his first son. But don't judge him—a lot of us may have done the same. Think about it: God called him into the land of Canaan when he was 75. When he was 86 years old—and not getting any younger—he still saw no evidence of God's promise. Wanting to help God out, his wife Sarai had what she thought was a great idea. She would give her Egyptian maidservant to Abram in order for him to birth a son.[15]

But God hadn't asked for any help. Think about that the next time you are waiting on one of His promises. He's pretty capable of bringing about a miracle all on His own, isn't He? Abram and Sarai's solution was the way of the flesh, not God's way. The result is what we call "birthing an Ishmael"—the name of the son the maidservant bore. Anytime we try to help God out in a way that He doesn't direct us to, we birth a problem rather than a fulfilled promise.

When Abram was 99, the Lord appeared to him again. It had been 24 years since God first told him that he would have a son. God wanted to confirm His covenant and told Abram that He was going to greatly increase his descendants. God changed his name to Abraham, saying that he would be a father of many nations. He changed Sarai's name to Sarah because she too would be a mother of many nations.

Now 90 years old, Sarah was way past the age of becoming pregnant. But by faith she received strength to conceive because she believed that God was faithful to His promises. From this one man, even though Abraham's ability to reproduce was dead, there were going to be born as many descendants as the stars of the sky in multitude—innumerable as the sand which is by the seashore (Hebrews 11:11-12).

We must be patient and wait upon the Lord. Dennis and I are grateful that we learned this early in our Christian walk, as there have been many times we've been tempted to help God out. I can't stress this too much. Do what God tells you to do when He tells you to do it, but make sure that you really wait for God's perfect timing.

Death to a Vision

Many years after the birth of Isaac, God gave Abraham yet another test. He was told to go to the region of Moriah and sacrifice Isaac there. Isaac was older than most of us think; rabbinic commentators estimate that he would have been around 25 or possibly in his late 30s at this time. In any case, he was old enough to stop Abraham, who was at least 125 years old. Even though this was the son God had promised, Abraham concluded that God was able to raise him up, even from the dead, if he indeed died (Hebrews 11:17-19).[16]

Think about that. Would God actually put us through a test like this? Well, He put Abraham through quite a battery of tests, didn't He? It had been about 50 years since God first told him that he would have a son, and now the test of all tests came upon him. But Abraham wouldn't fail. By this time, he had a history with God and knew that God was faithful. But to sacrifice his son—this, my brothers and sisters, was probably one of the hardest tests that any human ever had to go through. Abraham had never even heard of God doing a miracle like that before.

You too may be going through a very difficult test. Just remember that even though you're being stretched, God knows you'll pass if you remember to put your trust and faith in Him and not in yourself.

If God gives you something and then asks you to sacrifice it, just trust Him and do it. Many times before we actually see the birth of our promise, we must die to it. This means that things might look absolutely dead. But think about it: it needs to be this way. God brings resurrection power to the things that are dead to give them life so that people can see His glorious, miraculous power. Otherwise, we can take the credit for it. But God gets glorified in our weakness, for when we're weak, then we're desperate for His strength. So if you are in need of a miracle, you are in a good place! Now God can work. Just remember to keep your faith in Him, and don't be double-minded. Without faith, we cannot please God.

Abraham had many tests, as did all of the heroes of faith. Remember, though, that God is the best teacher. And like the great teacher that He is, He won't give you the test unless He knows that you know the material and can pass. It may stretch you; I can tell you that God is stretching me and so many others in this season. I feel like I'm in over my head—but that's a good thing! I can't do what He has promised me and called me to do, I must lean into Him and allow Him to do it through me. This way, He gets all the credit.

The key to the walk of faith is to trust in the Lord with all your heart and to lean not on your own understanding. In all your ways acknowledge (*yada*—get into close intimate contact) with Him and He will direct your paths (Proverbs 3:5-6). As we take our place of intimacy with God, faith will be birthed in our hearts!

CHAPTER 11: Pressing In for the Victory

I want to encourage you in this chapter to grab hold of God's promises and make them your own so you'll be able to move forward with an unshakable faith. In order to press in for the victory, you must believe the Word of God with all your heart. I want to share with you some of the things I've learned in my personal walk of faith that will help you understand how and what to do in order to stand firm until you receive the manifestation of your victory.

I believe the main battleground for us is whether or not we believe the promises of God. Peter said God has given us His exceedingly great and precious promises, and that through them we can become partakers of His divine nature (2 Peter 1:4). God has given us promises that relate to every area of life. He has promised us abundant provision, healing, and many other blessings. But when we open the Bible and begin to claim these promises, we discover that the battle is engaged. When we go after something God says we can have, the enemy will try to stop us in every way he can. Satan's goal is to frighten and discourage us so we turn back and don't press on.

When adversity comes against us, we can usually tell when it's Satan because he overplays his hand. Storms come against us to intimidate us and try to get us to turn back. When this happens we must *increase intercession*. We must let go of a victim mentality and "get up offa that thang" while declaring the Word of God. You must have a warrior mentality, and stand up and fight. You must remind the enemy that you're in charge and he's not!

Don't fall for the lies of the enemy when he tries to make you feel insignificant and puny. Remember, God loves to use the weak things of this world. That way He gets *all* the glory. Like David, who was tiny compared to the giant Goliath, whom he killed with a small stone, we must all keep this at the forefront of our minds: faith is not in ourselves but in our all-powerful God!

Faith of David

If you can believe God and remember how big and wonderful He is, warring becomes easy because our faith is in what He has already done, not in ourselves. We just need to step out in radical faith like David did and see the giants in our lives topple to the ground.

Faith is a feeling of absolute confidence. It's David laughing as he ran to meet the giant. He's fully assured that God is with him. He isn't pretending to be bold, hoping that God is with him; neither is he confessing the Word to himself, hoping to build his faith. No! He's full of confidence because he *knows* his God. David had a great love relationship with God and this made him dangerous to the enemy. David knew beyond a shadow of a doubt that he was looking at a dead giant and that he had the victory. Goliath's head would be cut off in no time, and he felt triumphant. David made history that day. He showed us that faith with feeling surely works. It's an attitude you have within you when you know (experience) your God!

Brain Cancer Healed

Before moving to Georgia to start Healing Rooms, I was on a Healing Room team in Minnesota for a couple of years. One young man we prayed for every week—let's call him Rob—had been diagnosed with stage four brain cancer. He was weak and warring for his life. He had a young wife and three small children. My children were toddlers at the time, and I empathized with how his wife must have felt, seeing her beloved husband get weaker and sicker as the days passed.

Sickness, disease, and pain are *awful!* It's so hard to see those you love go through tragedies like this. My sister Gina had also been diagnosed with this condition, so I took it as a personal mission to help Rob receive his healing. Gina wasn't open to prayer, but I figured Rob receiving his healing for the same illness might cause her to listen. God gave me love for him and his family, so that was my main reason for wanting to see him restored and healed. My heart was so burdened for him and his family. I knew that cancer was not God's will and that God wanted him to live and not die.

I spent time with Rob's family over the weeks and months and became friends with them. He traveled a couple of hours each week to the Healing Rooms for prayer, and we saw him getting stronger and better over time. One week I noticed that he didn't come to the Healing Rooms, so I called to see how he was doing. His wife told me he had gotten worse and that he was in hospice care, so a few of us went to his home to pray for him. I talked with his wife over the phone and continued to encourage her to stand despite what she was seeing in the natural realm.

Just like others who go through a major battle, they were weary of fighting and knew it would be better for him to go home to be with the Lord than to suffer. I agreed—it would be better for all of us to be in heaven with the Lord. But I asked her if she wanted to see her husband get healed and live, and of course she did, not just for herself but also for their children. So we continued to look to Jesus and the work that He finished by taking cancer upon Himself so Rob could be made whole. And Rob did receive his miracle. He got out of his bed and no longer needed hospice care. We were so excited!

Folks, let me tell you that the battle zone is fierce. It's hard work to be in a war, ask anyone in our Armed Forces. The truth is that you are in the war whether you like it or not, so you might as well learn how to fight to win. As more and more people come to know the truth about healing, we'll see more and more people healed. Sadly, many of the people fighting against us right now are actually born-again Christians who have a form of godliness but deny the power of God. The Bible says that we should stay away from people like that (2 Timothy 3:5 NLT). We need to continue to love them, but not allow them to steal our faith. Remember my friend Cherí? I pressed into God's Word and got healed myself and later this brought healing to her baby Hannah.

My precious Jesus wasn't beaten for nothing! He went through all the scourging so that *everyone* in the world could receive healing today. As the testimony of Jesus continues to go out, the truth that Jesus still heals will become widely known, accepted and *expected*. Then we will have more troops on the frontline fighting with us. I can hardly wait for that day!

Warrior

In my Christian walk, I have noticed that sometimes we have to wait patiently as we continue to war for our inheritance. Yes, it is free. But we have to fight to apprehend it as well as to keep it. The enemy will try to get us to go by our natural senses rather than the Word of God. This truly turns into a fight.

When the enemy comes back to attack you once you have received the manifestation of your healing, you must stand firm. Tell the pain or the sickness to leave and declare the truth that "by Jesus stripes you are healed." The enemy is trying to get you to go by what you see, feel, or experience in the natural realm. This is where many people lose the battle. So when the enemy comes against you and bombards you with fear, you must use your authority over him and command him to leave. When the pain or sickness tries to resurface, you must command it to go in the name of Jesus and call forth the healing virtue of Jesus to restore your health. Remember, if you stand up in your authority when the enemy comes in to attack, the Spirit of the Lord will come in like a flood and will lift up a standard against him (Isaiah 59:19).

Have you ever seen an army go to the front line and lie down and relax? No, they go up armed to win and must continue to fight until they do. The good news for us is that we know we win! But we still have to stand up and do our part. As the army of the Lord, we must all take our place and engage in battle, for there are many whose lives are depending on us. Remember that healing is a sign for the unbeliever. So as we testify of what He has done for us, others who are lost and in pain will also believe and step into the kingdom.

I think David was probably the first youth to think about taking on a giant. But after he did it, I'm sure faith rose up in many other people. They figured if David could do this by putting his faith in God, then they too could see the impossibilities of this earth bow their knee to the name of our God.

I believe there are a couple of different mindsets we need to have in order to receive our inheritance and keep it. The first is having the mind of a warrior. We're in a daily spiritual battle, and some days it's more intense than others. It doesn't take long to understand that the enemy does *not* like followers of Jesus and will do whatever he can to stop us from advancing God's kingdom on the earth. The enemy counts on the fact that many Christians don't understand that they have the keys to the kingdom. He will fight those who know this truth to try to make it look as if it isn't true. As a result, many Christians believe for a while but give up when the battle gets fierce. Friends, we must press in for our victory and for those around us.

Remember to KISS—Keep It Simple, Saint! Let's keep believing God's Word so we can bear fruit and bring forth an abundant harvest. We should have no less than 100 percent of people getting healed, not through ministers alone but through the nameless, faceless army that the Lord is raising up—YOU! It's those who have childlike faith in their God like David who will see Him do mighty miracles through them!

Armor of God

It's so important to cover ourselves with the armor God has provided for us. He has given us a wardrobe to wear as we enter into battle each day. As you dress in the morning, you need to suit up in God's armor as well.

A well-known passage in Ephesians says,

"Finally, be strong in the Lord and in his mighty power. Put on the full armor of God so that you can take your stand against the devil's schemes. For our struggle is not against flesh and blood, but against the rulers, against the authorities, against the powers of this dark world and against the spiritual forces of evil in the heavenly realms. Therefore put on the full armor of God, so that when the day of evil comes, you may be able to stand your ground, and after you have done everything, to stand. Stand firm then, with the belt of truth buckled around your waist, with the breastplate of righteous-ness in place, and with your feet fitted with the readiness that comes from the gospel of peace. In addition to all this, take up the shield of faith, with which you can extinguish all the flaming arrows of the evil one. Take the helmet of salvation and the sword of the Spirit, which is the word of God. And pray in the Spirit on all occasions with all kinds of prayers and requests. With this in mind, be alert and always keep on praying for all the saints" (Ephesians 6:10-18).

Putting on the armor of God includes:

The Belt of Truth: Buckle it securely around your waist. Know that God is with you every step of the way. He alone is the truth in life. Spend time in His Word and learn His truth!

Breastplate of Righteousness: As you put on your breast-plate, thank God for His never-ending mercy toward you. When our heavenly Father looks at us, He sees us through the blood of Jesus. Therefore He sees us like He sees Jesus, just as if we never sinned.

Sandals of Peace: Without God in our lives, we could not have peace. The "peace that transcends all understanding" (Philippians 4:7 NIV) is available to us only as we give our lives entirely over to His control. As you strap on your sandals each day, give your cares and concerns to God and ask Him to carry them. Then God's peace will come in their place.

Shield of Faith: Faith is another defensive weapon in our arsenal. We use this piece of armor to guard against the constant assaults by the enemy. Each morning as you pick up your shield, thank God for your faith—faith that comes in knowing He will never leave or forsake you (Deuteronomy 31:8).

Helmet of Salvation: When we accept Jesus as our Lord and Savior, we are given this piece of armor to protect us. We know that we have been saved to battle along with Him here on planet Earth. We can do so willingly, knowing we will spend eternity with Him.

The Sword of the Spirit: This is our only offensive weapon mentioned in this passage. Our sword is His Word, the Bible. With it we can slay the evil in the world as it presents itself to us. Read your Bible and memorize His Word, keeping it deep in your heart and mind. Then speak it with confidence each day.

As you dress in this armor daily, you are prepared to enter the world. Without it you will be prey to attack. Think about each piece as you put it on and thank God for supplying you with His armor of protection.

Be Proactive

We must not only take a defensive posture against the enemy; we also need to be on the offense. We do this by not waiting to respond to the fiery darts that come our way. We should start every day by warring with the sword of the Spirit, which is the Word of God. For the Word of God is living and powerful and sharper than any two-edged sword (Hebrews 4:12). Remember, don't base your faith on what you've seen or have personally experienced, but on God's Word that "it is finished."

Farmer

Another mindset we need is to think like a farmer. God's Word is seed, and as we plant it we must be faithful in order to receive the harvest. Think about it: If you were a farmer and planted seed, you would definitely expect a harvest, right? You wouldn't plant the seed today and expect to get up the next day to harvest the crop, would you? But that's exactly what we do when we pray and expect things from the Lord right away. Let me remind you that God is not sitting up in heaven wringing His hands in fear, wondering what's going to happen. He can see the whole picture from beginning to end and has your best interest at heart. We need to learn about seedtime and harvest, and we also need to understand that many things in life are on a seasonal schedule. The truth is that healing belongs to you today, but warfare may delay the arrival of your victory.

We can gain some amazing insights by examining the life of a farmer. First of all, he tills his fields in order to prepare them for the seed. Have you tilled your land, which is your heart, to loosen up the soil to prepare it for the truth of the Word of God? By tilling your heart, you're breaking up hard ground and uprooting any weeds that have been planted. It's important to prepare your heart by allowing God to soften it with His love. Then it's easier to dig up any roots of unbelief, doubt, or fear and get rid of anything that would block the seed from growing. After the ground is prepared, you would plant the seed, cover it up, water it, and wait for the harvest.

During the season that the seed is starting to germinate, it's important that your seed receive sunshine—God's presence—so it can grow. Your seed also needs water—our continued prayers being spoken over it. Remember, since our words are seed and we will have what we say, it's important to watch over our confessions and remember that life and death are in the power of our tongues. If you or anyone around you speaks fear, doubt, or unbelief, cut off those word curses that are trying to cause death to your seeds. Remember to grab hold of your thoughts and think upon God's Words and thoughts about you.

Like a farmer who understands seedtime and harvest, we need to believe that the seeds were planted and that they will come up. If the farmer doesn't see anything after a couple of months, he doesn't dig up the ground to see if the seed was growing. He's totally convinced that it will come up one day if it gets the right nourishment. But when we doubt that we will receive the promise of God's Word, it's like digging up our seed. We will see a harvest as long as we don't lose heart. The key is to not grow weary while waiting for the appointed season. We will reap if we don't give up (Galatians 6:9 NIV).

Understand the Battle

As we have been sharing, God has paid the price for everyone to receive healing and to walk in divine health while on the earth. Yet it's true that we have seen some casualties. We live in a broken world, and the enemy will steal, kill, and destroy whatever we allow him to. I personally believe that sometimes people die before their time because the battle gets so intense that they give up. I say this because my first mentor, Herb Mjorud, had cancer attack his body five different times. On two separate occasions he was told that he wouldn't make it until the morning, but he and his family refused to accept death. They continued to believe God's Word as absolute truth and declared that he would live! They weren't disappointed either because both times the Lord completely healed him in the eleventh hour. So though he was hit with cancer five times, God healed him every time. Like Herb and his family, we must press in and not give up! God's Word doesn't lie, and He doesn't change His mind either about our inheritance.

Several years ago, a young boy in a wheelchair came up to me and asked if he would ever be healed. I told him that if he continued to stand on the Word of God, I believed he would receive his healing because it's God's will for him. I said, "I believe the reason we aren't seeing everyone get healed is because there are casualties of war, and so few people are fighting the fight for people to receive healing." As I said that, I saw a picture of the Empire State Building in my mind. I asked him if he had ever seen how big the Empire State Building was, and he said yes. So I told him, "Let's just say that the body of Christ is the size of this building. If that were true, the number of people who are currently fighting for others to be healed would maybe fit in the janitor's closet in the basement."

I believe this was a word of knowledge because these words came out of my mouth without even thinking about them. After I said this, I instantly asked God if that was true. I checked with my pastor when I got home, and he said that it was a good picture of what's happening in the United States. Though this was several years ago, and I know more of the body of Christ is waking up now, we still have a long way to go. But when His body gets this knowledge down and learns to fight, we'll see fewer and fewer people die and more people walking out of wheelchairs. We'll see those who have been diagnosed with terminal illnesses healed, and the world will be a much better place!

I want to see God heal everyone and clear out hospitals. I have the privilege of helping raise up an army of God's people who will walk in so much resurrection power that even the dead will be raised.

When Jesus told us we could heal the sick, He said in the same sentence that we are to raise the dead (Matthew 10:8). For some of you, healing the sick may be all you can believe for. You may be thinking, *Angela, are you serious? Do you really believe that we can raise the dead? That's crazy—and impossible!* Yes, my friend, that *is* impossible—for us, but so is healing the sick. With God, all things are possible. After all, He's the one who does the healing and the raising.

I've prayed for three people to be raised from the dead. While I haven't seen anyone rise yet, that's not going to stop me from stepping out again on God's Word for the dead to be raised. If you don't pray for people to get healed, you'll never know if they are going to receive their healing or not. So if you want to be used to raise people from the dead, you must start praying for people who have died and commanding life back into their bodies.

Have you heard any testimonies of God still raising people from the dead? It's happening all over the world, people just don't hear much about it. But it won't be long, and we will be seeing it happen much more frequently.

I've received quite a few prophetic words that I'm going to raise the dead. I totally believe that will happen as three of four of my mentors have actually seen the dead come back to life. But do you want to know what I'm more excited about? The army of God raising the dead—and that includes YOU! As you learn to believe with the faith of a child you will be doing this and so much more!

Needless Casualties of War

The Bible declares that our struggle is not against flesh and blood, but against the rulers, against the authorities, against the powers of this dark world and against the spiritual forces of evil in the heavenly realms (Ephesians 6:12). In his book *Needless Casualties of War,* John Paul Jackson tells us about a dream God gave him that changed his understanding of spiritual warfare. He saw several figures standing on circular platforms and preaching to small groups of people. They shouted at the moon and encouraged others to do this as well. As the crowds grew larger, their platform rose higher. Instead of guns in their holsters, they were hurling hatchets at the moon. But they never hit the moon, and their hatchets fell into the darkness. After some time, the leaders grew weary, lay down on their platforms, and fell asleep. Then several dark figures dropped off the moon's surface and attacked the leaders with extreme viciousness. Since the platforms were large and lofty, no one had been alerted to the coming devastation. Soon blood-curdling cries came from the leaders—cries for their families, their children, their churches, and their ministries. "Somebody help me, I'm dying," someone pleaded.

It was a terrifying sight and sound. Then the dream faded to black. In the stillness that followed, God spoke to him: "To attack principalities and powers over a geographical area can be as useless as throwing hatchets at the moon. And it can leave you open to unforeseen and unperceived attacks."[17]

These leaders thought they were doing something great for God. What they failed to realize was that God alone reserves the judgment of Satan and the heavenly realms for Himself. They tried wrestling against principalities without sufficient instruction about how to do it and about Satan's counterattacks. This left them and their churches open to unforeseen and unperceived attacks. The seriousness of these attacks even got to the point that women were having miscarriages and other people died.

It has become apparent that many of these casualties of war were not simply a cost of war. Rather, they were unnecessary costs of warfare that was fought too often without wisdom. In our zeal to advance the Kingdom of God, we can often lack discernment in staging spiritual battles. If God leads someone into high-level spiritual warfare, it is best to address our prayers about demonic principalities *directly to God.* Then He will remove them.

What are principalities? The word "principality" means: chief or principle ruler. Principalities and powers are high-ranking demonic spirits of wickedness in Satan's kingdom and are responsible for ruling over territories and geographical regions from the 2nd heaven. The 2nd heaven is a spiritual place assigned to Satan and his co-horts where they are allowed to operate at this time.

The Bible declares that we are destroyed by a lack of knowledge (Hosea 4:6), and the truths shared in *Needless Casualties of War* will prevent some of the heartbreaking tragedies that have plagued so many Christians.

It's important to be careful so that we don't pay too much attention to evil spirits. When we focus on them more than God we elevate them above Him. We need to keep our focus on what God is doing because He has all power, and the enemy is subject to the name of Jesus. It's not that we shouldn't do spiritual warfare, but the temptation is to be so caught up in it that Satan and his hosts become a greater focus than God. Anytime we spend more time addressing anything or anyone more than God, our priorities are out of balance.

Jesus is high above all rulers and principalities, and as we worship Him and enthrone Him on our praises, we achieve victory and find protection (Eph. 1:19-23; Eph. 2:13; Ps. 22:3). Again let's look to see what Jesus did when He was upon the earth. His focus was always on God. Jesus demonstrated for us how to cast out devils and gave us authority to do so in Mark 16:15-18. We do have authority over demons, but we need clear direction from God when dealing with higher level satanic forces.

Even when the principalities and powers tried to drown Jesus and His disciples when they were on the Sea of Galilee, Jesus didn't speak to them at all. He rebuked the wind and spoke to the sea (Mark 4:35-41). Jesus' authority over the earth was greater than Satan's authority, so He didn't have to address the principalities. We have the same power and authority Jesus had, and we can rebuke storms and speak to the sea to be at peace.

When we are ministering, we've noticed that it's important to keep our focus on God and His power. We can rest in Him to do the work rather than fearing what the enemy has been doing in a church or even in a region. Recently we went to Columbia, South Carolina, to do a Healing Rooms conference and were told by friends in the ministry about how bad the warfare is in South Carolina. We decided not to even think about that and went full of faith, with our eyes on God. We had wonderful results. We didn't feel warfare until the morning after the conference was over. Then when we were attacked, we used our authority and commanded the oppression and the sickness to leave in the name of Jesus, and it left. Our trip was so easy that I forgot we sometimes feel the effects of the battle.

If you've stepped out of your realm of authority and gone into a place of high-level spiritual warfare without God's specific instructions and direction, the first thing that you should do is repent. Tell God that you're sorry for overstepping your area of authority and ask for His forgiveness. Then ask Him to cleanse you from the demonic attacks. You may also want to read John Paul Jackson's book, *Needless Casualties of War* to learn more about this topic.

Pressing In For Your Victory

Our Heavenly Father desires to do super-abundantly over and above all we could ever dare ask or think (Ephesians 3:20). We need to take God out of the boxes that we try to fit Him in because He just doesn't fit. Let your mind grasp that He loves you and really does desire to give you more than you can ever get your mind around. Remember, God doesn't think the way we do, and His ways are different and higher than ours. "As the heavens are higher than the earth, so are My ways higher than your ways, and My thoughts than your thoughts" (Isaiah 55:9).

God is so awesome, so start daydreaming about the abundance that He wants to give you, His precious child. He says, "Fear not, for I have redeemed you; I have called you by your name; You are Mine. When you pass through the waters, I will be with you; and through the rivers, they shall not overflow you. When you walk through the fire, you shall not be burned, nor shall the flame scorch you. For I am the Lord your God" (Isaiah 43:1-2).

I encourage you to press in today for your healing because as Jesus said, "It is finished!" Be willing to trade your sickness and pain for the truth of the Word of God, and by faith reach out and grab hold of your healing. It's a free gift, and with the simple faith of a child, you can receive it today because He loves you.

God Will Always Do His Part

Everyone who asks receives (Matthew 7:8). Jesus told his disciples a parable of a persistent widow to show them that they should always pray and not give up. The widow kept coming to the judge and asking him to grant her justice against her adversary. Now this judge was unjust. He didn't fear God, and he didn't even care about people. He refused for some time, but finally he decided that even though he didn't fear God or care about her, he would make sure she got justice. She was so persistent, he was fearful that she would wear him out. And the Lord said, "Listen to what the unjust judge says. And will not God bring about justice for his chosen ones, who cry out to him day and night? Will he keep putting them off? I tell you, he will see that they get justice, and quickly" (Luke 18:1-8 NIV).

It's a fundamental principle taught throughout the Bible that God answers the prayers of His people (James 5:16; John 16:23). We need to pray radical prayers using the Word of God because His Word will not return void (Isaiah 55:11). We need to believe for the unbelievable. Our radical faith attracts God and His angels. My pastor Johnny says it's like spikenard, the fragrance that catches God's attention. The Bible declares that His eyes roam all over the earth looking for those whose hearts are loyal to Him (2 Chronicles 16:9). "The Lord God is a sun and shield . . . no good thing does he withhold from those whose walk is blameless" (Psalm 84:11).

You can press in to take your place of victory by applying the following steps:

1. By faith, declare God's blessing as your portion. Come into agreement with Him that because He is your shepherd, you will not lack anything He has intended for you. Declare that He took your sickness and infirmity so that you could walk in divine health.
2. By faith, set your eyes on the goal and begin to move forward. Don't be hindered by the arrows. Set your heart in position to advance and know that you have a big shield. Take hold of it with both hands and hold it up with confidence. Find your place in God's army and stand shoulder to shoulder with others who are moving forward in the Lord.
3. Start using your sword and call forth your inheritance by speaking the Word of God. Take your stand in faith and declare that every arrow is being quenched and that you are victorious.
4. Thank Jesus for hanging on the cross for you. Thank Him that He has become your shield and that He took sickness for you so that you can receive healing today. Then receive the truth that by His stripes you are already healed!

CHAPTER 12: Enter His Rest

When the Lord told me to go to Florida to start writing this book, He instructed me to rest for seven days first. I thought, "Wow, God you love me that much, that you would allow me to rest and have fun before I start writing this book?" His answer was yes! I've had seasons in which I've worked day and night without breaks, but that's not what he wants. It's the enemy who is a taskmaster, not the Lord. God wants to show us the easy way to get filled and pour out.

Thankfully, God wanted me to rest. I wasn't allowed to write this book unless I had first rested. I had to be filled by Him and have His mind in order to write. Now God doesn't want us to be lazy and do nothing; we have to find balance. But we are to rest first and do all things from this position of leaning into Him, like the picture at the beginning of chapter 4.

Now that you've learned what it means to "take your place," I want to emphasize how important it is to do the works of Jesus from this place of rest. As we learned earlier, intimacy with God is the wellspring of our lives. Without it, we will be empty of Him and operating out of our own strength. Spending time in His presence is not something we should do out of obligation but out of pure joy—just as we spend time with a spouse out of desire rather than obligation. That's how our time with the Lord should be.

If we try to do the works of Jesus in our own strength, we'll become stressed out and burned out, and our fruit will dry up. We must abide in Him and allow His works to be done from the overflow of love that He has deposited within us. This means that we can be effective for the kingdom of God all from a place of rest. That way He gets all the credit and all the glory. He wants us not to be workhorses but extravagant lovers who are on a joy ride!

Learning to do this has been a journey, and I can't say I've arrived. I still have to decide on a daily basis if I'm going to do things because they need to be done or if I'm going to first sit in the presence of my lover, Jesus. You'll have to make this decision on a daily basis too. My recommendation is that you prioritize spending time alone in His presence. Don't make it an option; diligently practice it, or the enemy will slowly get you back into a place of striving. If you'll put your time with Him first, everything else will fall into place. Remember, Jesus told us to seek first His kingdom, and everything else will be given to us (Matthew 6:33).

Rest, Please

Let's take a look at what Jesus said about rest. "Come to Me, all you who labor and are heavy laden, and I will give you rest. Take My yoke upon you and learn from Me, for I am gentle and lowly in heart, and you will find rest for your souls" (Matthew 11:28-29).

The words "will give" and "rest" are from the same word: *anapauo*. If Jesus uses the same word twice in one sentence, He must really want us to get what He is saying. So what does it mean? To cease from any movement or labor in order to recover!

If we break down this passage, we hear Jesus saying this to us: "Come toward me, everyone who has grown tired and exhausted and who has a heavy burden or grief. And I will cause you to cease from any movement and labor so you can recover and collect your strength. You (insert your name here) will gain rest and refreshment and have a patient expectation of what I am going to do."

Where does all this come from? It comes out of abiding. The way we abide in Jesus is to remain as one with Him, to continue to be present with Him continually, and to wait for Him. It's out of this that we know (experience) Him, as we discussed some in the chapter on seeking God face to face. It's important first to get into His presence and get filled up so we can then do the work of the kingdom from a place of rest.

I've had to learn how to enter the Lord's rest this year more than any other year. Like most people, I always have more to do than I feel I can comfortably get done. That's been particularly true this year with the increasing demands of building a ministry and having increasing visions of things to do. I've learned that not everything needs to be done to match my desires, though. I've had to learn to let go and let God do what He wants whenever He wants to—and His timing rarely seems the same as mine. But as I mentioned in an earlier chapter, my friend Elizabeth reminds me often that I can't care more about this than God does. He is Jehovah-Jireh, and He will provide everything I need when I need it, and usually not a second sooner! Oh, how I love Him, He is so faithful.

The Rest of God

We don't have to strive to get healed or to get others healed. We are to put our faith in the work Jesus completed on Calvary. His body was broken for us, and by His stripes we were healed. The enemy pushes many people into striving not only to get things done but into trying to receive their healing. I know—I used to be that way. But we need to know that God is pleased in our just being with Him. After all, we are called human *beings*, not human *doings*. Life isn't about doing things for Him. Although there's a lot of work that needs to be done in the kingdom of God, we must enter into His rest in order to do them without getting burned out.

God has given us His Holy Spirit to live within us, and along with Him comes His fruit. This fruit is inside of us and is available whenever we need it—which is all the time. Many people feel that they need to work up the fruit of the Spirit, but it's residing inside of us. We can pick and eat it anytime we desire. Contrary to the way of the world, which is full of striving and chaos, God's plan is easy and very peaceful. I much prefer His way!

I once heard a great teaching on Hebrews 4 on how to enter the rest of God through believing. "Anyone who enters God's rest also rests from his own work, just as God did from his" (Hebrews 4:10). Many of us in the body of Christ haven't learned or accessed this principle in our own lives. God rested from His creative work, but what kind of work are we to rest from? When we come to faith in Christ, what is it that we're to quit doing? It's trying to receive our salvation, healing, and deliverance through works. We must stop trying to qualify for these free gifts that He's willing to lavishly pour out on His sons and daughters. We need to get our eyes off ourselves and onto Jesus, for all these gifts come through Him alone.

The writer of Hebrews goes on: "Let us, therefore, make every effort to enter that rest, so that no one will fall by following their example of disobedience" (v. 11). Friends, let's use our childlike faith to receive this rest from God. Though it requires effort, it's available to those who will focus their belief on Him and His truth. If we disobey God by refusing His Son, we will fall. It's all about receiving Him.

Have you received God's "Sabbath rest?" In chapters 3 and 4 of Hebrews, we see the importance of making sure that we've entered into the Sabbath available to all believers. The Israelites constantly failed to understand this simple principle of resting in the sufficiency of our Lord. The "rest" in Hebrews is ceasing from one's self-effort and then doing everything by faith and trust in God, who resides within us. Remember, our job is to believe and receive.

The author of Hebrews gives us a clear call to stop "trying" to serve God and instead to rest in dependence upon Him. This principle of Sabbath rest is key for us as we seek to understand the ways of God.

We began our life as a Christian by surrendering our lives, our souls, and our desires to Jesus. This is not a one-time surrender but a daily surrendering to Him of all that we are. Every day that we walk with Jesus, we're growing deeper in understanding Him and His ways, which are so different than our own. Just as a baby must learn to stand before she can walk, and walk before she can run, so we use our spiritual muscles to learn to discern the deeper things of God. Each day our faith and confidence gets exercised, the more we grow in Him.

C. S. Lewis put it this way: "Give up yourself, and you will find your real self. Lose your life, and you will save it. Submit to the death of your ambitions and your favorite wishes every day, and the death of your whole body in the end, submit with every fiber of your being, and you will find eternal life. Keep back nothing. Nothing that you have not given away will ever be really yours. Nothing in you that has not died will ever be raised from the dead. Look out for yourself and you will find, in the long run, only hatred, loneliness, despair, rage, ruin, and decay. But look for Christ, and you will find Him, and with Him, everything else thrown in."[18]

Bearing Fruit for the Kingdom

We need to remember that in order to bear fruit in the kingdom, we must abide in Him. He is the vine, and we are the branches. We get our power and everything we need from Him (John 15:5). Just this week, I was feeling overwhelmed and pushed, so I just stopped. I decided that everything could just fall apart if it needed to, but I wasn't going to do another thing until I spent at least one hour with the Lord. And my time with Him was so precious! I realized that nothing in life matters more than Him. Spending time with Him really helps put everything in proper order. He needs to come first, and everything else needs to just wait.

So the key to bearing much fruit, then, is remaining in Jesus. We can do nothing without Him. If we try to do the work of the kingdom in our own strength, we'll burn out and be fruitless. I've tried doing things in my own strength, and it's not what it's cracked up to be. It's a lot of hard work for little or no reward.

Jesus warned His disciples of the results of relying on their own effort. "If anyone does not remain in me, he is like a branch that is thrown away and withers; such branches are picked up, thrown into the fire and burned" (John 15:6). Jesus tells us to abide in Him, and that if we do not remain in Him, we're like a branch that is picked up and thrown into the fire and burned. I don't know about you, but I don't want to wither! I want to be like the tree that remains by the river of life so I can truly live.

Doing the Works of Jesus

Many of you are like me—a mover and a shaker. If something needs to get done, I'm the person they give things to. Because I'm so passionate, I give 100 percent of my heart and effort to everything I do. Dennis says my passion is one of the things that caused him to fall in love with me. While it's a wonderful characteristic and definitely a gift from God, it can swing the other way and can cause a person to get into striving and self-effort. There needs to be balance.

You are interested in "taking your place"—otherwise you wouldn't be reading this. So I want to share from my own experience how important it is to find the balance between your passion and your rest. It's important to have God's heart in order to do the works of Jesus, but you can't carry the weight of it. For example, I wanted to lead everyone I could find to the Lord. I saw what He had provided and felt His heart for those who were lost, sick, and in pain. But God wanted to teach me a few things. First He wanted me not just to learn some things about His love but to experience it for myself. He wanted me to let people know they can experience His love on this side of eternity. He taught me that pouring out His love is the drawing card for people to come to Him, not getting them to come to Him out of fear of going to hell. I needed to be able to show people who He is and what His benefits are, not just give them a "Get out of hell free" card.

I felt horribly responsible for everything and everyone! I carried people's burdens and couldn't stand to see anyone hurting or poor. I thought God needed me and depended on me. I was even afraid to have children because I didn't want to be at home having babies while people who didn't know God were on their way to hell. I felt pressure from all that responsibility.

I came to realize that this was a lie of the devil. Yes, God wants to pour His love through us. Yes, He wants each one of us to take our place. But when we step out not understanding Him and His ways, it will burn us out and we won't have a lot of fruit. I did lead people to the Lord and saw many instant miracles, but thank God that He held me back with His reins. My friend Elizabeth calls that the harness of the Lord—I guess that's what God uses on us wild horses!

She also told me one day when I was feeling stressed, "Angela, if you're feeling pushed, turn around and look to see who's pushing you." I thought that was interesting. God would never push me, so why did I feel this way? Because I wasn't handling my responsibility to be a good steward from a place of rest. It has taken me many years to learn this, but finally I'm starting to understand. It's not that I'm able to rest all the time and lounge in God's presence all day like

I sometimes want to do. It's just that now I can do the things He has called me to do in His strength as I prioritize His presence.

The greatest news about this is that I don't feel overwhelmed. This comes from carrying false responsibilities, but we aren't called to do that. Jesus is the one who heals and saves people. Healing the sick is only hard when we think we have something to do with it. The truth is that we simply partner with God. If we will do what He says by laying hands on people, then He will heal them. It's that simple. If they don't receive their healing, we're not responsible. We're just the vessel He pours through, not the healer.

Recently, I went to Florida with a couple of friends from the Healing Rooms. Brenda was going to stay in Florida for a while with her friend Britt who lived there. Britt had been sick and in pain and Brenda desperately wanted us to pray for her healing. The gift of faith rose up in me, and I knew deep down inside that Britt was going to receive the manifestation of her healing, so I told Brenda she would be completely healed. Britt's testimony tells the rest of the story:

> I had been ill for three years with shingles and PHN (post-herpatic nerve damage), which resulted from shingles. I suffered a staph infection after having a TENS [Transcutaneous Electrical Nerve Stimulation] machine implanted into my spine for the severe pain and burning. This infection can be paralyzing. My treatment involved eight weeks of strong antibiotics infused two times a day. I was hospitalized, and the doctors surgically implanted a Pic Line [catheter] to protect my veins.
>
> Two weeks after the injections were finished, another driver rear-ended me going 60 miles an hour. My injuries included painful migraines, a concussion, confusion, brain fog, memory loss, fatigue, a neck injury, a sprain, whiplash affecting the occipital lobes, causing severe eye pain with nausea, carpal tunnel, nerve damage, and a frozen shoulder.
>
> I had to retire as a music teacher. My driving was very limited, as it became too difficult. I couldn't do simple tasks and household chores. My therapy included four medica-

tions daily for pain, a TENS unit and pain patches, additional medication for anxiety, hot and cold packs, physical therapy three times a week, doctor visits two times a week, seeing a specialist once a week and my primary care doctor once a month for MRIs, CAT scans, braces on both forearms, and TENS machine at night. I never slept all night, and could not stay up more than two or three hours at a time.

As I entered into the hotel room, Angela greeted me with the words, "Welcome to the Healing Rooms." The atmosphere immediately changed as Angela prayed and Marla and Brenda interceded. First, there was a release of burdens and self-condemnation that I had carried. Then as they prayed for my neck injury, all of a sudden a terrific pain came into my head and neck that was more severe than it had ever been. Angela explained that this was the enemy trying to hold on and that it would go away as they kept praying. My entire body became extremely hot, and then all the pain left. Praise God!

Next I received prayer for the nerve pain in my back from the shingles. The nerve inside my back became hot, starting at my neck and going all the way down my spine and into my hips. Tremendous joy was bursting out of me—laughing and crying at the same time. I looked in the mirror and saw bright color return to my face and I saw life come back into my eyes. I was glowing!

Angela had me run down the hall to check out my healing. I bent my head over, touched the floor, and raised my arms over my head, and there was no pain or dizziness! I had been unable to read anything because of the concussion, so I sat down and read for ten minutes without eye or head pain. As I went to the computer, I found out that my coordination and ability to process information had returned.

Since that day, I have been performing normally in every activity. I can read labels in grocery stores without nausea and can work on my computer again, and I am amazed. I remember directions and remember where I am. I have been outside at the beach in the heat without the itching and burning of the nerve in my back where the shingles had been. I have energy to enjoy my grandchildren. I have eaten foods that I have not been able to tolerate. I can raise my arm without pain. My husband had been raising my arm for me five times per day, and there had been terrible pain, but now I am healed. I haven't used the TENS unit, pain patches, or hot or cold packs, and I have not needed the medications for the shingles.

I am forever grateful to Jesus Christ my Savior for my incredible healing. I have the deepest appreciation for those who serve in the Healing Rooms, as I now have my life back. My husband really thanks you. My family, friends and my ministry have all been affected by this healing. God bless you!

Friends, this is what it's about! Taking your place is about being available to help others and showing them the love of God everywhere we go. Not only has Britt's life been divinely changed, but so have the lives of those around her—her husband, children, grandchildren, neighbors, those in her church, and all her friends. Because of her physical condition, the enemy had been stealing their finances, but now she can return to work again and to the calling the Lord has on her life. Britt has learned that now she needs to share her testimony with those around her, and then to be a conduit to bring healing to others as she goes about her everyday life. This will affect multitudes, as the testimony of how Jesus healed her will draw others into believing for their inheritance of healing as well.

Brenda told me that Britt was so excited about what God did in her that when she saw a sick dog a couple days later, she jumped out of the car like a wild woman to the rescue. She gave the dog some water and then laid hands on it and prayed for it to be healed. Within a few minutes, the dog was up and walking. It works on animals just as it does humans. Did you know that if you are in need of healing, you can lay hands on yourself and claim your healing? It's true, I do it when I get attacked and it works!

There is a domino effect in this. It's not just about who you lead to the Lord or who you pray for to be healed. If those who receive ministry do what they are supposed to do, they will go pray for others to be healed and saved as well. When we lead others to the Lord or pray for someone and they receive the manifestation of healing, we need to tell them that they are to do the same thing we did. Matthew 10:8 says that we're to heal the sick, cleanse the lepers, raise the dead, and to cast out demons. Freely we have received, and freely we need to give it away.

Just as Adam and Eve walked in the glory of God, now we can too. We need to become radical lovers who are not consumed with our own desires, but are willing to be poured out in order to be a light in this dark world in which we live. Remember, we are to be the hands and the voice of Jesus in the world.

Take Your Place

As I have taught, you know that the first step to *Take Your Place* is to show others God's love. We all can do that, can't we? Everyone wants to know that they are loved and cared about, and most people love to talk about themselves. Then share a testimony of what God has done for you or someone else so they can see what God has available for them. If they are having a difficult time or need healing, I encourage you to ask them if they would like prayer. Then pray for them, showing them God's love in action. This may be a little scary at first, but you will find as you love them with His love that this is as easy as tying your shoe. Remember, He just needs our availability so He can pour through us. As you pray for them, listen to Holy Spirit as He will lead you and show you how to pray. If they have a healing need expect a miracle and pray for them as if everyone you have ever prayed for was healed instantly.

This week, my friend Debby—a person that I met and prayed for on the beach in Florida 5 years ago—told me that she has been taking her place and prayed for an elderly couple in Walmart, just like my story. Only she was in the soda aisle, not the beer and wine aisle like I had been. This couple was so blessed by the love of God that flowed through her that the wife cried. I was so excited when Debby told me her story because she is the "fruit" of what I teach in this book. Debby said it was a little scary at first, but she decided to put into action what I have taught her. She said that they felt so loved that she can't wait to reach out to someone else again. I know this is only the beginning of what God will do through her—and through you when you step out. So let go of all fear, and just step out and take your place.

However, if you aren't bold enough to pray for them, start by telling them about the Healing Rooms until you gain the boldness to pray yourself. To find a Healing Room near you, go to www. healingrooms.com. If there isn't a Healing Room near you, ask God to raise one up in your city. If there is a Healing Room in your city, I highly recommend that you join the team. It is a great place to be trained so you can do the works of Jesus everywhere you go, as well as participate in a city-wide healing ministry that is healing the sick and bringing in the lost. Remember we should all give out ARKS (acts of random kindness) everywhere we go. Each of us can be a ray of Son-light to those around us and release the glory of the Lord on the earth.

Each One Reach One

Recently I preached the "Take Your Place" message at a church on a Sunday morning. There were about 300 people there. I challenged each of them to step out of their church pew and to take their place. If each one reached one that *week* there would be 300 people by the following Sunday who would have experienced the love and power of God for themselves. In one month 1,200 people would have been reached. I told them that if they were serious about this and reached out to 1 person a *day* that there would be 2,100 people in one week, 8,400 people in one month and in one year there would be 109,200 people reached with His love and power. This town's population was about 100,000. Can you see that if each of us take our place, that we can reach our cities and our communities for Jesus! It's so easy. Just take your place and do what you've learned in this book. Remember, it's about knowing Him and making Him known.

Many times I have considered the advancement of the kingdom of God from a network marketing point of view. Then it's not just about our efforts, but about the power of multiplication as we teach others to do what we do. Actually, that's what I am doing with you.

Years ago, God told me that if I would submit to His ways, I would be able to reach way more people than I could on my own. All I had to do was let Him pour through me and release what He placed in my heart, and He would raise up His army in the earth.

What would happen if we didn't just share our light with people, but taught those we reach to do the same? Do you know what would happen if each of these 300 people shared with 3 people in the first month, and then taught those people to share with 3 people the next month? By the end of the second month there would be 2,700 people reached. Here's what would happen if this cycle continued:

Month 3	8,100
Month 4	24,300
Month 5	72,900
Month 6	218,700
Month 12	159,432,300

By the end of 15 months the number would rise to over 4 billion people who would have been reached for Jesus. *Really? Yes Really!* That's the power of multiplication. So instead of each one, reach one, it would be — each one, reach three and teach them to do the same.

Recent estimates indicate that the world's population is around 6.8 billion people. So can you see how we can really reach the world if each of us take our place and give away what we freely received? Truly as we carry His glory and release it, His glory will cover the earth.

Saints, now it's time for you to *Take Your Place!* Will you join the army of radical laid-down lovers of the King of glory? He is calling for saints who are lit on fire with His love and His passion. You will be releasers of the river of God to bring abundant life everywhere you go.

Will you respond to His calling to you today? If so, we want to hear from you so we can continue to encourage you to *take your place*. If you're interested in receiving our *"free"* Take Your Place quarterly newsletter, visit our website at www.AngelaKline.com to sign up.

Two Visions of Running the Race

On the Elijah List (March 6, 2008), Kelry Green wrote about a vision she had involving two different groups of people. In the first vision, she saw a company of people running a race. Their faces were shining like the sun, as they carried God's presence. Their hearts were full of peace and joy. Then the scene suddenly changed to the second vision. She saw another company of people who were also running a race. This group was a little different from the first one. They were always looking around them as they ran. They looked to their left and to their right, as well as behind them. They ran swiftly, and most of them were smiling. But when their hearts were shown, they had intense pain and were bleeding.

When she asked God who the people were, 1 Corinthians 9:24–25 was impressed on her heart: "Do you not know that those who run in a race all run, but one receives the prize? Run in such a way that you may obtain it. And everyone who competes for the prize is temperate in all things. Now they do it to obtain a perishable crown, but we for an imperishable crown."

Then God showed her that the first company was running the race for the imperishable crown. They accepted and experienced His unconditional love daily. They loved God with all of their heart, mind, soul, and strength. They also understood that they were God's sons and daughters, not orphans. They lived a lifestyle of loving selflessly, seeking meekness, thirsting and hungering for righteousness, and being poor in spirit. They had an understanding of their eternal inheritance. They related to God with the same intimacy that Jesus had with the Father.

The second group was running the race for the perishable crown—the crown that man can give them. While they smiled on the outside, they really hurt on the inside. They competed with each other and lived their lives striving for people's acceptance. Though they were not orphans, they had an orphan mentality. They didn't believe they could have their promised inheritance, and they fought for all they could get in this life. Men crowned them often, but every crown would decay. There was no eternal significance. Our Father was extremely sad and wanted to pour out His everlasting love upon them. He longed to heal their hearts and to spend time with them, but they were running so hard for the perishable reward that they did not stop to spend time with Him in order to receive His love, kindness, and acceptance towards them.

God revealed that He is raising up a company of people in the nations of the earth that will not run the race for the perishable crown but for the imperishable crown—the one that will last forever. He is the One who gives the crown that does not fade. In Revelation 2-3, we see the rewards that will be given to those who "overcome." These rewards are imperishable and cannot decay.

Paul tells us that he didn't run aimlessly or with uncertainty (1 Corinthians 9:26). Uncertain runners run without a vision of the reward because they can't envision the finish line. But those who run with certainty hold a picture of eternity in their hearts. In order to run with certainty, our hearts and minds need to be set on the imperishable reward while rejecting the lust of the flesh and the spirit of this age.

What would it be like if we as the body of Christ chose to live in obedience and faithfulness to the voice of God? What if we embraced the great commandment of loving God with all our heart, all our soul, and all our strength while loving our neighbors as ourselves? What would our world be like if we chose to give freely what we have received, blessed those who have persecuted us, and laid down our lives for others and for King Jesus? This, my friend, is the heart of God and how we are to live our lives. Won't you take your place and love others as He has loved you?

God is calling *every* Christian to take their place and that includes YOU! Cal Pierce says that the only requirement is to be able to "fog a mirror." That means that if you're breathing and you call yourself a Christian, then you ought to live up to the name. Remember, being a Christian means that you do the things that Jesus the Anointed One did. It's time for you to step up, get out of the pew, and take your place! So what are you waiting for? Revival isn't out there somewhere, it's in you. It's time to release the love and power of your God to those around you in *your world*.

Parting Words

You are important, and everything you do is important. I once heard a minister say that every time you forgive, the universe changes; every time you reach out and touch a heart or a life, God's purposes are accomplished and nothing will ever be the same again. You are a world-changer, and a history maker. As you take your place wherever the road takes you, the world will be a better place because you were there!

Let's Pray

Father, I pray that you will burn passion in my heart so that I would seek you above all else. I want to love you the way you love me. Help me to keep my relationship with you as the priority of my life! I yield to you, Father, and ask you to pour yourself through me so that I might *re*-present you to the world. I want to be a light for you in this world and I ask for boldness as I step out and do the things that Jesus did while He was on the earth. Give me revelation of who I am in you, and of the amazing inheritance you've given to me. I desire to lean into you so that I can do everything in my life from a place of rest. I hear you calling me to take my place and to step into a life of miracles and I say "Yes" to you today. As you pour through me to do the works of Jesus, I promise to give you all the praise, all the honor, and all the glory! Thank you for your love for me. I want to be like you! *In Jesus Name I pray, Amen.*

NOTES

[2] *The Meal that Heals,* by Perry Stone, Charisma House, 2008.

[2] *The Secret Place: Passionately Pursuing His Presence,* by Dale Fife, Whitaker House, 2002.

[3] "The Battle for Intimacy," by Patricia King, April 23, 2006, http://www.extremeprophetic.com/archivesitem.php?art=366&c=0&id=11&style=

[4] "Soaking: the Key to Intimacy," by Gary Oates, http://www.elijahlist.com/words/display_word_pf.html?ID=4272

[5] *Journal of the Unknown Prophet,* by Wendy Alec, Warboys Media & Arrow Publications, 2006, p. 123.

[6] John Wimber and Kevin Springer, *Power Healing,* excerpts from pp. 48, 49, 50, 51, 52.

[7] *The Supernatural Ways of Royalty: Discovering Your Rights and Privileges of Being a Son or Daughter of God,* Bill Johnson and Kris Vallotton, Destiny Image Publishers, 2006.

[8] Story is summarized from Luke 15:11-31.

[9] From "The Eagle Christian" by Glen Clifton, www.ancientpath.net/bible/topical/top_eaglechristian.htm

[10] Much of the information in the next few paragraphs is taken from "A Lesson from the Life of an Eagle" by Jimmy Oentoro, www.jimmyoentoro.com/?p=91

[11] Elijah List, *www.elijahlist.org,* Feb. 22, 2007.

[12] *The Anointing,* © 1997 by Ian Peters, CityLights Ministries International.

[13] *These Walk on Water: The Gospel with Power—Returning the Church to the Destiny God Intended,* © 2007 by Danny Steyne, MOW Books.

[14] Genesis 12

[15] Genesis 16

[16] The full story of the sacrifice of Isaac is told in Genesis 22.

[17] *Needless Casualties of War,* © 1999 by John Paul Jackson, Streams Publications, p. 33.

[18] C.S. Lewis, Mere Christianity, © 1980 by Arthur Owen Barfield, Simon & Schuster 1996, p. 191.

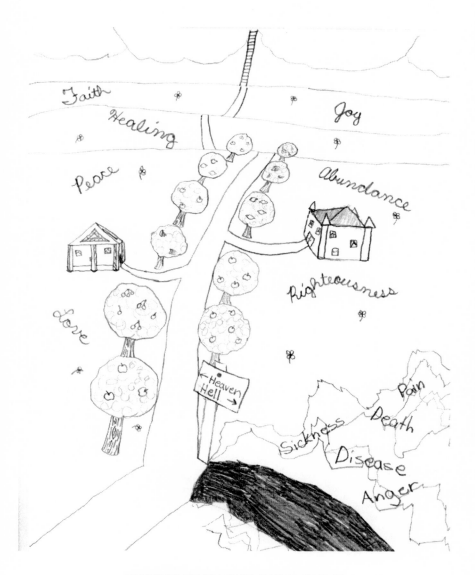

WHICH KINGDOM
WILL YOU CHOOSE?

RECEIVING JESUS

Some of you may have been in church most of your life, like I had been, but have never personally asked Jesus to come into your heart. Maybe you're new to learning about Jesus, or maybe you have received Jesus, but want to rededicate your life to the Lord. If so, I want to walk you through that now. God has a wonderful, abundant life planned for you, and this is the first step in the right direction. Jesus is real, and He wants you to know Him in an experiential way, this side of eternity. Whatever your story, there's no time like the present. Let's get started today.

Jesus took all of your sins upon Himself and hung on the cross for you so that you can be forgiven. Not one of us is righteous before God, but the blood of Jesus cleanses us from all of our sins so that our Father views us as if we have never sinned. You must recognize your need for Him as your Savior and Lord. Believe that He died on the cross to pay for your sins. Then come before Him and ask Him to forgive you for all your sins. When you *receive* the free gift of Christ through faith, you will experience a new birth. He's just waiting for you.

If you are ready to receive the Lord or to rededicate your life to Him, pray this prayer out loud:

"Lord Jesus, I need you. I have done many things wrong in my life, and I ask you to forgive me for all of my sins. I ask you to come into my heart. Thank you for dying on the cross for my sins. I want to follow you and let you take control of my life. I open the door of my heart to you and receive you as my Savior and my Lord. Thank you for giving your life for me so that I can experience an abundant life here on earth. Make me the kind of person you want me to be. I

ask that you baptize me with your Holy Spirit now. Fill me with your love, your presence and your power. In your name I pray, Amen."

Now it's important to find a good church where you can grow and learn more about Him and His plan for your life. Try to find someone in the church who can mentor you and teach you about the love of your Father. Start reading the Bible every day. I recommend starting in the New Testament, preferably in the book of John. Listen to good worship music and allow your love to grow for the Lord.

I remember going to a Christian bookstore soon after I became a Christian, and I had no idea what kind of music to buy. The lady behind the counter asked me what kind of music I liked to listen to. I told her that Whitney Houston was my favorite and she recommended that I get a CD by Cici Winans. If you aren't familiar with good Christian music, ask someone to help you find artists whose style you prefer.

Start talking to God every day to build your relationship with Him. You don't need to feel ashamed for your sins because He has forgiven you and forgotten about them already. Choose to forgive yourself. Remember the scripture verse, "freely you received, now freely give"? Well, now it's your turn to tell someone else about Jesus and what He's done for you.

RECEIVING THE BAPTISM OF THE HOLY SPIRIT

If you are a Christian, you can ask for the baptism of the Holy Spirit. Jesus is the One who baptizes us with the Holy Spirit (Mark 1:8). Remember, you are asking Jesus for the promised gift of the power of the Holy Spirit in order to live the victorious life and to be able to take your place as a child of the King. But also remember that speaking in tongues is the *result* of receiving the power of the Holy Spirit, not the goal.

As I've shared in the book, just as you received salvation by faith, you also receive the baptism of the Holy Spirit by faith. When you ask Jesus to do this for you, believe in faith that you have received it (just as you believe in faith that you have received salvation).

If you're ready to receive the gift of the power of the Holy Spirit, then pray out loud and ask Him for it right now:

"Heavenly Father, I thank you so much that you sent Jesus here to save me. Lord Jesus, I ask that you baptize me now in the Holy Spirit. I receive your love, your power, and your anointing now so that I might be a carrier of your glory. I want to be empowered for service from this day forward so my light will shine brightly for you. I want to take my place in the earth so that you may be glorified. In your name I pray, Amen."

Now that you have asked for and received the baptism of the Holy Spirit, you can begin to practice your new spiritual gifts. A great place to start is with your heavenly prayer language just like the first apostles did. To do this, begin praising God by telling Him how much you love Him. Begin to speak out loud in whatever words come to you. As you begin to make small sounds, you will find that words come out of you that you have never said. Sometimes you may only get a couple of words. That's okay—you are a new Spirit-filled believer, and the more you pray in tongues, the more words will come forth. Just as a baby only gets a couple of simple words when he first starts to speak, so it may be with you. I have seen many different things experienced by believers. Some may only get a couple of simple words or syllables, where others speak a mighty prayer that flows like a river. Either way, continue to speak in your heavenly prayer language every day. If you want to pray for a specific situation or a certain person, just tell God what you want to pray for and then step into your new prayer language. Holy Spirit will then be praying perfect prayers through you as He hooks your heart up with the perfect will of our Father.

If you didn't speak in your heavenly prayer language, remember what happened to me. I couldn't speak in tongues, but when Herb commanded fear, doubt, and unbelief to leave, I started speaking in my heavenly language immediately. And so will you! So command fear, doubt and unbelief to leave in Jesus name and thank God for His free gifts. Then open your mouth and enter into your heavenly prayer language.

If you need someone to pray for you, find a local Spirit-filled church to see if there is someone there who can pray with you. Or go to www.healingrooms.com and find a Healing Room in your area. They would love to pray for you to receive the baptism of the Holy Spirit. Then you can always join the team and pray for the sick in your community as well.

PRAYER FOR THE SICK

I can't show you exactly how to pray for people. Holy Spirit shows us because only He knows how to minister to each person exactly the way they need ministry. But I will attempt to show you a basic prayer model.

It's not the prayer that heals the sick anyway, it's His power that will flow through you as you release His presence into them. In the Healing Rooms we have a plaque in each room that says, "His Presence", so get into His presence and release it.

If you or someone around you needs healing I want to walk you through how to pray. Remember there may be some reasons why certain individuals have a hard time receiving the manifestation of their healing. God wants people totally healed, not just receiving their physical healing. Some individuals could be held in bondage because they are captives or prisoners. This has to do with lies they have believed or sin that may block healing. A person may receive physical healing with sin in their life, but if the sin stays, it can be an open door for pain or sickness to return.

After reading this book you should have *no* question about God's desire to heal you. You've heard about things that can block healing, example: fear, unbelief, doubt, unforgiveness, or possibly other sin issues. You must let go of all condemnation and victim mentality in order to reach out and grab hold of your inheritance that Jesus paid for 2000 years ago.

Let me ask you a few questions:

1. Is there anyone in your life that has hurt you that you are having a hard time forgiving? If so, choose to forgive them

251

so that you can get free. Remember I chose and am free today because I made that choice.

2. Has anything bad happened in your life that has made you angry at God or that you are blaming Him for? Sometimes things happen in life where people actually blame God for what happened. Remember God is not the author of sickness, disease or accidents, that is the job description of the enemy. As you have learned in this book, God allows what we allow. As you and I grow in our knowledge we will be able to block what the enemy throws at us or those around us, but we each must take our place. It's also true, we live in a fallen world and sometimes bad things happen to good people. But put blame where it belongs- the devil. He's the one who steals, kills and destroys. Tell God you are sorry for blaming Him and ask Him to forgive you for believing the lie. Release all the unforgiveness and bitterness from your heart.

3. Do you find that you have a hard time forgiving yourself and beat yourself up for things that you have done in the past? If so, choose to forgive yourself and forget about it as God does. Command condemnation to leave you in the name of Jesus. Then receive His love and forgiveness, while choosing to love yourself.

4. Is there any unconfessed sin in your life that is between you and God? Know that God already knows what it is and desires to forgive you right now. Ask Him to forgive you for any sins and receive His forgiveness and unconditional love now. This is always the way to get free. Submit yourself to God, resist the devil and he will flee (James 4:7).

If you answered yes to any of those questions let's start there before praying for healing. Tell God you are sorry for holding bitterness in your heart towards someone, Him or yourself and tell Him that you choose to forgive them. Ask Him to come into your heart and give you love for the person you were hurt by, or for yourself. If there was sin, ask Him to forgive you.

Laying Hands on the Sick

Remember you are the vessel that God will work through so it's important that you release the power of God through your hands as you pray. Place your hand on the area of your body that needs healing. If praying for someone else, have them lay their hand on or near the area that needs healing and you lay your hand gently over their hand. Whatever the problem is: pain, sickness, disease or bondage, you will command it to leave in Jesus' Name and call forth healing in the Name of Jesus.

If you have your heavenly prayer language, pray in the Spirit for a few minutes to see if Holy Spirit wants to show you anything before you begin praying. If you are praying for someone else and feel that Holy Spirit showed you something, the best way to address it would be to ask them if they have ever had a problem with that. If they do, have them pray and ask God to forgive them for it and then command it to leave them.

You must pray audibly, remember the enemy can't hear you when you pray in your head. Let's pray:

"Come Holy Spirit! We ask for your presence to come now and touch (say... me, or the name of the person you are praying for.) In the Name of Jesus I bind (say... the pain, sickness, disease or bondage) and command it to leave right now. You have no right to attack any longer and I command all damage to be restored now. I speak complete healing now in Jesus Name."

Now pause and release the power of God into the affected area. It's important to wait to see if Holy Spirit wants to show you anything else. Sometimes thoughts will come to your mind, so if they do, ask the person you are praying for if the thought means anything to them. If so pray it through.

Have them check out the problem that they had to see if and how much of the manifestation of healing they have received. If the condition is still there or is not completely gone, pause a minute and ask Holy Spirit if there is anything you missed. Then pray again praying a similar prayer to above, commanding it to leave and calling forth their healing in the Name of Jesus.

Sometimes you may need to pray a few times before they receive the total manifestation of healing. Sometimes they will notice that they have been healed at a later time. If not, see if you can find a Healing Room in your area for more prayer: www.healingrooms. com. For more information on healing, I highly suggest Cal Pierce's book: *Healing in the Kingdom.* Since faith comes by hearing the Word of God, listening to cd's with healing scriptures on them is very powerful.

When you are done, thank God for healing this person and seal their healing in the Name of Jesus. If they have been totally healed it is important for them to speak that God has healed them as this seals it. We overcome the enemy by the Blood of the Lamb and the word of our testimony (Revelation 12:11). If symptoms return, it's just the enemy trying to get them to believe his lies, so they lose their healing. They must resist them because Divine Healing is their inheritance.

PICTURE ACKNOWLEDGEMENTS

Picture on page 88 by Dana Hanson, Lord Warmington Studio, www.lordwarmingtonstudio.com

Picture on page 186 by Moriah Kline

Picture on page 245 by Moriah Kline

Take Your Place Overview

Chapter 1: My Story

Take your place and start sharing your testimony of what God has done for you. As you share those things with others you will be showing people who God is and what He is like. Your testimony will encourage others that God can heal them and also use them to be a light and release supernatural power to heal the sick and even raise the dead. This will point people to Jesus in order to bring them back home and to help them receive all of His benefits.

Chapter 2: The Kingdom of God

Take your place in the kingdom of God by telling people that the kingdom of God is near them and that they can experience it on this side of eternity. The gospel we are to share with people is the full gospel of the kingdom, not just the gospel of salvation. Romans 12:2 says that we must not think as those in the world think, but we need to be transformed by having our minds renewed. Then we will be able to prove what is the good, acceptable, and perfect will of God. If our minds aren't renewed, the enemy will be able to use us to continue his work of destruction in the earth. In order to be a gatekeeper for the kingdom of God, we must have our minds renewed to think as God thinks.

Do you practice God's will every day? If not, don't feel condemnation over it, but recognize the challenge God is putting before us. It's always good to ask yourself, "What did Jesus do?"

Jesus told us that we are to pray and ask for the kingdom of God to come on earth as it is in heaven. Are you experiencing this? If not, realize that as His body we are called to take dominion in the earth and take back everything that the devil has stolen from us. As princes and princesses in the royal kingdom, we are to give out an ARK—Act of Random Kindness—everywhere we go as we *re*-present Him. As we reach out with the love of God and share the gospel of the kingdom, we will see the lives of those around us changed and our cities transformed. For those who are outside the kingdom, the light will show them the way in. For those who are just in the doorway, you can show them how to come in and eat all of the delicacies in the kingdom, for the kingdom of God is at hand.

Chapter 3: The Healing Word

Take your place by learning the foundation of His healing Word. It's important to know the written Word, but it is even more important to know the "Living Word"—Jesus and all He has so abundantly provided for you. Hosea said that God's people are destroyed for a lack of knowledge (Hosea 4:6). What you and those around you don't know can kill them. God's children are living like they are orphans and beggars. Many of them are sick, in pain, and full of death and disease. Jesus was not beaten and nailed to a cross just so you can have a ticket to go to heaven one day but to live like hell on the earth. He was beaten to take your guilt, your shame, and your pain. He took all sickness and disease and by His stripes you *were* healed. He said, "It is finished!" He did all this so you could receive healing and live an abundant life here on earth as it is in heaven. Choose to let go of all the lies of the enemy and believe God's Word. According to your faith, may God's will of healing come to you today!

Chapter 4: Face to Face with God

Take your place by prioritizing your face-to-face time with the Lord. After all, this is your purpose in life. The Creator of the universe, our loving Father God, desires relationship with you above all things. Be someone who is in love with Him, for out of this you will bear much fruit so that our Father may be glorified. We must be Mary-Marths who first sit at the feet of Jesus prior to doing the works He said we should do. God is pouring out His anointing on those who seek His face and His heart just because they love Him, not because they want something from Him. We can't pull anything over His eyes. He sees all. So prioritize your alone time with Him and ask Him to give you a heart of passion for Him and for the things that concern Him. Remember, He doesn't want to use you, but He does desire to have relationship with you because He loves you very much! After you have been seasoned with His love and His anointing, then He will pour through you to reach those around you. Remember, first things first and intimacy with Him must be the priority!

Chapter 5: The Commission and Assignment

Take your place as a kingdom ambassador and share the full gospel with those you meet. You are in full-time ministry and called to be a light to all those around you. Remember, it is as easy as loving those around you and telling them the wonderful things that God has done for you and through you. This, my friend is preaching (sharing) the gospel (good news). As you do this, you are being a light in the world to show other people what God is like. Your testimony will not only help others know that they can be healed but that God wants to pour through them as well. As you step out and fulfill the assignment of sharing the good news of God's kingdom, signs and wonders will follow you because you believe.

Chapter 6: Holy Spirit

Take your place by getting to know precious Holy Spirit. He is the third Person of the Godhead who created everything in the earth, and He lives within you. This is why it is true that greater is He who lives inside of you than he (the devil) who lives in the world (1 John 4:4). He desires to have relationship with you so that you know Him just like you know Father God and Jesus. Holy Spirit is our great Comforter when we need comforting. He teaches us and leads us into all truth. He gives us "high fives" in the spirit when we pass the tests and trials we find on our journey. If we blow it, He picks us up, brushes us off and says, "You can do this, let's try again." He truly is our Great Reward, and we can experience Him and His help on this side of eternity. We can experience heaven on earth because He lives inside of us. Jesus spent alone time with Holy Spirit and Father God often and so must we. Have you received Holy Spirit? He longs for you to know Him.

Chapter 7: Understanding your Identity

Take your place as a prince or princess in the kingdom of God because you are royalty. Everything is under the rule of King Jesus, and He has transmitted His authority to you. It's important to see yourself from His viewpoint as more than a conqueror because He already won the war! You are an eagle Christian, not a turkey. Instead of running and hiding like a turkey or a chicken, you can be like the eagle and fly directly into the face of the storm, focusing on the last place you saw the Son. He will teach you how to put out your wings and learn to catch the thermal currents so that you can fly above the storm. Just as an eagle helps encourage other eagles who are in the wilderness going through a time of transformation, you are called to help feed and encourage those who are in need around you. God gives strength to the weary and increases the power of the weak. "Even youths grow tired and weary, and young men stumble and fall; but those who hope in the LORD will renew their strength. They will soar on wings like eagles; they will run and not grow weary, they will walk and not be faint" (Isaiah 40:28-31).

Chapter 8: The Authority of the Believer

Take your place as a sheriff on duty and enforce the rule of God on the earth. Jesus defeated the devil and took away the keys of the kingdom and gave them back to us. This gives us *all authority* over the enemy and his works. The enemy counts on our not knowing the facts and drives people by getting them to operate only by what they are experiencing with their physical senses. Therefore if he can cause problems to occur, if he causes sickness, or if he steals from us, we often just lie there and take it instead of standing up to fight. Let me remind you, we are not victims, we are *victors*. So when the enemy knocks you down, instead of thinking that when it rains it pours, "get up offa that thang" and command him to leave in the name of Jesus. Stay on guard against the devil and grab hold of all your thoughts. If they are negative and destructive, pull them down and cast them from your mind. Think upon God's thoughts. Life and death are in the power of your tongue, so start declaring *victory* and take the kingdom by force. You're in charge! Go ahead and take dominion, stop the work of the enemy, and enforce and release the kingdom of heaven upon the earth.

Chapter 9: Anointing

Take your place by learning to go to the river in order to receive His anointing. Many times we try to do things in our own strength, but as Zerubbabel learned, it's not by might, nor by power, but by the Spirit of the Lord (Zechariah 4:6). As we lean into Holy Spirit because of our desire to be close to Him rather than to get something from Him, He will pour His love, power, and presence into us. After He has filled us, His gravy boats, He will flow out of us to touch those around us. The key here is that we must prioritize time with God because we can't give out what we don't have. His anointing will remove burdens and destroy yokes for ourselves and those around us as long as we allow Him to do it through us.

The foundation of the kingdom and everything we do must be built on love. It's extremely important that we *examine the motives of our hearts* to make sure that we aren't doing anything to bring honor or glory to ourselves. If we try to take credit for what the Lord does, we will lose our rewards. We must continually wrap ourselves with the plain mantle of humility and give Him all the glory for all He does as He pours His anointing through us.

Chapter 10: Faith

Take your place by believing God with the simple faith of a child. It's easy to do the work of the kingdom because you are just the vessel He flows through. Without faith it is impossible to please God. As you put your belief and simple trust in Him, you will truly see that all things are possible. Just as you believe in Him though you cannot see Him, so you must believe His Words even when you can't see what it is you are asking for. This is the confidence we have in Him, that if we ask anything according to His will we know that He's heard us and that we will have what we are asking of Him (1 John 5:14). This is our title deed to the object we are waiting for. We must have absolute, 100 percent, walking-on-water faith that believes in the midst of the storm. The key to staying in faith is to keep your eye on what He says and by focusing on what He is doing right now. Then praise Him for it. As you do this, you will see your request come to pass. Praising Him is like applying miracle-grow fertilizing water onto your seed to make it germinate and grow up more quickly.

Chapter 11: Pressing in for the Victory

Take your place by pressing in for the victory no matter what problem or storm comes your way. Dress yourself for battle using God's armor. Then like David, who was able to laugh as he ran toward the giant, knowing that Goliath was as good as dead, run toward the giants in your life expecting them to topple. As you engage in the battle, know that no matter how long the battle is, you're going to win. Understand that just as a farmer completely believes that he will have a harvest from the seeds that he has sown, so you will reap as you sow God's Word, for His Word doesn't return void but will accomplish the thing it is sent to do. Just as apple seeds produce apples, so healing scriptures will produce healing. Stand in confidence, for He who promised is faithful!

Chapter 12: Enter His Rest

Take your place by entering His rest. Now that you know how to war, you need to learn how to do it from a place of rest and abiding in Him. This is so important, and I hope you can learn from my mistakes and victories. You, my friend, will have the wonderful opportunity of learning how to walk this out yourself, as we all must. Bearing fruit for God is about resting and abiding (staying close) to Him, for a branch cannot bear fruit unless it abides in the vine. Out of this place of abiding in Him, He will birth His heart in you. It is important that we learn the balance between carrying the passionate heart of God for those around us while not carrying the responsibility of it. You must learn how to rest in Him and His timing for the things of the Kingdom to be established in your life. Let me remind you, you *will* have the opportunity for patience to be established and for your spiritual muscles to be strengthened in the process. Oh, the process! Life is all about process, not just getting to the finish line. Learn to appreciate every part of your life and to stop long enough to smell the roses and enjoy the blessings that are all around you every day. Our lives are like beautiful, multicolored, stained glass windows. Each little piece is designed individually. By themselves they don't look like anything, but when you put them together, they make a beautiful masterpiece. Trust the Lord and enter His rest no matter what season you are in. It has been my experience that His timing rarely ever meets up with how and when I'd like Him to do things. Trust Him, fall back in His arms, and just let go. He who holds the world in His hand never slumbers or sleeps, and He has your best interests at heart. If you can't see His hand, you can always trust His heart.

Remember, it is His good pleasure to give you the kingdom. That you can trust!

Final Words

Now you are going to be taking your place in the race in order to receive the prize of the imperishable crown. Learn to accept and experience God's unconditional love for yourself daily. Your wonderful Father in heaven loves you as much as He loves His son Jesus. Your relationship with Him is more important than any other thing! Press into your love relationship with the Lord and pour your love out on Him. Understand that you are a son or a daughter, a prince or a princess of God, not an orphan or a beggar. Everything that belongs to Him belongs to you. This life is only preparation for eternity!

Take Your Place as a light set up on the "High Place" while loving selflessly and helping all those around you. Then help those who are running for the perishable crown. They are hurting, competing, and not understanding the ways of the kingdom. Your light will show them the way of hope and that our Father freely gives only "good and perfect gifts" to His children. Extend your love to them that they might know His love; this will be the drawing card for them. Even though they are fighting for the prize, believing that there's not enough, you can show them that God lavishes His gifts upon His children and that there is no end to His supply.

As you run forward in this race, you will hold a picture of eternity in your heart as you learn to love God with everything that is within you. Out of this place of relationship with God, you will learn to love yourself with God's love and to see yourself as He sees you, His beautiful creation. This will enable you to lay down your life for others and to love your neighbor as yourself, giving freely what you have received.

It's time for you to stand up, get out of the pew, and take your place saints! So what are you waiting for? Revival isn't out there somewhere, it's in you. Be a releaser of His kingdom and see His supernatural power change your life and the lives of those around you. Certainly the world will be a better place because you were here!

Arise my friend, it's Time to Take Your Place!

ABOUT THE AUTHOR

Angela Kline has been preaching and in ministry for over 10 years. She carries the heart and compassion of the Lord for all those who are sick, in pain and are lost. She desires to help raise up the army of the Lord to cover the earth with His glory to bring in the final harvest.

Angela, Dennis, and their two children, Moriah and Israel, moved to Atlanta in 2002 with a vision to start Healing Rooms in Georgia. Together they direct the Healing Rooms of Greater Atlanta. Angela is the Georgia Director, South Carolina Advisor, and a Regional Director for the International Association of Healing Rooms. She travels throughout the southeast and is going to the nations in order to raise up the saints to do the works of Jesus in Healing Rooms and in the marketplace.

If you'd like to invite Angela to speak at your church or ministry, email us at: *conferences@AngelaKline.com*.

If you've received the Lord, the baptism of the Holy Spirit, been healed, prayed for others and seen them healed, or your life has been touched positively by reading this book, please send us your testimony: *testimonies@AngelaKline.com*.

If you'd like to receive more indepth training on how to take your place, please visit our website for upcoming conferences or you can also order CDs and DVDs of "Take Your Place Training."

Last but not least, if you'd like to respond to His calling to *Take Your Place* and receive the Take Your Place Newsletter, please visit our website at: *www.AngelaKline.com.*

Printed in the United States
214845BV00002B/1/P